1989

Chaucer and the Law

# CHAUCER
# AND
# THE LAW

by

Joseph Allen Hornsby

Pilgrim Books
Norman, Oklahoma

By Joseph Allen Hornsby

Library of Congress Cataloging-in-Publication Data

Hornsby, Joseph Allen.
    Chaucer and the law / by Joseph Allen Hornsby.
      p.  cm.
    Bibliography: p.
    Includes index.
    ISBN 0-937664-79-0
    1. Chaucer, Geoffrey, d. 1400—Knowledge—Law.  2. Law in
literature.  3. Law, Medieval.  4. Law—Great Britain—History and
criticism.  I. Title.
PR1933.L38H67   1988
821'.1—dc19                                  88-2316
                                                                   CIP

ISBN: 0–937664–79–0

For Anne

# Contents

# Acknowledgments

This book began as a hunch — one spawned from ignorance as much as inspiration — that Chaucer's works were full of law and that a project exploring law in Chaucer was worth pursuing. I am deeply grateful to Denton Fox for his willingness to direct the doctoral thesis that resulted out of that hunch. His scrupulous reading of its drafts and judicious advice saved me from stylistic infelicities and many wrongheaded and petulant positions — shortcomings I have resisted the temptation to reintroduce into this book. Any errors that remain in that work and in this are my own. My colleague John Pat Hermann generously gave of his time and interrupted work on his own book to read and comment upon this project at crucial stages in its transformation from thesis to book. His advice has been invaluable to the completion of this work. Many others too have been generous with moral support and encouragement: my father, a lawyer, and mother, a teacher, who never suggested insanity as the motive for my dropping out of the practice of law to chase a Ph.D. in English and write about law and Chaucer; and countless friends in Toronto and Tuscaloosa who humoured me while I babbled on about obscurities of fourteenth-century English law. Much thanks goes as well to Howard Schless who read this work in thesis form and was kind enough to recommend it for publication. Financial support for this project in its final stages was provided by the Research Grants Committee of the University of Alabama. Pennsylvania State University Press has granted permission to include in Chapter One material that was published in the *Chaucer Review*, vol. 22: "Was Chaucer Educated at the Inns of Court?" Finally, one person has contributed more to the completion of this work than I will ever be able to acknowledge: my wife, Anne, to whom this book is dedicated.

# Chaucer and the Law

# Introduction

The prevalence of law in Middle English literature, and the importance of the study of law to an understanding of the literature, was brought home in John A. Alford's groundbreaking article "Literature and Law in Medieval England."[1] Alford convincingly demonstrated that law, a dynamic force in medieval culture, played a prominent role in the developing poetics of Middle English writers. There is a wealth of critical literature on a scattered variety of Old and Middle English poems and their relation to law.[2] But until now there has been no concentrated study of law in the work of a major figure in Middle English poetry—a study that acknowledges the diversity of legal systems at work in medieval England and the impact those various systems might have on a poet's representation of law in literature.

On the surface, the most likely candidate for such a study is Chaucer. It is commonly assumed that he had a legal background.[3] Indeed, the records of his life show that he held positions as an employee of the crown and as a private citizen that would have brought him in contact with different aspects of the law. For example, he was controller of customs and a justice of the peace, two positions that required some degree of acumen in the law to be performed competently. Apart from what the records of his life lead one to assume about his knowledge of law, Chaucer is traditionally thought to have been formally trained in

---

[1] J. A. Alford, "Literature and Law in Medieval England," *PMLA* 92 (1977): 941–51.
[2] See the entries in J. A. Alford and D. Seniff, *Literature and Law in the Middle Ages: A Bibliography of Scholarship*, pp. 45–98.
[3] See, for example, D. Brewer, *An Introduction to Chaucer*, pp. 48–50.

law, possibly at the Inns of Court.[4] But the obvious reasons one might turn to Chaucer to make a study of law in Middle English poetry are the wrong ones. The evidence that he was a lawyer is problematic, and there is little highly technical legal material in Chaucer's poetry. Chaucer's work is a fertile source of law, but its existence there is not self-evident. To understand Chaucer's poetry, it seems to me, one must also understand the law that infiltrates it — what institutions that law stems from and how it worked in day-to-day life.

Chaucer was writing at a time when English law did not stem from a single system of uniform rules but was a conglomerate of different legal systems with overlapping and often conflicting rules and jurisdictional claims. Although the royal courts were gradually imposing something of a national legal system on England in the fourteenth century, the common law remained primarily the king's law and was not nearly as common to all of England as it became in later centuries. A large part of the burden of legal business in medieval England was still shouldered by the local courts, both secular and ecclesiastical; these courts adhered to their own idiosyncratic rules when managing the legal affairs of their communities. The courts of towns, boroughs, and manors followed customary law, while church courts observed canon law.

In this book I attempt to place Chaucer's works in the perspective of the legal milieu of the late fourteenth century. I consider what that legal material means in relation to the legal realities it reflects, and how it operates in the fictions Chaucer creates. I concentrate on two primary areas of law: contract and crime. This limitation is not arbitrary, but has been imposed on the study by the material itself — these are the two areas of law Chaucer appears to have used most often in his poetry. One area of law glaringly absent from this book, and from Chaucer's work, is property law, the stuff from which the common law developed. What little explicit reference to it I have found in Chaucer's work is treated in chapter 3. The absence of such a major area of law from a body of work by a poet quite willing to depict his culture in detail is understandable given Chaucer's position in society — he was bourgeois. Private real property was the possession of the aristocracy, though Chaucer's Franklin is evidence that that would not be the case much longer.

The chapters reflect the method of inquiry outlined above. Chapter 1 is a consideration of Chaucer's legal background. It tests the case

---

[4] See E. Rickert, "Was Chaucer a Student at the Inner Temple?" in *The Manly Anniversary Studies in Language and Literature*, pp. 20–31.

for Chaucer's education at one of the Inns of Court and then looks for other ways Chaucer might have learned about law. Chapters 2 and 3 deal with the language of agreements in Chaucer's poetry and how that language reflects different legal traditions about contracts—those of canon and secular law. Chapter 4 deals with the criminal law of the age. While my study of law in Chaucer and its relation to the practices of the legal institutions of fourteenth-century England has only scratched the surface of the field, I hope a start has been made at sharpening our understanding of the function of law in the poetics of Chaucer and his contemporaries.

# 1

## Chaucer's Legal Background

Although the records of Chaucer's life are silent concerning the circumstances of his education, his early biographers proposed an impressive educational pedigree for him. It has been said that he studied at Oxford, at Cambridge, in France, and at the Inns of Court.[1] While most of the traditions concerning Chaucer's education were relegated to the realm of myth by nineteenth-century scholars, many Chaucerians continue to take Chaucer's education at the Inns of Court as within the region of probability. The tenacity of the Inns of Court

---

[1] The early accounts by John Bale and John Leland of Chaucer's life had him educated at Oxford, in France, and at the Inns of Court. Speght's biography of Chaucer in his 1598 edition of the poet's works added that he was educated at Cambridge and specified the Inner Temple as the Inn of Court where he was educated. These accounts are reprinted in E. P. Hammond, *Chaucer: A Bibliographical Manual*, pp. 1–2 (Leland), 10 (Bale), 21–22 (Speght). By the nineteenth century most of these theories of Chaucer's education had been dismissed as legend; see T. R. Lounsbury, *Studies in Chaucer*, 1:155, 164–72. New life was given to the notion that Chaucer was educated at the Inns of Court by E. Rickert in "Was Chaucer a Student at the Inner Temple?" in *The Manly Anniversary Studies in Language and Literature*, pp. 20–31.

tradition on Chaucer's biography is due in part to Edith Rickert's influential article "Was Chaucer a Student at the Inner Temple?" and J. M. Manly's adoption of her finding in *Some New Light on Chaucer*.[2] In her article, Rickert argued that Thomas Speght's report about Chaucer's education at the Inner Temple in his 1598 edition of the poet's works had been based on a reliable source. Speght had written: "It seemeth that both these learned men [Chaucer and Gower] were of the inner Temple: for not many yeeres since, Master *Buckley* did see a Record in the same house, where *Geoffrey Chaucer* was fined two shillings for beating a Franciscane fryer in Fleetstreete."[3] Rickert discovered that Buckley was the chief butler and records keeper of the Inner Temple and was therefore in a position to have seen such a record.[4] After establishing the reliability of Speght's source, and thus the probability of Chaucer's education at the Inner Temple, she suggested that Chaucer attended that inn between 1360 and 1366, a period unaccounted for in records of his life.

Rickert went on to describe vividly the education Chaucer might have received there. Her scenario depicting Chaucer's probable education at the Inns of Court has proved attractive to Chaucerians for many reasons. It not only provides a tantalizing glimpse of an obscure area of Chaucer's life but also invests that vision with an aura of verifiability. Relying on John Fortescue's description of education at the inns, Rickert argued that Chaucer would have received instruction there in a variety of matters other than law. According to her, the Inns of Court were a sort of finishing school for well-to-do young gentlemen where they learned to polish their courtly manners through instruction in etiquette, singing, and dancing, and where they also shaped their souls and honed their business and legal skills through a regimen of spiritual, historical, and legal readings, law lectures, and mock trials. With such a background, Rickert posited, it was no wonder that Chaucer was awarded the civil service positions he occupied during his life, positions which required a certain degree of acumen in business and in law.

  [2] J. M. Manly, *Some New Light on Chaucer*, pp. 7–18. Scholars continue to include the legend of Chaucer's education at the Inner Temple among the probable facts of his biography. Among those who most recently have done so are D. S. Brewer, *An Introduction to Chaucer*, pp. 48–50; J. H. Fisher, "Chaucer in His Time," in *The Complete Poetry and Prose of Geoffrey Chaucer*, ed. J. H. Fisher, p. 957; S. S. Hussey, *Chaucer: An Introduction*, p. 3; G. Kane, *Chaucer*, p. 12; R. O. Payne, *Geoffrey Chaucer*, 2d ed., p. 7.
  [3] See Speght's "biography" of Chaucer in *The Workes of Ovr Antient and lerned English Poet, Geffrey Chavcer, newly Printed*, ed. Thomas Speght; reprinted in Hammond, *Chaucer*, pp. 19–35.
  [4] Rickert, "Was Chaucer a Student at the Inner Temple?" pp. 22–23.

The shame of it is that this tidy scenario is stretched across the flimsiest of frames, and few Chaucerians have taken the trouble to look behind the grand tableau of Chaucer's intellectual and social development at the inns to inspect the evidence supporting it.[5] Those who have done so have been largely ignored. Two years after Rickert's article appeared, Aage Brusendorff maintained that Buckley's report of Chaucer's fine was another of the "spurious traditions" and was probably invented to explain why "the poet's 'hands ever itched to be be revenged, and have his pennyworths out of friars.'"[6] While D. S. Bland's reexamination of the evidence failed to uncover new proof to strengthen Rickert's hypothesis, the negative results of that study failed to dissuade Chaucerians—Bland among them—of the plausibility of Chaucer's education at the inn.[7] Bland, however, like Manly and Rickert, was laboring under the assumption that the Inns of Court had been offering training in law since the early fourteenth century.[8] Recent work by J. P. Dawson and E. W. Ives, largely neglected by Chaucerians, has shown this assumption to be mistaken.[9] According to them, the Inns of Court in the fourteenth century served only as places of lodging for lawyers—not places of education for law students. This later information about the function of the Inns of Court in the fourteenth century makes further attempts to bolster Rickert's hypothesis about Chaucer's Inner Temple education exercises in futility. Instead, the later material on the early history of the inns makes it necessary to assess the

[5] A notable exception is R. F. Green, *Poets and Princepleasers*, pp. 71–77. Green, following the suggestion of S. E. Thorne in "The Early History of the Inns of Court, with special Reference to Gray's Inn" (*Graya* 50 [1959]: 79–96; reprinted in *Essays in English Legal History*, pp. 137–54) that the Inns of Court probably did not perform an educational function until a late stage in their development, concluded that Chaucer most likely was educated in the king's household rather than at the Inns of Court, as was suggested by T. F. Tout in "Literature and Learning in the English Civil Service in the Fourteenth Century," *Speculum* 4 (1929): 382–86.

[6] Aage Brusendorff, *The Chaucer Tradition*, pp. 27–28.

[7] D. S. Bland, "Chaucer and the Inns of Court: A Re-Examination," *ES* 33 (1952): 145–55.

[8] Recent work by Chaucerians demonstrates how pervasive is the misconceptioin about the Inns of Court in the fourteenth century; see N. Orme, "The Education of the Courtier," in V. J. Scattergood and J. W. Sherborne, eds., *English Court Culture in the Later Middle Ages*, pp. 76–78; E. Salter, *Fourteenth-Century English Poetry*, p. 31. Both writers assume that the Inns of Court were providing education in the fourteenth century.

[9] E. W. Ives, taking Thorne's findings as a point of departure, has made a thorough study of the available records and has also concluded that the Inns of Court did not provide a legal education until a time later than the fourteenth century; see his "The Common Lawyers," in C. H. Clough, ed., *Profession, Vocation and Culture in Later Medieval England*, pp. 197–209; and *The Common Lawyers of Pre-Reformation England: Thomas Kebbell, a Case Study*, pp. 36–59. Ives's studies are examined in greater detail later in this book. See also J. P. Dawson, *The Oracles of the Law*, pp. 36–47.

case for Chaucer's education at an inn once again, this time with an eye
to putting that notion in its proper place, with other spurious traditions
about Chaucer's life and learning. The place to begin is with the actual
evidence for Chaucer's presence at the Inner Temple, the evidence upon
which Rickert built her case and which Bland did not undercut. Then
one must consider discoveries made by Dawson and Ives about the
function of the Inns of Court in the fourteenth century. By following
this course of inquiry, perhaps we can establish a truer picture of the
fourteenth-century Inns of Court and shed some light on both the form
of legal training Chaucer may actually have received in the fourteenth
century and how he might have received that training.

## CHAUCER AND THE INNS OF COURT

Apart from the paucity of evidence that the Inns of Court were educational facilities during the period in which Chaucer is reputed to have
attended the Inner Temple, several other factors, considered together,
further weaken the validity of Rickert's findings about Chaucer's osten-
sible Inns of Court background. Among these factors are the questionable reliability of her chief witness, Speght, and the dubious value of
Fortescue's account as evidence of fourteenth-century activity in the
inns.

Speght is the only direct evidence for Chaucer's membership in the
Inner Temple. His reputation as a reliable and unbiased witness,
however, can be impugned on several counts. First, as Brusendorff
suggested, Buckley's report about Chaucer's fine for flogging a friar may
have been attractive to Speght because it supported the relatively
common assumption of his era that Chaucer was something of a pre-
Reformation Protestant, not because of its value as evidence for Chaucer's educational background. [10] In fact, Thomas Fuller, in *The Church-
History of Britain* (1655), an account cited by Brusendorff, viewed
Speght's story of Chaucer's fine precisely as evidence of Chaucer's anti-
Catholic sentiments:

> I finde this *Chaucer* fined in the Temple two shillings, for striking a Franciscan Frier
> in *Fleet-street*, and it seems his hands ever after itched to be revenged, and have his
> penniworths out of them, so *tickling* Religious Orders with his *tales*, and yet so

---

[10] For sixteenth- and seventeenth-century statements of Chaucer's anti-Catholic bias, see C. F.
E. Spurgeon, *Five Hundred Years of Chaucer Criticism and Allusion, 1357–1900*, vol. 3, index,
s.v. *Chaucer* II(f)g, *Anticlericalism*.

*pinching* them with his *truths*, that Friers in reading his books, know not how to dispose their faces betwixt *crying* and *laughing*.[11]

The notion that Chaucer had an anti-Catholic bent was bolstered by the attribution to him of two blatantly anti-Catholic works during the sixteenth century, both of which were included in Speght's 1602 edition of Chaucer's works: *The Plowman's Tale* and *Jack Upland*.[12] Among writers on Chaucer during this period who viewed Chaucer as something of an *ante facto* Protestant, the statements of John Foxe and Francis Thynne are representative. In 1570, Foxe recorded in his ecclesiastical history of England that Chaucer "saw in Religion as much almost, as euen we do now, and vttereth in hys works no lesse, and semeth to be a right Wicleuian, or els was neuer any, and that all his workes almost, if they be thoroughly aduised will testifie."[13] Foxe especially singled out *The Plowman's Tale* as a work which exposed the fraud perpetrated by officers of the Catholic church.

Francis Thynne, in his *Animadversions*, argued for the inclusion of the "pilgrymes tale" in Chaucer's canon of works, a work "moore odious to the Clergye, then the speche of the plowmanne" and in which "did Chaucer most bitterlye enveye against the pride, state, couetousnes, and extorcione of the Bysshoppes, their officialls, Archdeacons, vicars generalls, comissaryes, and other officers of the spirituall courte."[14] The common opinion of the age concerning Chaucer's religious prejudices suggests that Speght's motive for including Buckley's report of Chaucer's fine was probably to indicate the similarities between Chaucer's attitude toward friars and their religion and that of his own day, rather than to prove that Chaucer studied at the Inns of Court.

If one looks to Speght for evidence that Chaucer attended the Inns of Court, his statements to that effect must be considered in the context of the historical inaccuracies which riddle the rest of his account of Chaucer's education. On the basis of earlier statements by John Leland and John Bale, Speght reports that Chaucer attended Oxford and describes the education he received there.[15] Also following Leland and

---

[11] Ibid., 1:230.

[12] For a discussion of the inclusion of *The Plowman's Tale* and *Jack Upland* in early editions of Chaucer's works, see Hammond, *Chaucer*, pp. 430–31, 444–46.

[13] Spurgeon, *Five Hundred Years of Chaucer Criticism and Allusion*, 1:106.

[14] Francis Thynne, *Animadversions upon Speght's First (1598 A.D.) Edition of Chaucer's Works*, ed. G. H. Kingsley, rev. F. J. Furnivall, pp. 7–9.

[15] Hammond, *Chaucer*, p. 21. For an examination of the historical accuracy of the sources for Speght's claims that Chaucer was educated at Oxford, at Cambridge, at the Inns of Court, and in France, see Lounsbury, *Studies in Chaucer*, 1:155–96.

Bale, Speght asserts that Chaucer traveled extensively in France, was educated there, and returned to England in the last days of the reign of Richard II to be educated at the inns of court:

> About the latter end of King Richard the seconds daies he florished in Fraunce, and got himselfe great commendation there by his diligent exercise in learning. After his returne home, he frequented the Court at London, and the Colledges of the Lawyers, which there interprete the lawes of the lande, and among them he had a familiar frend called Iohn Gower.[16]

To the accounts of Leland and Bale, Speght adds two more "facts" about Chaucer's education. First he states that Chaucer also attended Cambridge University. This assertion is based on a statement made by the narrator of *The Court of Love*, a poem included in Speght's editions of Chaucer but no longer attributed to him, who calls himself a clerk of Cambridge.[17] The second "fact" Speght adds is that a Master Buckley saw a record of Chaucer's fine at the Inner Temple.

Under close scrutiny, much of Speght's account of Chaucer's education proves to have little factual basis. Since the nineteenth century, Speght's claims for Chaucer's education at Oxford, at Cambridge, and in France have been rejected.[18] Since part of his evidence for Chaucer's education at the Inns of Court is based on the same sources on which he founded most of his other claims about Chaucer's educational experience, Leland and Bale, that claim may be fallacious as well. Of course, there is the matter of Buckley's apparent corroborative evidence.

Before considering Buckley and his report of Chaucer's fine more closely, I would first like to consider certain factors extraneous to the substance of that account which tend to weaken its value. For instance, one problem in accepting Speght's account as evidence that Chaucer attended the Inns of Court between 1360 and 1366, as Rickert argued, is that Speght stated that Chaucer was a member there in the latter days of Richard II's reign, rather than the latter days of Edward III's reign. In his *Animadversions* on Speght's 1598 edition of Chaucer's works, Francis Thynne rejected Speght's claim for Chaucer's membership in the Inner Temple for precisely that reason, since in the latter part of Richard II's reign Chaucer was far too old to have been a student

---

[16] Hammond, *Chaucer*, pp. 21–22.
[17] See Lounsbury, *Studies in Chaucer*, 1:496–503; W. W. Skeat, ed., *Chaucerian and Other Pieces*, pp. lxxii–lxxx.
[18] Lounsbury, *Studies in Chaucer*, 1:164–72.

there.[19] It is also noteworthy that Thynne, a contemporary of Speght and a member of one of the Inns of Court, Lincoln's Inn, was not swayed by Buckley's testimony to accept the theory of Chaucer's membership in an inn as fact.

Rickert took Thynne's failure to question the identity of Buckley as positive evidence that Thynne knew who Buckley was and that, therefore, he was a reliable witness.[20] Yet Thynne's doubts about Chaucer's association with the Inner Temple seem to contradict the conclusion Rickert drew from his silence. Inferring Chaucer's membership in the Inner Temple from Buckley's statement and from what Speght gives us about Buckley's identity is at best a dubious enterprise. First, apart from mentioning his name, Speght never identified the source of his information about Chaucer's fine. Rickert herself acknowledged that there were a number of other Buckleys who could possibly have been Speght's source.[21] Certainly, had Speght's Buckley been chief butler of

[19] Thynne, *Animadversions*, pp. 21–22. Thynne's doubts about Chaucer's membership at the Inner Temple are of some interest. He cites Speght's account in full and then frames his rebuttal as follows: "This is a harde collect[i]one, to prove Gower of the Inner Temple, althoughe he studyed the lawe. for thus yoᵘ frame youʳ argumente. 'Mr Buckley founde a recorde in the Temple that Chaucer was fyned for beatinge the fryer, Ergo Gower and Chaucer were of the Temple.' But for myne owne parte, yf I wolde stande vppon termes for matter of Antiquytye, and ransacke the originall of the lawiers fyrst settlinge in the Temple, I dobte whether Chaucer were of the temple or noe, vnlest yt were towardes his latter tyme, for he was one olde manne, — as apperethe by Gowere in Confessione amantis — in the xvi yere of R.2: when Gower wroote that Booke. And yt is most certeyne to be gathered by cyrcumstances of Rercordes, that the lawyers were not in the temple vntill towardes the latter parte of the reygne of kinge Edwarde the thirde; at whiche tyme Chaucer was a grave manne, holden in greate credyt, and employed in embassye; so that me thinkethe he sholde not be of that howse; and yet, yf he then were, I sholde iudge yt strange that he sholde violate the rules of peace and gravytye yn those yeares" (pp. 21–22). Thynne's statements regarding the issue of Chaucer's education at the Inner Temple may be more trustworthy than Speght's. R. F. Roxburgh, *The Origins of Lincoln's Inn*, pp. 1, 8, notes that Thynne was a member of Lincoln's Inn and something of a historian on the beginnings of the Inns of Court. Around 1600, he delivered a paper on the history of the inns, "Discourse of the Antiquity of the Houses of Law," to the Society of Antiquarians; this paper can be found in Thomas Hearne, ed., *A Collection of Curious Discourses*, 1:66–77. It is possible that Thynne's appeal to "Rercordes" to support his assertion that the Inner Temple was founded as a society of lawyers at a date too late for Chaucer to have been a member there may have been based on his investigation of the records of that inn. If that is the case, then Thynne's conclusions about the plausibility of Chaucer's membership in the Inner Temple should be given more serious consideration than they have been granted in the past.

[20] Rickert, "Was Chaucer a Student at the Inner Temple?" p. 21; see also Manly, *Some New Light on Chaucer*, pp. 8–10.

[21] See Rickert, "Was Chaucer a Student at the Inner Temple?" p. 22 nn. 1, 5; she admits that other Buckleys were associated with the Inns of Court during the last half of the sixteenth century; however, she disregards these extraneous Buckleys because they were not associated with the Inner Temple and including them would, no doubt, weaken her argument. She thinks that her Buckley was Speght's informant because Speght called him "Master," a common title of respect used when

the Inner Temple, an identification of him as such would surely have been appropriate to bolster the veracity of his report. But then, Speght often does not seem to have been concerned about the quality of his evidence.

A more troublesome matter is that the information attributed to Buckley does not categorically state that Chaucer was a member of the Inner Temple. Instead, Speght states that Buckley saw a record of Chaucer's fine at the Inner Temple. From this information Speght concluded that Chaucer was a member. One, however, should exercise a certain degree of caution before accepting the fragment of information attributed to Buckley as incontrovertible evidence.[22] As H. Cohen pointed out in his study of the early history of the English legal profession, Chaucer may have been fined for beating the friar because the incident occurred while he was a visitor to or guest of the Inner Temple, and his violent behavior was a violation of house rules.[23]

More damaging to an attempt to use Buckley's evidence to support an argument placing Chaucer at the Inner Temple between 1360 and 1366 is the evidence presented by a recent study which indicates that the New Temple was not divided into the Inner and Middle Temples until after its destruction by Wat Tyler's mob in 1381.[24] Only after the

---

referring to a member of the Inns of Court (Rickert's Buckley the butler became a member in 1572). She also sees the fact that Buckley was not more specifically identified by Speght as positive evidence of Buckley's association with the Inner Temple. She reasons that he was not identified because Speght thought that he was so well known that further identification was unnecessary.

[22] For evidence that can be construed as corroborative of Speght's, see *The Text of the Canterbury Tales*, ed. J. M. Manly and E. Rickert, 1:182; R. A. Caldwell, "Joseph Holand, Collector and Antiquary," *MP* 40 (1943): 295–301. In describing Cambridge University Library manuscript Gg.4.27, Manly and Rickert observed that the sixteenth-century owner of the manuscript had a paraphrase of Speght's 1598 biography of Chaucer added to it. The entry in the addition claiming Chaucer's membership in the Inner Temple substituted a direct statement, "There is a record in the same howse," for Speght's reference to Master Buckley. On the basis of this evidence, Manly and Rickert proposed that the manuscript owner may have seen the record that Buckley saw. Caldwell identified the manuscript's owner as Joseph Holand, who had attended the Inner Temple in the sixteenth century and still kept chambers there in the early seventeenth century. Caldwell, pp. 300–301 and nn., argues that Holand's membership in the Inner Temple and his interest in Chaucer, as attested by ownership of the manuscript, would have led him to seek out the record of Chaucer's fine and confirm Buckley's statement for himself. Thus the direct statement of the existence of the record substituted for the reference to Buckley would indicate that Holand saw the record and corroborated Buckley's account. No one seems to want to acknowledge that the direct statement of the record's existence was merely the result of the scribe's paraphrase of Speght's account and probably never was intended to have the significance that Manly, Rickert, and Caldwell have attached to it.

[23] H. Cohen, *A History of the English Bar and "Attornatus" to 1450*, pp. 486–97, 487, n. f.

[24] See R. F. Roxburgh, "Lawyers in the New Temple," *Law Quarterly Review* 88 (1972): 414–30, esp. pp. 424–29; Roxburgh, "Lincoln's Inns of the Fourteenth Century," *Law Quarterly*

New Temple was rebuilt did it split into the Inner and Middle Temples. With this information in mind, it seems highly unlikely that any document that Buckley saw would have placed Chaucer at an inn named the Inner Temple as a student before 1381. After 1381, records exist to indicate that Chaucer was engaged in business other than learning law at Inns of Court. If there was indeed a Master Buckley who did see a record about Chaucer at the Inner Temple, then the surest conclusion that can be drawn from the substance of that record, as reported by Speght, is that Chaucer was fined by the inn, not necessarily that he was a member of it.

Finally, when all of the inadequacies of Speght's account of Chaucer's membership in the Inner Temple are recognized, and when one considers, for example, the inaccuracy of his sources as well as Speght's tendency to accept evidence with little concern for its validity, Speght's reliability as a source for Chaucer's education at the Inner Temple is questionable.

## EDUCATION IN THE INNS OF COURT

The general assumption has been that Chaucer was a member of the Inner Temple and that therefore he received a legal and indeed a courtly education. I have attempted to show that the first part of this assumption is probably not true. It is necessary now to take up the second part of the assumption and consider what sort of education, if any, the Inns of Court provided in Chaucer's time.

The greatest obstacle confronting anyone wishing to place Chaucer at the Inns of Court is the absence of extant records of any inn earlier than those of Lincoln's Inn, which start in 1422.[25] Apart from these records, which provide little information about the form of education offered, evidence of the early activity of the inns comes from a limited number of sources. The major description of the educational activity in the inns is Fortescue's account in his treatise in praise of the laws and lawyers of fifteenth-century England, *De laudibus legum anglie*. According to Fortescue:

---

Review 94 (1978): 363–82, esp. p. 373. Roxburgh thinks that lawyers may have resided at the New Temple, also known as the Temple Barr, as early as 1338 and that by 1346 these lawyers had organized themselves into an educational hierarchy of apprentices and masters. The only evidence, however, to indicate that there was indeed some sort of organization of the lawyers in the New Temple is Thomas Walsingham's brief reference to the apprentices living there in his account of the destruction of the Temple Barr in 1381 (see below).

[25] See Roxburgh, *The Origins of Lincoln's Inn*, p. 28.

... since the laws of England are learned in these three languages [English, French, and Latin], they could not be conveniently learned or studied in the Universities, where the Latin language alone is used. But those laws are taught and learned in a certain public academy, more convenient and suitable for their apprehension than any University. For this academy is situated near the king's courts, where these laws are pleaded and disputed from day to day, and judgements are rendered in accordance with them by judges, who are grave men, mature, expert and trained in these laws. So those laws are read and taught in these courts as if in public schools, to which students of the law flock every day in term-time. [26]

In the next chapter, Fortescue continues his description of the educational curriculum of the inns:

In these greater inns [the Inns of Court], indeed, and also in the lesser [the Inns of Chancery], there is, besides a school of law, a kind of academy of all the manners that the nobles learn. There they learn to sing and to exercise themselves in every kind of harmonics. They are also taught there to practise dancing and all games proper for nobles, as those brought up in the king's household are accustomed to practise. In the vacations most of them apply themselves to the study of legal science, and at festivals to the reading, after the divine services, of Holy Scripture and of chronicles. [27]

From Fortescue's account, one can gather that students received most of their legal education from observing the legal procedure and practice of lawyers in the king's courts and not from any systematic program of legal education provided by the inns. As for the education provided by the inns, Fortescue describes lessons in singing, dancing, and social graces along with private reading of Scripture and chronicles undertaken by students on festival days. He also mentions the study of legal science undertaken by most of the students during vacations. This perhaps meant the explication of statutes by older lawyers, as well as moots, or practice courts, which Inns of Court records indicate were held during vacations. [28] These two activities seem to have constituted the greater part of the legal education provided by the inns in the fifteenth century.

The primary problem with using Fortescue's account of the Inns of Court to describe the inns in the fourteenth century is that Fortescue's account was written more than one hundred years after Chaucer ostensibly was educated there. Also, Fortescue's report may not be completely reliable. Roxburgh, in *The Origins of Lincoln's Inn*, offers this

---

[26] Sir John Fortescue, *De laudibus legum anglie*, ed. and trans. S. B. Chrimes, pp. 117; this work was composed between 1467 and 1471. For more on the date of this work and biographical information on Fortescue, see the General Preface to the edition and Chrimes's Preface and Introduction, pp. ix–cxiv.

[27] Ibid., p. 119.

[28] See Ives, "The Common Lawyers," pp. 199–200.

caveat: "In assessing the historical value of Fortescue's description of the Inns, it is well to remember the title of his work. His praises seem to be too fulsome and lacking in discrimination."[29]

E. W. Ives also thinks that Fortescue's account of the educational activity of the Inns of Court may be misleading.[30] For example, there is no evidence in the records of the inns to corroborate Fortescue's report that the inns were not only an academy of laws but also an academy of courtly etiquette. Ives concludes that any instruction of singing, dancing, and manners was extracurricular. More important, Ives observes that Fortescue's chapters on the education provided by the inns indicate that most legal instruction was occurring in the law courts.[31] In fact, except for the study of legal science during vacations, there is little mention of legal education provided by the inns or the professional organization of the members into a hierarchy of benchers and barristers according to educational advancement. Yet by the sixteenth century, there was a systematic legal education being offered by the inns as well as an organization of members into ranks. From the absence of these details in Fortescue, Ives concludes that Fortescue's description was of a group of organizations in the process of developing into highly structured institutions of legal education, a process not complete until the sixteenth century.

Ives's interpretation radically changes our notion of the stucture of the Inns of Court in Chaucer's day, for if what Fortescue described were educational institutions in their formative stages, then the inns of one hundred years earlier may conceivably have had nothing at all to do with education.[32] Although some historians persist in arguing that the

---

[29] Roxburgh, *The Origins of Lincoln's Inn*, p. 29.

[30] Ives, *The Common Lawyers of Pre-Reformation England*, p. 38.

[31] Ives, "The Common Lawyers," pp. 197–99.

[32] This account of the Inns of Court in the fourteenth century is based on the reconstruction of their history in both Ives's article and his book. Ives considers the evidence available from fourteenth- and fifteenth-century records concerning the various Inns of Court. J. P. Dawson, *The Oracles of the Law*, pp. 36–47, gives a similar account of the development of the Inns of Court. Both Ives and Dawson are following Thorne's suggestion that the Inns of Court did not begin educating lawyers until a late stage in their development. These studies of the early history of the inns reject the traditionally held notion that they taught law in the first half of the fourteenth century, as put forward, for instance, by W. S. Holdsworth in *A History of English Law*, 4th ed., 2:493–509; see also the survey of the different theories proposed for the early history of the Inns of Court in C. Carr, ed., *Pension Book of Clement's Inn*, pp. xvi–xvix. Of the other more recent examinations of the history of the inns, Roxburgh's *The Origins of Lincoln's Inn* argues for an early-fourteenth-century date for the origin of educational activity at the Inns of Court; but his later articles, "Lawyers in the New Temple" and "Lincoln's Inns of the Fourteenth Century," more cautiously argue that lawyers were living in the inns in the early fourteenth century and do not

Inns of Court were educational institutions in the fourteenth century, more recent studies take the absence of evidence supporting such a claim to indicate that they were not.[33] Until the early fifteenth century, the inns were merely residences for practicing lawyers during the court term; only gradually did they evolve into places where young men went to live and learn the law.

What can be reconstructed from the scraps of available evidence suggests that the inns of the early fourteenth century were no more than communal living arrangements made by provincial lawyers who needed to be near Westminster during the law terms.[34] Throughout the fourteenth century, scattered references to buildings housing apprentices-at-law can be found in various records. The earliest record documenting this is found in a yearbook from 1329 which refers to "the apprentices in their hostels."[35] By 1381, a group of apprentices seems to have established permanent residence at the "Temple Barr." The reference by Thomas Walsingham, the chronicler of Saint Albans, to the destruction of the "Temple Barr" by Wat Tyler's rebels in 1381 describes the place as a residence for apprentices at law and indicates that by that year they had formed themselves into some form of residential society.[36] Walsingham's "Temple Barr" is apparently the New Temple, which, as we have seen, was rebuilt and divided into the Inner and Middle Temples.

Although fourteenth-century references to the residents of these inns describe them as apprentices, this denomination does not mean

---

press the claim that law was being taught there at such an early date. A. W. B. Simpson, "The Early Constitutions of the Inns of Court," *Cambridge Law Journal* 28 (1970): 241–56, has examined the early constitutions of the inns for hints on their development and reaches a conclusion similar to those reached by Ives and Dawson.

[33] For a survey of possible references to the Inns of Court in fourteenth-century legal sources, see Dawson, *The Oracles of the Law*, p. 36 and nn.

[34] See generally the works of Ives and Dawson.

[35] Ives, *The Common Lawyers of Pre-Reformation England*, p. 39.

[36] For a list of fourteenth-century references to apprentices at law, see Dawson, *The Oracles of the Law*, p. 36 n. 4; see also Roxburgh, "Lawyers in the New Temple." The only possible reference to the Inns of Court in Chaucer is found in the Manciple's portrait in *The General Prologue* to *The Canterbury Tales*: "A gentil Maunciple was ther of a temple, / Of which achatours myghte take exemple / For to be wise in byyng of vitaille" (lines 567–69); "Of maistres hadde he mo than thries ten, / That weren of lawe expert and curious, / Of which ther were a duszeyne in that hous / Worthy to been stywardes of rente and lond / Of any lord that is in Engelond" (lines 576–80). Except where noted, all references to Chaucer's works are to *The Works of Geoffrey Chaucer*, ed. F. N. Robinson, 2d ed. The temple referred to in the Manciple's portrait is apparently one that housed lawyers, but these lawyers are "of lawe expert" and not students. There is no way, of course, to ascertain whether this temple was the New Temple, before or after being rebuilt to form the Inner and Middle Temples, or any other Inn of Court.

that they were students. Instead, apprentices-at-law were lawyers competent to plead in most courts of law, including the king's courts.[37] This privilege was curtailed only slightly in the fifteenth century, when sergeants-at-law gained exclusive right to plead in one of the king's courts, the court of common pleas. A. W. B. Simpson notes that "the significance of the expression *apprenticius ad legem (apprentice de ley)* was presumably that such apprentices were in the unusual position of having no particular master—they were not apprenticed to anyone except the law itself, and so they remained until they became *servientes ad legem (serjeants del ley)*."[38] An apprentice was simply a junior practitioner working through the ranks of the legal profession toward becoming a sergeant-at-law.

In view of this conception of apprentices-at-law, a 1388 listing of newly appointed sergeants-at-law and the inns from which they came can be construed not as proof that these men received their education from one of the inns of court but rather as an indication that a group of apprentices from different inns had been elevated to the rank of sergeant.[39] Interestingly, this list, found in a yearbook of 1388, is the first concrete evidence of the fourteenth-century existence of the Inns of Court under the names by which Fortescue would have known them. The sergeants of 1388 come from the Inner Temple, the Middle Temple and Gray's Inn.[40] As evidence of a specific time when the Inns of Court can positively be said to have been operating, this list is quite important; however, in no way does the list prove that the Inns of Court were performing an educational function at that time.

In all likelihood, they provided lodging, while legal training was obtained in the law courts, where students observed the practice of the law from a special place reserved for them called the crib. Also, some men learned law by serving an apprenticeship under an established lawyer. Apart from the training in canon law and civil law offered at the universities, the only formal legal education provided to students in fourteenth-century England was that offered by the clerks of the chancery.[41] These clerks lived in hostels, Inns of Chancery, governed by

[37] Ives, *The Common Lawyers of Pre-Reformation England*, pp. 17–19; Dawson, *The Oracles of the Law*, pp. 30–32.

[38] Simpson, "The Early Constitutions of the Inns of Court," p. 250; see also T. F. T. Plucknett, *A Concise History of the Common Law*, 5th ed., pp. 223–25.

[39] This list was published by J. H. Baker in "The Inns of Court in 1388," *Law Quarterly Review* 92 (1976): 184–87.

[40] Ibid., p. 184.

[41] For an account of the early development of the Inns of Chancery into educational institutions and the subsequent usurpation of that function by the Inns of Court, see Ives, *The Common Lawyers of Pre-Reformation England*, pp. 39–41.

senior clerks. By the middle of the fourteenth century, they were giving instruction in drafting legal documents and managing writs. By the fifteenth century, the clerks were teaching legal procedure: the mechanics of pleading and nuances of writ writing. At this time, the Inns of Court also were beginning to offer legal education.

At some point during the first half of the fifteenth century, although no one knows why, the Inns of Chancery abandoned the law school business, and the Inns of Court took over. Even in the early part of the fifteenth century, though, this transition was not complete. The earliest records of Lincoln's Inn show that all that was necessary for one to become a fellow there was attendance at three successive Christmas celebrations.[42] Although moots and readings were held at different periods during the year, attendance was voluntary and did not influence one's status in the society. In other words, the primary function of the inns in the early years of the fifteenth century was still social.

In light of the new evidence about the function of the Inns of Court in the fourteenth and fifteenth centuries, it is not very likely that Chaucer was educated there. If he had been a member of one of the inns, it would have been as a practicing lawyer and not as a young law student. There is, however, no evidence suggesting that Chaucer ever practiced law.

## POSSIBLE SOURCES OF CHAUCER'S LEGAL KNOWLEDGE

One of the more attractive aspects of Rickert's vision of Chaucer's education at the Inns of Court was that, according to Fortescue, the Inns of Court were more than mere law schools; they were places where young men could get a general education. Thus, by placing Chaucer at the Inner Temple, Rickert could partly account for his educational background. An alternative to the Inns of Court theory was proposed by T. F. Tout, who suggested that, as a valet in the royal household, Chaucer probably received a basic education.[43] Tout also suggested that during the period of Chaucer's service in the royal household he was trained to be a civil servant. This training probably consisted of an apprenticeship when he was taught the fundamental skills required of

[42] Ives, "The Common Lawyers," pp. 202–203.
[43] Tout, "Literature and Learning in the English Civil Service in the Fourteenth Century," pp. 382–86; see also Tout, *Chapters in the Administrative History of Mediaeval England*, 3:202.

a lower-level bureaucrat in the royal corporation, the most important of these being reading and keeping accurate business records. Tout thought that this was the normal way men of Chaucer's rank were educated and the way Chaucer could have qualified for the various government positions he was awarded during his life.

Tout's theory about Chaucer's education provides a plausible alternative to the Inns of Court theory. It has received support in R. F. Green's *Poets and Princepleasers*.[44] Another candidate for Chaucer's place of education is the Inns of Chancery, which do appear to have been providing education during Chaucer's life. Any possible site of Chaucer's education, though, is a subject for speculation but not, unfortunately, verification. However, while the process by which Chaucer received his basic education may never be fully accounted for, it seems necessary to look somewhere other than the Inns of Court if our picture of that process is ever to become clearer. The logical places to consider are the various positions Chaucer held as a civil servant and the duties required of him. For instance, Chaucer had to become familiar with certain rules of law and legal procedure to gain many of the positions he held in the civil service. The records of his life also indicate that he came in contact with law in various other ways. A survey of the different government posts Chaucer occupied along with the work required of him in them and an examination of the records of his private life demonstrate how easily Chaucer could have obtained a working understanding of legal principles and procedure.

At different periods in his life, Chaucer served as a diplomat and traveled to various European countries to further the crown's interests abroad.[45] The primary purpose for two of these overseas missions seems to have been to negotiate some form of treaty or agreement with a foreign power. Between 1372 and 1373, Chaucer traveled to Italy.[46] Although no records documenting the purpose of that journey survive, Chaucer probably participated in the negotiation of a trade agreement with Genoa and, possibly, the securing of a loan for Edward III. Between February, 1377, and March, 1381, Chaucer made several trips to France to negotiate a peace treaty between England and France.[47]

[44] Green, *Poets and Princepleasers*, pp. 71–72.

[45] See D. Brewer, *Chaucer* 3d ed., pp. 13, 34, 40, for his interpretation of the records documenting Chaucer's diplomatic activity.

[46] See M. M. Crow and C. C. Olson, eds., *Chaucer Life-Records*, pp. 32–40; hereafter cited as *LR*.

[47] Ibid., pp. 44–53.

Even if Chaucer played a minor role in negotiating and drafting these treaties and agreements, he could have learned a good deal about contracts. Since a peace treaty is nothing more than a contract obliging two nations to maintain peaceful relations with one another and a trade agreement is a contract delineating the terms by which two nations can carry on trade with one another, if Chaucer observed the mechanics of negotiating and drafting terms acceptable to both parties or saw the final documents, he learned the contractual formulas that created binding agreements.

From 1374 to 1386, Chaucer served as controller of the wool customs.[48] His primary duty as controller was to keep records of the duty on wool collected by the customs collectors. This was done to verify the accuracy of the collector's records.[49] In that position, Chaucer was exposed to law in several ways. Since he dealt daily with wool merchants, he probably gained a certain degree of familiarity with the "law merchant,"[50] a special set of legal rules governing mercantile transactions and particularly applicable to mercantile agreements. These rules determined what kinds of contractual formalities must be included in a mercantile contract for it to be legally binding. Chaucer's knowledge of the law of contracts would have been augmented by other aspects of his work.[51] As controller, Chaucer dealt with various kinds of bonds and agreements. For instance, as part of his regular duties, Chaucer handled indentures recording a merchant's payment of the wool custom and sealed the indentures with the cocket, the official seal of the controller, as proof of payment. There is also evidence that Chaucer dealt with contracts of credit between the king and his creditors during his tenure as controller.

As controller, Chaucer also had important dealings with one of the major administrative offices of the royal bureaucracy, the exchequer.[52] This institution not only managed the financial affairs of the government but also functioned as a law court whose purpose was to hear cases involving royal financial transactions, especially those dealing with money owed by or to the crown.[53] The exchequer would occasionally

[48] Ibid., pp. 148–270.
[49] Ibid., p. 173.
[50] G. W. Dunleavy, "Natural Law as Chaucer's Ethical Absolute," *TWA* 52 (1963): 183–85.
[51] *LR*, pp. 177–80, 184.
[52] For Chaucer's encounters with the exchequer and an outline of the various functions of the institution, see *LR*, pp. 209–68, 384–87.
[53] See H. Jenkinson and B. E. R. Formoy, eds., *Select Cases in the Exchequer of Pleas*; for evidence that Chaucer was acquainted with this function of the exchequer, see *LR*, pp. 384–87, where an exchequer action against Chaucer to recover a debt is recorded.

audit Chaucer's accounts of the expenditures and receipts of the collectors of the wool custom. M. M. Crow and C. C. Olson thought it likely that Chaucer was familiar with all stages of the audit, including the issuing of writs to summon the controllers and collectors to the audit and the procedural steps involved in proving the veracity of the records of the customs duty collected.[54] In his capacity as controller, Chaucer probably also instigated proceedings in the exchequer for seizure of the wool, woolfells, and hides of those merchants who attempted to cheat the king by failing or refusing to pay customs duty on their wares.[55] Chaucer's dealings with the exchequer would have given him a fairly thorough knowledge of its procedural practices, practices very similar in many ways to those observed by the royal courts.

By virtue of his association with the various men who held the position of collector of customs during his term as controller, Chaucer had the opportunity to become acquainted with officers of the local courts of London and, possibly, the practice of those courts. Several of these men, John Barnes, Nicholas Brembre, William Walworth, John Warde, and John Philipot, served as mayors of London coterminous with their tenures as collectors.[56] One of the functions of the mayor was to preside over trials in two of the city courts — the court of hustings and the mayor's court — the latter being a court convened when the court of hustings was not scheduled for session. These courts determined the outcome of a wide range of legal matters, including disputes over title to land, contractual quarrels, and disputes between foreign merchants which had to be decided by reference to the law merchant.[57] From his association with these men, Chaucer could easily have become familiar with the workings of the London law courts and the nature of legal disputes decided therein.

From 1389 to 1391, Chaucer served as clerk of the king's works.[58] Among the duties of this position was the procurement of labor and materials necessary for the building or repair of buildings owned by the crown. He also had to keep accounts of the expenditures made by his office. In both aspects of the job, the spending and the accounting, he had to work closely with the exchequer, which coincidentally gave him

---

[54] *LR*, p. 267.

[55] Ibid., pp. 186–88.

[56] See ibid., pp. 171–73; J. R. Hulbert, *Chaucer's Official Life*, pp. 44–47.

[57] See A. H. Thomas, ed., *Calendar of Early Mayor's Court Rolls*, A.D. *1298–1307*, pp. xvi, xxi–xxiii; H. M. Cam, "The Law-Courts of Medieval London," in *Law-Finders and Law-Makers in Medieval England*, pp. 85–94.

[58] See *LR*, pp. 402–76; for a list of the duties of the clerk of the king's works, see ibid., p. 412.

a further opportunity to familiarize himself with the procedures of that office. To obtain the funds needed to carry out the various construction projects supervised by his office, Chaucer had to petition the exchequer for money.[59] This entailed the issuing of writs by his office to the exchequer. These writs usually simply authorized the withdrawal of funds for financing particular projects. At times, though, the writs authorized that an assignment tally be granted. The tally was a legal instrument which recorded a debt owed the king. It served as legal proof that the person in possession of the tally had the right to collect the debt. Chaucer's accounts of expenditures were also subject to periodical audit by the exchequer, a process he had become familiar with as controller of customs.[60]

As clerk of the king's works, Chaucer had the power to enter into contracts with workmen for the repair and construction of buildings under his jurisdiction.[61] Furthermore, he had disciplinary jurisdiction over laborers working under him, including the power to bring back workers who deserted their jobs without permission and the power to imprison those who refused to work. His position also empowered him to make sworn inquests regarding stolen building materials and to effect their restoration. A sworn inquest was a common form of legal inquiry involving gathering a panel of jurors, whose number varied according to the kind of inquest, and charging them under oath to gather evidence by inquiring throughout the community about particular matters put before them.[62] From the different duties associated with the post, it is clear that in his position as clerk of the king's works he had to exercise legal skills and a degree of judicial power.

From an analysis of the skills required of him as a civil servant, it is clear that Chaucer worked with many aspects of the law. During the last two decades of his life, Chaucer in his capacity as a private citizen was appointed to a number of positions in which he had to work with the law. From 1385 to 1389, he served as a member of a commission of laymen and lawyers who sat as justices of the peace for Kent. In 1387,

[59] For the procedure to be followed to obtain funds from the exchequer, see ibid., pp. 443–45.

[60] For records relating to the exchequer's audit of Chaucer's accounts as clerk of the king's works, see ibid., pp. 445–62.

[61] For an example of the type of agreement the clerk of the works might handle, see ibid., pp. 470–72, and the discussion on pp. 474–75.

[62] For a discussion of the function and uses of the sworn inquest as a means of judicial procedure in medieval England, see B. H. Putnam, ed., Introduction, *Proceedings Before the Justices of the Peace in the Fourteenth and Fifteenth Centuries*, pp. xxxii–xxxv.

he was appointed justice *ad inquirendum* regarding a case of abduction.[63] Although no records survive to verify that Chaucer actually sat as justice of the peace during the term of his appointment, there are records which indicate that he did sit as justice *ad inquirendum*.[64] If Chaucer did have the opportunity to sit as justice when a commission of the peace was in session, he worked closely with a number of serjeants-at-law. All six of the lawyers who served on the two commissions of the peace to which Chaucer was appointed were serjeants-at-law, and all later became justices in the royal courts. One of these lawyers, William Rickhill, also served as justice *ad inquirendum* with Chaucer.[65]

The duties of the justices of the peace were to keep the peace and to take surety of the peace and surety of good behavior from those who threatened others with bodily harm or arson.[66] When the requisite number of justices were present, they were to gather evidence by sworn inquest about the perpetration of any crime or violation of any labor statute. Under certain circumstances, the justices also tried those accused of matters uncovered in the course of their inquests. The procedure followed by the four justices *ad inquirendum* regarding the abduction of Isabella Hall was essentially the same as that observed by the justices of the peace: they conducted a sworn inquest to uncover the facts surrounding the case and then submitted their findings to the court of the king's bench, where it was determined whether there was sufficient evidence to bring the alleged abductors to trial.[67] Chaucer's duties were limited to sitting on the commission inquiring into the facts of cases and did not include serving as justice to try cases.

In 1390, Chaucer served on another judicial commission as commissioner of walls and ditches.[68] This commission, composed of four laymen and two lawyers, was empowered to empanel a jury composed of knights of the community to inquire by sworn inquest into the condition of walls, ditches, and other structures erected to control flooding along the Thames between Woolwich and Greenwich. The

---

[63] For records and commentary regarding both positions, see *LR*, pp. 348–63, 375–83; M. Galway, "Geoffrey Chaucer, J.P. and M.P.," *MLR* 36 (1941): 1–36; for a thorough account of the function of the justice of the peace in Chaucer's day, see Putnam, ed., Introduction, *Proceedings Before the Justices of the Peace*, pp. xiii–cxxxii.

[64] See the discussion in *LR*, p. 378.

[65] For a list of the men who served as justice of the peace and justice *ad inquirendum* with Chaucer, see ibid., pp. 359–63, 378.

[66] These duties are listed in ibid., pp. 348–50.

[67] See ibid., p. 378.

[68] For the terms of the commission appointing Chaucer to this position and a discussion of the duties, see ibid., pp. 490–93.

commission also had the power not only to try those persons who damaged or failed to maintain these structures and, consequently, caused flooding but also to order the repair of damaged defenses. Although no legal training was required of citizens appointed as justice of the peace, justice *ad inquirendum*, or commissioner of walls and ditches, by serving on these various judicial commissions Chaucer could have become familiar with the legal procedure followed in holding sworn inquests and, in his service on peace commissions, the variety of crimes punishable by English law.

Apart from his duties as civil servant and his service on various judicial commissions, as a private citizen Chaucer had his share of experiences with various aspects of English law. On several occasions, he was called upon to serve as mainpernor for someone.[69] That is, he stood as surety to ensure that someone who incurred a legal obligation to perform some duty would in fact fulfill that obligation, for example, that a person who had been arrested and released would return to stand trial. It is likely that Chaucer was aware of the obligations and liabilities that one incurred upon agreeing to become a mainpernor. As legal guardian of the heir of Edmund Staplegate and the heir of John Soler, Chaucer must have been aware of the legal duties concomitant with that office.[70] Also, at various times of his life, Chaucer executed several leases and personal loan agreements, witnessed deeds of land, and was appointed attorney to take seisin of land in place of the actual feoffee.[71]

Perhaps, though, where Chaucer learned the most about law and legal procedure was through his numerous encounters with the court system as litigant or witness in particular matters. In 1379, a plea of trespass and contempt was brought against Chaucer before the court of the king's bench.[72] In 1380, Cecily Champaign released Chaucer from a charge of raptus and enrolled the release in the records of chancery and the mayor's court.[73] With regard to both of these matters, Chaucer knew more about the legal issues involved than we do, for the records are very vague about what he actually did to be accused of trespass and raptus. Actions of debt were brought against Chaucer several times: in

[69] Ibid., pp. 276–93.
[70] Ibid., pp. 294–302.
[71] For records of various leases and loan agreements which Chaucer executed, see ibid., pp. 144–47 (lease to Chaucer by the city of London for residence over Algate); pp. 384–401 (actions against Chaucer for recovery of debts); pp. 500–503 (record of loan to Chaucer in account book of Gilbert Mawfield); pp. 510–12 (Chaucer appointed attorney to take seisin); pp. 535–40 (lease for home at Westminster).
[72] Ibid., pp. 340–42.
[73] Ibid., pp. 343–47.

the exchequer in 1388 and in the court of common pleas in 1388–90, 1394–95, and 1398–1399.[74] Of the cases mentioned in this paragraph, it seems that none went to trial but were settled out of court. In dealing with these legal actions Chaucer, however, would have been introduced to the jurisdiction of various courts, the initial procedure in having an action brought against one in the different courts of London, and the means of preventing the action from proceeding to trial.

Chaucer was involved in at least one legal matter that did go to trial, though he was not the principal litigant. During his tenure as clerk of the king's works in 1390, Chaucer was robbed by highwaymen. Because part of what was taken from Chaucer was money belonging to the royal treasury, criminal proceedings were begun in the name of the crown.[75] A commission *ad inquirendum* was appointed in October, 1390, to investigate the robbery. Criminal proceedings were brought against Chaucer's assailants in the court of the king's bench in 1391. Although the records do not reveal Chaucer's role in the legal proceedings against the men, if he participated in the trial in any fashion, he would have had the opportunity to observe the procedure of conducting criminal trials in the court of the king's bench.

Chaucer also appears to have been familiar with at least one of the more specialized law courts, the court of chivalry, whose function was to handle litigation of a military nature and that having to do with the right to bear a particular coat of arms.[76] Chaucer appeared before the court of chivalry in 1386 as witness in the Scrope-Grosvenor dispute, a conflict between two families over the right to bear a set of arms claimed by both.

From the preceding survey, it seems clear that Chaucer was familiar with several different secular law courts ranging from the courts of the city of London to those administering the king's justice. Also, as both civil servant and private citizen, Chaucer associated with justices and lawyers working in these courts. For example, Chaucer was often joined with a lawyer as mainpernor for a particular individual.[77] Apart from

[74] Ibid., pp. 384–401.

[75] See ibid., pp. 477–89, for the records documenting the various legal proceedings regarding the robbery of Chaucer and a discussion of those documents.

[76] See ibid., pp. 370–74; for a concise description of the jurisdiction of the court of chivalry, see C. T. Allmand, "The Civil Lawyers," in Clough, ed., *Profession, Vocation and Culture in Later Medieval England*, p. 156.

[77] Thomas Marchant, attorney of the court of common pleas, served with Chaucer as mainpernor for Matilda Nemeg, 1388–89, *LR*, pp. 289–92; William Norwich, an attorney practicing in the court of common pleas, served with Chaucer as mainpernor for Simon Manning, 1386, ibid., pp. 285–89; Ralph Strode served with Chaucer as mainpernor for John Hende, ibid., pp. 281–84.

those officers of the court who were business associates of Chaucer, a few lawyers seem to have been more intimately acquainted with him. Ralph Strode, mentioned with John Gower in the closing verses of *Troilus and Criseyde*, was common sergeant and common pleader for the city of London. If this is the same Ralph Strode who was a fellow of Merton College at Oxford from 1359 to 1360, he was, perhaps, versed in canon as well as common law.[78] Another lawyer with whom Chaucer also had personal dealings was Richard Forester, who appears to have been a professional attorney and was, along with John Gower, appointed by Chaucer to serve as his general attorney while he was abroad in 1378.[79]

Chaucer was also associated with a group of highly literate knights and civil servants who, though not lawyers per se, probably had a more substantial knowledge of the law than the average layman. These were among the men who made up Chaucer's audience and whom he would have expected to understand any legal references in his poetry. Among these men were Gower (who perhaps had some formal legal training), Henry Scogan, Thomas Usk, Thomas Hoccleve, Richard Sturry, Lewis Clifford, John Clanvowe, John Montague, and Phillip de la Vache.[80]

The evidence offered by the records of Chaucer's life suggests that he could have acquired a respectable knowledge of the law observed by the various secular courts in London. As well, there is evidence that Chaucer knew something about canon law. For example, the opening verses of *The Friar's Tale* (lines 1301–13) offer a fairly accurate summary of the different matters over which courts of the archdeacon had jurisdiction:[81]

> Whilom ther was dwellynge in my contree
> An erchedeken, a man of heigh degree,
> That boldely dide execucioun
> In punysshynge of fornicacioun,

[78] See ibid., p. 284; E. P. Kuhl, "Some Friends of Chaucer," *PMLA* 29 (1914): 270–76; A. B. Emden, *A Biographical Register of the University of Oxford to* A.D. *1500*, 3:1807–1808; all of the above thought it likely that the Oxford Strode and the London lawyer Strode were the same man.

[79] *LR*, p. 60 n. 5; it has not been positively established that Chaucer's acquaintance was the same Richard Forester who was a professional attorney.

[80] See P. Strohm, "Chaucer's Fifteenth-Century Audience and the Narrowing of the 'Chaucer Tradition,'" *SAC* 4 (1982): 7–14; for the possibility that Gower had some legal training, see J. H. Fisher, *John Gower: Moral Philosopher and Friend of Chaucer*, pp. 55–57.

[81] For examinations of the jurisdiction of English ecclesiastical courts, see N. Adams and C. Donahue, eds., Introduction, *Select Cases from the Ecclesiastical Courts of the Province of Canterbury c. 1200–1301*, pp. 72–103; B. L. Woodcock, *Medieval Ecclesiastical Courts in the Diocese of Canterbury*, pp. 79–92.

> Of wicchecraft, and eek of bawderye,
> Of diffamacioun, and avowtrye,
> Of chirche reves, and of testamentz,
> Of contractes and of lakke of sacramentz,
> Of usure, and of symonye also.
> But certes, lecchours dide he grettest wo;
> They sholde syngen if that they were hent;
> And smale tytheres weren foule yshent,
> If any persoun wolde upon hem pleyne.

*The Parson's Tale* is another of Chaucer's works which deals in part with various aspects of the canon law. One of the sources for this work was the *Summa de casibus de poenitentia et matrimonio* of Raymond of Pennaforte,[82] which deals with aspects of the canon law on subjects ranging from homicide and usury to confession, penitence, and marriage.[83] Through Raymond's work, Chaucer could have learned a good deal about canon law without having access to the various collections of papal decrees which form the *Corpus juris canonici*. Moreover, W. A. Pantin has observed that many manuals for the instruction of priests circulating in fourteenth-century England offered condensed and digested treatments of the major principles of the canon law.[84] Among these works were William of Pagula's *Oculus sacerdotis*, John de Burgh's *Pupilla oculi*, and John Mirk's *Manuale sacerdotis*. Chaucer's use of Raymond's *Summa* and the availability of other treatises which presented canon law in a digested format show that Chaucer could have acquired a knowledge of the principles of canon law without studying the actual decretals and their glosses.

Finally, several scholars have suggested that laymen in Chaucer's time were well acquainted with the workings of both ecclesiastical and secular courts. Dorothy Owen thinks that, because the power of the ecclesiastical courts to regulate spiritual affairs gave them tremendous influence in communities under their jurisdiction, laymen were well aware of both the kinds of matters considered by those courts and the

---

[82] See G. Dempster, "The Parson's Tale," in W. F. Bryan and G. Dempster, eds., *Sources and Analogues of Chaucer's* Canterbury Tales, pp. 723–29.

[83] For a general account of this work and Raymond's other canon law works, especially his role in compiling the *Decretals* of Gregory IX, see S. Kuttner, *Repertorium der Kanonistik (1140–1234)*, pp. 438–52; T. B. Schwertner, *Saint Raymond of Pennafort*, ed. and rev. C. M. Antony, pp. 90–104; A. Teetaert, "Raymond De Penyafort," *Dictionnaire de théologie catholique*.

[84] W. A. Pantin, *The English Church in the Fourteenth Century*, pp. 189–219. See also L. E. Boyle, "The Fourth Lateran Council and Manuals of Popular Theology," in T. J. Heffernan, ed., *The Popular Literature of Medieval England*, pp. 30–43; J. Shaw, "The Influence of Canonical and Episcopal Reform on Popular Books of Instruction," in ibid., pp. 44–60.

fundamental principles of canon law used to resolve disputes coming before them.[85] This theory is supported by D. J. Guth's account of patterns of litigation during Henry VII's reign.[86] Guth notes that the overlap in jurisdiction among the many different courts in England offered the potential litigant a variety of places to begin his lawsuit. For instance, a man could bring suit on a debt in the local bishop's court, the mayor's court, or before the king's justices. Guth also observes that, because of this proliferation of courts in medieval England, the layman not only was much more willing to turn to law courts to settle all sorts of disputes but also was more knowledgeable of certain technical aspects of law and legal procedure than the layman of today.

There is a considerable amount of evidence to indicate that Chaucer could have acquired knowledge of legal principles and legal terminology without having been trained formally as a lawyer. Since most available information points toward the conclusion that the Inns of Court were not operating as law schools until very late in Chaucer's life, the most logical foundation upon which one can build a case for Chaucer's having had any knowledge of law is from the evidence provided by the *Life-Records*. As I have attempted to demonstrate, those records provide sufficient proof to support the proposition that Chaucer was exposed to law in various ways throughout his life and could have learned much about it from that exposure. The following chapters explore aspects of contractual law, criminal law, and criminal procedure found in Chaucer's works in an effort to show some of the kinds of law with which he was familiar.

[85] D. Owen, "Ecclesiastical Jurisdiction in England, 1300–1550: The Records and Their Interpretation," *Studies in Church History* 11 (1975): 199–221; see also T. Hahn and R. W. Kaeuper, "Text and Context: Chaucer's Friar's Tale," *SAC* 5 (1983): 67–102; this article suggests that many of the details presented in *The Friar's Tale* about the practice and jurisdiction of ecclesiastical courts and their officers were common knowledge. Hahn and Kaeuper pay particularly close attention to the portrait of the summoner in the tale and examine the correspondence between the conduct of Chaucer's summoners and that of actual fourteenth-century summoners.

[86] D. J. Guth, "Enforcing Late-Medieval Law: Patterns in Litigation during Henry VII's Reign," in J. H. Baker, ed., *Legal Records and the Historian*, pp. 80–82.

# 2

# Chaucer and the
# English Canon Law
# of Agreements

Chaucer's characters often make promises. Consider Dorigen's hasty promise in *The Franklin's Tale* to become Aurelius's lover if he moves rocks from the harbor. Aurelius considers the promise binding when he fulfills the condition Dorigen imposes on the promise. Other promises exchanged by Chaucer's characters also seem binding; yet little work has been done to determine the extent to which Chaucer actually uses vocabulary associated with legal agreements to give these promises the vestments that would make them similar to those regarded as binding at law.[1] What work that has been done on the language of agreements

---

[1] Much of the work on contracts and agreements in Middle English literature has centered around *Sir Gawain and the Green Knight* and the works of Chaucer. For studies dealing with promises and agreements in Gawain, see R. L. Blanch and J. N. Wasserman, "Medieval Contracts and Covenants: The Legal Coloring of *Sir Gawain and the Green Knight*," *Neophil* 68 (1984): 598–610; W. R. J. Barron, *"Trawthe" and Treason: The Sin of Gawain Reconsidered*; J. A. Burrow, *A Reading of Sir Gawain and the Green Knight*; R. J. Spendal, "The Fifth Pentad in 'Sir Gawain and the Green Knight,'" *N&Q*, n.s., 23 (1976): 147–48. For studies dealing with promises and agreements in Chaucer, see N. Bøgholm, "A Rash Promise," *SN* 15 (1942): 41–42; A. T. Gaylord,

in Middle English poetry relies almost exclusively on common law rules to provide the legal interpretation of that language. Such heavy reliance on the common law may distort our understanding of Middle English contractual language, however.[2] In the fourteenth century the common law of contract was woefully underdeveloped, and most disputes involving oral agreements, like those in *The Franklin's Tale*, were handled by local church and customary courts.[3]

---

"The Promises in *The Franklin's Tale*," *ELH* 31 (1964): 331–65; L. S. Johnson, "The Prince and His People: A Study of the Two Covenants in the *Clerk's Tale*," *ChauR* 10 (1975): 17–29.

    [2] This problem is illustrated in Blanch and Wasserman, "Medieval Contracts and Covenants." Although they write perceptively about the literary significance of the promises in *Gawain*, they muddle certain distinctions of law and, consequently, confuse our appreciation of the technical nature of the promises exchanged between Gawain and the Green Knight and Gawain and Bercilak. Chief among the problems with their handling of the law of contracts is their reliance on the common law, the law of the royal courts in medieval England, for the rules of contract that inform their analysis of Gawain's promises; see their discussion at pp. 598–600. Two points in the use of the common law in their legal analysis of contracts in *Gawain* are especially problematic: their reliance on the action of assumpsit and the doctrine of quid pro quo as the legal bases for the contractual elements that provide a veneer of validity for the oral agreements in the poem. First, the action of assumpsit was not recognized by the royal courts as a method of getting oral agreements adjudicated until *Slade's Case* in 1602. While assumpsit did provide a procedural means of getting oral agreements into the royal courts earlier, then, however, an action brought in assumpsit was for misfeasance or malfeasance in performing an undertaking rather than for breach of an agreement. Even in this guise assumpsit was a relatively rare procedural device until the fifteenth and sixteenth centuries. Thus it hardly seems likely that the law surrounding assumpsit can help much in understanding the legal elements in agreements in a fourteenth-century poem. For the most thorough examination of the development of the action of assumpsit, see A. W. B. Simpson, *A History of the Common Law of Contract: The Rise of the Action of Assumpsit*. See also S. F. C. Milsom, *Historical Foundations of the Common Law*, 2d ed., pp. 314–60; C. H. S. Fifoot, *History and Sources of the Common Law: Tort and Contract*, pp. 330–94. Second, quid pro quo is usually considered an element in agreements creating monetary debts like loans, not in agreements generating obligations to perform services or tasks; in fact, there is little talk in English legal records of quid pro quo as a necessary ingredient for the actionability of debt agreements until the fifteenth century, and there is some question whether lawyers actually thought it a rule of law that the legality of a debt agreement was contingent on the existence of quid pro quo. Although some sort of uncompensated exchange seems always to have been necessary for an action in debt to arise, where a bond or written agreement evidenced the debt, the presence of quid pro quo was irrelevant. There is some discussion of the term in fourteenth-century debt cases, but the meaning is vague, and the concept is never referred to as an absolute rule of law. Only in the fifteenth and sixteenth centuries does the concept of quid pro quo approach canonization as legal doctrine in the courts. Simpson, *A History of the Common Law of Contract*, pp. 193–96; and W. M. McGovern, "Contract in Medieval England: The Necessity for Quid Pro Quo and a Sum Certain," *American Journal of Legal History* 13 (1969): 173–86, think that the term functioned as a description of the usual circumstances under which an action in debt would arise rather than as a rigid rule of law; see also Fifoot, *History and Sources of the Common Law*, pp. 225–27. My own use of quid pro quo is for descriptive purposes only.

    [3] Oral agreements, like the agreements exchanged between Gawain and the Green Knight and Gawain and Bercilak, were generally excluded from adjudication by the common law courts unless they were debt agreements for a precise sum of money. But see W. M. McGovern, "The Enforcement of Oral Covenants Prior to Assumpsit," *Northwestern University Law Review* 65

The argument of this chapter and the next is that Chaucer borrows from the law of contracts and agreements of his day for the language of his promises. But it is important to distinguish between the types of agreements and contractual formalities recognized as valid by different courts. Thus one aim of the two chapters which follow is to relate the law of contracts recognized by the various courts in medieval England to Chaucer's use of legal contractual formulas and language. To set this examination in its appropriate context, general principles of the law of contracts applicable to canon and secular law courts will first be surveyed. Then the different rules recognized as binding agreements at canon law and particular works by Chaucer which reflect that system's law of agreements will be considered. Discussion of the secular law of contracts is deferred until chapter 3. By a careful examination of the terminology Chaucer uses for the agreements in his works, it can be determined whether Chaucer uses language clearly associated with agreements recognized by one legal system exclusively or, instead, terminology shared by both ecclesiastical and secular courts.

### GENERAL SURVEY OF CONTRACTUAL PRINCIPLES OF MEDIEVAL ENGLISH LAW

When, in the *Prologue* to *The Man of Law's Tale*, Harry Bailly demands that the lawyer tell a tale, the Man of Law replies with a legal maxim. He assures Harry that he will honor the promise he and the other pilgrims made at the Tabard Inn: "To breke forward is nat myn entente. / Biheste is dette, and I wole holde fayn / Al my biheste, I kan no bettre sayn" (lines 40–42).[4] The straightforward statement that "biheste is dette" is a common enough Middle English proverb meaning that a promise (*biheste*), more specifically the Man of Law's agreement (*for-*

---

(1970): 576–614, for examples of special types of oral covenants which were enforced by the king's courts. For a succinct discussion of the development of the law of contracts in the royal courts and the early restrictions on its jurisdiction over particular forms of contractual transactions, see Milsom, *Historical Foundations of the Common Law*, pp. 243–82, 314–60. For other studies dealing with the practice of the royal courts regarding contracts, see Simpson, *A History of the Common Law of Contract*; W. M. McGovern, "The Enforcement of Informal Contracts in the Later Middle Ages," *California Law Review* 59 (1971): 1145–93; McGovern, "Contract in Medieval England"; M. S. Arnold, "Fourteenth-Century Promises," *Cambridge Law Journal* 35 (1976): 321–34.

[4] For the meaning of the functional legal terms in these lines, see *MED*, s.v. *foreward* n.; *dette* n., 1.

*ward*) to tell four tales, creates an obligation (*dette*).[5] The words are a variation of a canon law maxim, "Pacta sunt servanda," "Agreements must be kept."[6]

The Man of Law's proverb embodies the basic premise behind rules governing the legality of agreements made in Chaucer's day: promises, even oral ones unattested by a deed or other form of documentation, ought to be binding — as long as they conformed to certain simple legal conventions.[7] Chaucer, in fact, alludes to this concept of contractual fidelity in his lyric *Lak of Stedfastnesse* when he reads the failure of Englishmen to maintain their obligations as symptomatic of a larger cultural malaise (lines 1–7):

> Somtyme the world was so stedfast and stable
> That mannes word was obligacioun;
> And now it is so fals and deceivable
> That word and deed, as in conclusioun,
> Ben nothing lyk, for turned up-so-doun
> Is al this world for mede and wilfulnesse,
> That al is lost for lak of stedfastnesse.[8]

This notion, "Biheste is dette," implies that consensual contracts as well as real contracts generate a legal obligation.[9] Although the differ-

---

[5] B. J. Whiting (with H. W. Whiting), *Proverbs, Sentences, and Proverbial Phrases from English Writings, Mainly Before 1500*, B214.

[6] See Harold J. Berman, *Law and Revolution: The Formation of the Western Legal Tradition*, p. 247.

[7] For evidence confirming that oral agreements were enforced by the local courts of medieval England, see F. W. Maitland and W. P. Baildon, eds., *The Court Baron*, pp. 115–18; M. Bateson, ed., *Borough Customs*, 2:lxxx–lxxxii; *The Liber Albus*, vol. 1 of *Munimenta Guildhallae Londoniensis*, ed. H. T. Riley, p. 214; H. M. Cam, ed., *The Eyre of London, 14 Edward II, A.D. 1321*, 1:lxix, cvi; see also R. L. Henry, *Contracts in the Local Courts of Medieval England*, pp. 209–12.

[8] In the first stanza of *Lak of Stedfastnesse*, Chaucer is in effect lamenting that men no longer honor the rule "Biheste is dette."

[9] For a discussion of the distinction between real and consensual contracts in the common law, see W. S. Holdsworth, *A History of English Law*, 4th ed., 2:275–77; F. Pollock and F. W. Maitland, *The History of English Law Before the Time of Edward I*, 2d ed., 2:185–86. For a view that challenges the traditional notion that the common law considered a debt a real contract, that is, a contract formed on the basis of a transfer of something of value rather than on an exchange of promises, see McGovern, "Contract in Medieval England: The Necessity for Quid pro Quo and a Sum Certain," pp. 173–75. McGovern argues that debt was actually founded on a promise to pay rather than on an exchange of value. This is probably how a layman understood the situation. A creditor no doubt believed that he had a right to recover money owed him because the debtor had promised to repay him, regardless of what the right to recover the debt arose because of the loan transaction instead of the promise to pay. Whether the lawyers and judges thought of debt in terms of a real contract or promise to pay is difficult to determine. McGovern points out that the real contract was an idea derived from Roman law's analysis of legal debts. Early commentators on the law of England, Ranulf de Glanville and Henry de Bracton, borrowed

ence between consensual and real contracts is academic, it is important both for understanding distinctions made by law courts in the fourteenth century and for grasping the form an agreement had to take if it was to be recognized as binding by church courts. A consensual contract is a contract made legally binding by the terms of the promises made by one person to another—for example, a covenant. A real contract, on the other hand, is one whose legally binding force is created by the underlying transaction generating the obligation—that is, by the transfer of something of value from one person to another instead of by the promise alone. A loan of money is one example of a real contract. With a loan, the legal obligation to repay the money is arguably created not by the promise to repay but by the transfer of money from the creditor into the hands of the debtor. To use terminology familiar to fifteenth-century common law analysis of debt litigation, with a real contract the obligation was generated by a quid pro quo—when something of value was exchanged between debtor and creditor. Usually that something was the loan given to the debtor in exchange for a promise to repay the loan and, perhaps, some form of security. Because a completed transaction was easier to prove than a promise, real contracts were given favored status in the royal courts and were subject to less stringent modes of proof than consensual contracts.

It is also important to note that *contract* and *covenant* were quite distinct legal terms in medieval England.[10] The term *covenant*—not, as today, *contract*—was the general term covering all sorts of agreements. *Contract* referred to specific types of covenants, what I have termed real contracts. *Contract* became generalized once *covenant* became identified solely with the common law action of covenant. This action could be brought in the king's courts only for breach of written agreements under seal. Before this confusion of terminology, however, *covenant* referred to any type of agreement and in many cases, whether oral or written, one which was legally binding.

---

terminology from the Roman law to describe the English law on debt. Legal historians have taken this as an indication that the common law conception of debt was analogous to the Roman law conception of debt. McGovern's study suggests that the description of debt in Glanville and Bracton was more a reflection of their reliance on Roman law for their definitions than one of contemporary legal practice. For the distinction between real and consensual contracts at Roman law, see B. Nicholas, *An Introduction to Roman Law*, pp. 161–89.

[10] For the legal distinction in the Middle Ages between *covenant* and *contract*, see S. F. C. Milsom, "Reason in the Development of the Common Law," *Law Quarterly Review* 81 (1965): 500–501; and Milsom, *Historical Foundations of the Common Law*, pp. 246–50, 260; see also Simpson, *A History of the Common Law of Contract*, pp. 5–6, 185–90.

That an oral agreement carried the same legal significance as a written one in some courts in the English Middle Ages probably violates our modern conception of the types of transactions that constitute binding agreements. Today a man is as good as his word only when you can get him to put it in writing and sign his name in agreement to the terms of the document. The inscription on paper, not uttered vows, seems to invoke the magical charm which makes the words binding. Certainly, even in Chaucer's day, a written document always made better proof of the existence of an agreement than an ephemeral exchange of spoken promises. Only in the king's courts, however, was a document required for a covenant to be actionable. This development came about because traditional modes of proof originating from procedural practices of local courts became ineffectual in the larger forum of the king's court. [11]

In a local court, when a plaintiff claimed that a covenant had been breached, if he had no evidence but his word to support his claim, he had to produce "good suit" to maintain his action. "Good suit" entailed producing persons (the plaintiff's secta) prepared to attest to that plaintiff's honesty and the good faith of his claim. If his secta were the only form of proof offered, the defendant could simply deny the plaintiff's claim and "wage his law." Wager of law was the process by which the defendant assembled a group of neighbors, called oath helpers or compurgators, who were willing to swear that the defendant's version of the facts was truer than the plaintiff's.

When the forum was a secular local court, the secta and compurgators were neighbors who lived and worked in close proximity. They were, therefore, in a position to know the truth of their party's claim and swear in good faith to its veracity, or they were in a position to know the falsity of the claim yet unite to assert its truth anyway. In ecclesiastical courts, witnesses to a disputed transaction were also friends and neighbors of the parties involved; their testimony was sufficient to support the truth of a claim of a breached agreement. In both situations, it was easy to find people who based their oaths upon actual knowledge of both the disputed transaction and the parties involved.

But in the king's courts logistics often made it impossible to have friends and neighbors present at Westminster to serve as witnesses, and

---

[11] The discussion that follows is based on Milsom, *Historical Foundations of the Common Law*, pp. 67–68, 247–49. For a detailed examination of the various rules of evidence applicable in local courts, see Henry, *Contracts in the Local Courts of Medieval England*, pp. 11–90.

witnesses local to the forum and with no firsthand knowledge of the agreement had to be found. Inevitably, owing to this sort of practice, the production of secta and wager of law were rendered ineffectual and patently absurd modes of proof. Thus, subject to exceptions,[12] a written document came to be regarded as the only logical means of proving the existence of a covenant and was therefore required if the king's court was to allow the suit to be heard.

Another reason for the proliferation of legal oral agreements in the Middle Ages was that in a predominantly nonliterate culture it was grossly inequitable to require that the legality of an agreement be conditioned upon a written document.[13] For example, if John the Carpenter were to agree to sell his sow to Robin the Reeve, it would be ridiculous to force John and Robin to have some clerk draw up a written document attesting to that agreement when neither man could decipher the significance of the words. In a society which afforded legal status to oral agreements, however, there had to be some objective means to distinguish promises made in earnest from those made in jest. Certain formalities and rituals were performed with the exchange of promises which indicated that a legally binding agreement had been formed.[14]

These rituals ranged in degree of formality. In situations where a great deal rested on performance of the promises, one party might be forced to find sureties or give the other party a piece of valuable property as security. More commonly, though, the bargain would be secured by simpler rituals symbolizing each party's intention to be bound and to perform his promise in good faith. The exchange of a rod or another object, termed a wed or festuca—symbolic objects of security—was one such ritual.[15] Other less elaborate rituals were pledg-

---

[12] The exceptions to this rule have to do with debt agreements and are considered in chapter 3.

[13] For a recent account of the predominantly nonliterate makeup of medieval society, see B. Stock, *The Implications of Literacy*, pp. 13–14.

[14] For examinations of the legal effect of the different formalities used to confirm and bind oral agreements, see Bateson, ed., *Borough Customs*, 2:lxxx–lxxxiii; Henry, *Contracts in the Local Courts of Medieval England*, pp. 202–204, 230–31, 245–46; Pollock and Maitland, *The History of English Law*, 2:185–95. These various formalities indicated to the parties to the bargain and their witnesses that a legal agreement had been formed, and they also served as collateral evidence in a court of law of the existence of that agreement.

[15] See *OED*, s.v. *wed* sb., Obs., 1; for a discussion of the legal definition of wed and festuca and their contractual use, see Pollock and Maitland, *The History of English Law*, 2:185–98, p. 185 n. 2. See also T. F. T. Plucknett, *A Concise History of the Common Law*, 5th ed., pp. 629–31; Henry, *Contracts in the Local Courts of Medieval England*, pp. 202–204, 230–31.

ing one's faith or taking an oath upon a promise, shaking hands and pledging one's faith into the hands of another, or having a drink on the bargain. Not only did these formalities serve as objective legal evidence of the parties' intention to keep their word but also, because they indicated an intention to act in good faith, they provided an ethical impetus for each promisor to maintain his promise. In essence, it was this element of good faith that made oral agreements binding in the fourteenth and fifteenth centuries.

In a nutshell, the moral principle behind English law governing agreements in the later Middle Ages was that every man should act in good faith upon the promises he made. The king's courts, however, required greater proof of the existence of a legally binding agreement before they would force someone to keep his promise. To understand the subtleties of the law of agreements in this period, it is necessary to examine how each court system applied this principle. While in both ecclesiastical and secular courts the law of agreements was based on the same concept, philosophical differences accounted for the divergence in their application of that concept. Ecclesiastical courts, which were concerned with the spiritual implications of breach of promise, fashioned their remedies accordingly. Secular courts, though, were concerned with the economic and social ramifications of breach of promise: potential chaos in the marketplace and potential vengeance in the streets. Thus secular courts constructed remedies that would punish the breacher as well as remunerate the injured party.

Although the theological issues related to the canon law doctrine regarding promises are rather complex, the application of that doctrine by ecclesiastical courts was quite straightforward. Unlike secular courts, where there were several different classes of agreements with different legal rules applicable to each class, in church courts all agreements were treated the same as long as a few simple conditions were met. Therefore, the canon law on agreements and elements of that law in Chaucer's works will be considered first.

Before proceeding further, I must warn that, since both church courts and secular local courts enforced oral agreements to a certain extent, many contracts in Chaucer's poetry (were they not fictitious) could have been actionable in either an ecclesiastical or a secular tribunal. Yet, as will become clearer as the legal policy of each forum is delineated, the canon law doctrine of agreements would have been applicable to most forms of agreements in Chaucer, and he may very well have wanted to make the promises in his poetry carry the implications associated with promises by canon law.

## CANON LAW AGREEMENTS AND CHAUCER'S POETRY

### GENERAL PRINCIPLES OF LAW

Would Chaucer have been familiar with the rules of canon law? While copies of the decretals and their glosses existed in England during this period, would he have had access to those collections of papal decrees and their interpretation? A more likely source for knowledge of aspects of the canon law would have been the commentaries I mentioned previously, like Raymond of Pennaforte's *Summa de casibus de poenitentia et matrimonio*, from which Chaucer translated portions of his *Parson's Tale*; John de Burgh's *Pupilla oculi*; William of Pagula's *Oculus sacerdotis*; and other manuals for the instruction of priests, most of which contained a fair amount of canon law in a digested format.[16] An even better source in which Chaucer could have learned something about the canon law of agreements would have been the day-to-day practice of the church courts in handling contractual matters.[17] Often, though, there were discrepancies between the canon law theory and its application.

The main line of the canonist position, in the *Corpus juris canonici*, can be found in C. 22, q. 5, c. 12 of the *Decretum* of Gratian and the glosses to that section.[18] The canon essentially states that God wishes there to be no difference between oaths and speech; just as there should

[16] As noted in chapter 1, W. A. Pantin has observed that many manuals for instruction of priests were circulating in fourteenth-century England which offered condensed and digested treatments of the major principles of the canon law. See his *The English Church in the Fourteenth Century*, pp. 189–219.

[17] As noted in chapter 1, several recent studies have indicated that the layman in medieval England knew a great deal about the law applied and the procedure followed by the different law courts in medieval England: see Guth, "Enforcing Late-Medieval Law, pp. 80–82; Owen, "Ecclesiastical Jurisdiction in England 1300-1550," pp. 199–221.

[18] Gratian, *Decretum Gratiani seu verius decretorum canonicorum collectanea*, cols. 1334–35. The subject matter of this section is dealt with in a general fashion by G. Le Bras in *The Legacy of the Middle Ages*, ed. C. G. Crump and E. F. Jacob, pp. 352–56. E. W. Kemp, *An Introduction to Canon Law in the Church of England*, pp. 20–23, provides an excellent brief introduction to the canon law on promises. A more comprehensive study of the development of the canon law of agreements in the decretals and the commentaries on them is that of F. Spies, *De l'Observation des simples conventions en droit canonique*, pp. 30–138.

be no perjury with regard to oaths, there should be no lying with regard to speech. From this, Johannes Teutonicus, in his gloss *distantiam*, extrapolated that a nude pact, a promise granted without the benefit of an oath or other formality, could give rise to an action to enforce that promise. According to the gloss, all that seems necessary to be bound by one's promise is the intention to be bound by the words spoken.

By considering simple promises legally as well as morally binding, the canonists abrogated a fundamental tenet of the Roman law of agreements. According to Roman law, a contract had to be clothed in proper legal formulas to be enforceable.[19] Since the canonists were interested more in the preservation of the soul than in the sanctity of contractual formulas, they determined that a man should be legally bound by his promises no matter how scantily they were clad. Innocent IV, however, advocated a less radical doctrine and argued that no action to enforce a breached promise could arise from the violation of a mere nude pact.[20] He ruled, instead, that the breacher of such a pact should be subjected only to disciplinary proceedings in the church court. This position seems to have reflected the minority opinion on the subject, for the majority of the commentators maintained that breach of a nude pact gave rise to its enforcement.

### THE PLEDGE OF FAITH

Despite the consensus of doctrinal opinion arguing for the actionability of nude pacts, there is little evidence to suggest that breach of a mere promise was actionable in English ecclesiastical courts in the fourteenth and fifteenth centuries. It is certain, however, that these courts regularly entertained actions involving violation of promises supported by a pledge of faith or a sworn oath. Such a case was known as *causa fidei laesionis seu perjurii*.[21] Possibly questions concerning the actionability

---

[19] See Fifoot, *History and Sources of the Common Law*, pp. 306–307; Le Bras, *The Legacy of the Middle Ages*, pp. 352–53; Kemp, *An Introduction to Canon Law*, pp. 21–22.

[20] Spies gives a detailed account of Innocent IV's modifications of the nude pact theory and the subsequent rejection of those modifications by later commentators. *De l'Observation des simples conventions*, pp. 40–94.

[21] This section on the jurisdiction of English church courts over actions of breach of faith and perjury is based on the following authorities and studies: W. Lyndwood, *Provinciale (seu constitutiones angliae)*, p. 315, s.vv. *perjurio* and *fidei transgressione*, for legal definition of these terms; Lyndwood's gloss for *perjurio* also contains an example of the accepted formulas to be followed in drawing up a libel for an action of perjury and indicates the facts which the libel must allege, the basic allegation being that the defendant violated a promise based on a pledge of faith or oath; N. Adams and C. Donahue, eds., Introduction, *Select Cases from the Ecclesiastical Courts of the*

of nude pacts never came before the courts. Since, as R. H. Helmholz points out, promises supported by oaths guaranteed the litigant an audience before the court, litigants wisely alleged the existence of an oath in their libel, the document that detailed the charge against the defendant.[22] In other words, the practice of the church courts seems to have been sufficiently well known to have alerted litigants bringing such actions that a pledge of faith or oath was an essential element in any agreement if the church courts were to hear the case.

Ostensibly the ecclesiastical courts had jurisdiction over the violation of any type of agreement as long as it was supported by an oath or pledge of faith. Very early in the development of jurisdictional boundaries of the English ecclesiastical courts, however, the king attempted to restrict their power to hear cases concerning purely secular agreements. In the Constitutions of Clarendon (1164), Henry II prohibited church courts from hearing causes where the underlying transaction was a secular debt. Helmholz reports yearbook dicta following Henry II's edict which indicate that, in the opinion of justices of the king's courts, church courts had no jurisdiction over disputes concerning secular debts. In his studies of fifteenth-century records from various church courts, Helmholz concluded that in reality the church courts heard litigation involving all kinds of sworn promises including actions to recover secular debts where the debt was created by a promise on an oath or pledge of faith.[23] In fact, studies by C. Donahue, Helmholz, and B. L. Woodcock indicate that *fidei laesionis seu perjurii* cases made up a substantial portion of the business of the church courts in the fourteenth and fifteenth centuries.

When someone made a promise upon a pledge of faith, he symbolically gave his faith, his hope of salvation, into the hands of another as security to bind that promise. By extension, when someone swore upon God, God became his surety.[24] The function of oaths and

---

*Province of Canterbury c. 1200–1301*, pp. 96–97; C. Donahue, "Roman Canon Law in the Medieval English Church: Stubbs and Maitland Re-examined," *Michigan Law Review* 72 (1974): 647–716; R. H. Helmholz, "Assumpsit and *Fidei Laesio*," *Law Quarterly Review* 91 (1975): 406–32; B. L. Woodcock, *Medieval Ecclesiastical Courts in the Diocese of Canterbury*, pp. 89–92.

[22] Helmholz, "Assumpsit and *Fidei Laesio*," pp. 408–409.

[23] Ibid., pp. 407–408; R. H. Helmholz, "The Writ of Prohibition to Court Christian Before 1500," *MS* 43 (1981): 297–314.

[24] Adams and Donahue, eds., Introduction, *Select Cases from the Ecclesiastical Courts of the Province of Canterbury c. 1200–1301*, p. 96; Pollock and Maitland, *The History of English Law Before the Time of Edward I*, 2:188–92, 197–98. Maitland pointed out that the synonymous terms "pledge of faith" and "plight of troth" were contractual formalities recognized by ecclesiastical and secular courts as creating legally binding agreements: see F. W. Maitland, ed., *Select Pleas in Manorial and Other Seignorial Courts*, p. 185, s.v. *affidare*; see also Bateson, ed., *Borough Customs*, 2:lxxx.

pledges of faith as forms of security was an extension of an older method used to formalize agreements, that of giving a wed, an object representing valuable security, to bind an agreement. The granting of faith as wed came to be substituted for the passing of an actual object from one party to another. The idea of a transfer of security from the person making the promise into the hands of the person receiving the promise was retained, however, as indicated by the ritual of granting one's faith or troth into the hands of another.

Since pledges of faith and oaths served as symbolic security, when one breached a promise, he lost his security, his hope of salvation, unless he took steps to remedy the default. The church's concern in enforcing breached promises was to provide some means by which the breacher could extricate his soul from the flames of eternal damnation. Although church courts had no coercive legal mechanism like distraint—the threat of confiscation of personal property used by the secular courts to force performance of a violated promise—the threat of excommunication was usually sufficient motivation to spur the recalcitrant into reconsidering and amending his breach.[25]

Apparently, the spiritual ramifications of breach of a promise made upon an oath or pledge of faith were very serious in the late Middle Ages. Fictitious pledges of faith or oaths sworn by characters in the poetry of the period are fraught with moral and symbolic significance. In Middle English works, the pledge of faith takes its form in the swearing, granting, or plighting of "feith," "fey," or "trouth." According to Middle English-Latin glossaries like the *Promptorium parvulorum* and the *Catholicon anglicum*, the Middle English term "trouth" was the equivalent of the Latin *fidelitas* and synonymous with the Middle English "faythe."[26] The Latin for "to plyhten trouthe" was *affidare*, which, according to Maitland, meant "to pledge faith."[27] The *Catholicon anglicum* also gives *disponsare*, "to betroth," as the Latin for "trowtheplight."[28] The possible meanings for these contractual terms are quite broad.

[25] For the forms of punishment at the disposal of the ecclesiastical authorities for the correction of faith breachers, see Woodcock, *Medieval Ecclesiastical Courts in the Diocese of Canterbury*, p. 90; Helmholz, "Assumpsit and *Fidei Laesio*," pp. 411–12.

[26] S. J. H. Herrtage, ed., *Catholicon Anglicum: An English-Latin Wordbook, Dated 1483*, p. 394, s.v. *trowthe*; A. Way, ed., *Promptorium parvulorum sive clericorum*, p. 503, s.v. *trowthe*.

[27] In the glossary to his edition of *Select Pleas in Manorial and Other Seignorial Courts*, p. 185, s.v. *affidare*, Maitland observes that the term as used in those plea rolls meant "to pledge faith" or "troth" and that it was not until the "end of the middle ages that 'affidavit' began to imply an oath." See also Way, ed., *Promptorium parvulorum*, p. 405, s.v. *plyghtyn truthe*.

[28] Herrtage, ed., *Catholicon Anglicum*, p. 394.

Though the plighting of troth was a significant aspect of affiancing, legally the pledge of faith was not exclusively associated with the betrothal or promise to marry. Just as often it secured a simple agreement. For example, in John Gower's *Confessio Amantis*, Mundus persuades two priests of the Temple of Ysis to lure Paulina there so that he can rape her. The priests agree to help him and pledge their troth on the agreement: "And thei here trowthes bothe plyhte, / That thei be nyhte hire scholden wynne. . . ."[29] In *Piers Plowman*, a knight plights his troth on an agreement to protect Piers while he labors to provide food for them both: "By my power, Piers, I pliȝte þee my trouþe / To fulfille þis forward þouȝ I fiȝte sholde."[30] The context of the plight of troth, the words expressed in the promise to which the pledge is attached, indicates whether that pledge effects an espousal or simply seals an agreement.

Most promises in Chaucer's works appear to be based on a pledge of faith, a plight of troth, or a sworn oath. On the simplest level, Chaucer's characters will form some sort of bond with one another, pledge constancy in that bond, and then seal their promises with pledges of faith. In other instances, the pledge of faith will seal material promises. Most commonly, one will vow to be faithful to another and then seal that promise with a pledge of faith. Criseyde affirms a promise of this nature to Troilus after their first evening together at Pandarus's house in book 3 of *Troilus and Criseyde* (lines 1510–12):

> "But herte myn, withouten more speche,
> Beth to me trewe, or ellis were it routhe;
> For I am thyn, by God and by my trouthe!"

The subject of their promise is an abstract rather than a material

---

[29] John Gower, *The Complete Works of John Gower*, ed. G. C. Macaulay, 2:58, lines 822–26.

[30] William Langland, *Piers Plowman: The B Version*, ed. G. Kane and E. T. Donaldson, p. 350, lines 33–35. See also the use of the plight of troth in *The Legend of Thisbe* (*The Legend of Good Women* 776–83); the promise exchanged by Piramus and Thisbe to meet outside the city walls is sealed with plighted troth, but it is obvious from the context that this "covenaunt" (line 790) is not an espousal but merely a promise to meet: "Unto this clyft, as it was wont to be, / Com Piramus, and after com Thysbe, / And plyghten trouthe fully in here fey / That ilke same nyght to stele awey, / And to begile here wardeyns everichon, / And forth out of the cite for to goon; / And, for the feldes ben so brode and wide, / For to mete in o place at o tyde, / They sette mark here metynge sholde be / There kyng Nynus was grave, under a tre, — / For olde payens, that idoles heryed, / Useden tho in feldes to ben beryed, — / And faste by this grave was a welle. / And, shortly of this tale for to telle, / This covenaunt was affermed wonder faste; / And longe hem thoughte that the sonne laste, / That it nere gon under the se adoun" (lines 776–92).

quantity. Yet, by clothing the promise in a pledge of faith, Criseyde secures her promise with a formula that Chaucer's audience would have recognized as important to the validity of a fourteenth-century agreement, a formula that created a moral and, according to canon law, a legal obligation. Of course, the canon law would never consider a promise to enter into an immoral relationship binding. Still it is important to acknowledge Chaucer's care in crafting the terminology of Criseyde's promise; when Criseyde breaches the "trouthe" she pledged on her promise to Troilus, she violates more than an idle promise to become Troilus's lady: she violates a promise vested with the formal trappings of an agreement recognized as binding by fourteenth-century English church courts, and one that Chaucer's audience might have considered too formally endowed to be regarded lightly.[31]

Lovers swear vows of faithfulness in Chaucer's works, and friends swear vows of brotherhood to one another. For example in *The Knight's Tale*, Palamon and Arcite become sworn brothers before their incarceration by Theseus. At the height of their dispute over Emelye, Palamon reminds Arcite of their bond (lines 1129–39):

> "It nere," quod he, "to thee no greet honour
> For to be fals, ne for to be traitour
> To me, that am thy cosyn and thy brother
> Ysworn ful depe, and ech of us til oother,
> That nevere, for to dyen in the peyne,
> Til that the deeth departe shal us tweyne,
> Neither of us in love to hyndre oother,
> Ne in noon oother cas, my leeve brother;
> But that thou sholdest trewely forthren me
> In every cas, as I shal forthren thee, —
> This was thyn ooth, and myn also, certeyn;...."

If one followed to the letter the canonical doctrine concerning agreements, Palamon and Arcite have a binding and actionable agreement. They have based their promise to "forthre" one another upon an oath, the requisite formality for generating the type of agreement recognized by canon law courts as legally binding. This sworn promise, like those sworn between lovers, is not of course of the type technically enforceable in an ecclesiastical court, despite the moral nature of the bond generated by the agreement.

---

[31] In a number of places in book 5, Criseyde's promise to return to Troilus and be faithful to him is referred to as her "trouthe." In his letters to her, Troilus reminds Criseyde of her promise: "'...and though no manere routhe / Commeve yow, yet thynketh on youre trouthe'" (5.1385–86). He also prays that "she wol come ayeyn and holde hire trouthe" (5.1586).

The promises are either to be true in love or to "forthre" one another. Nothing tangible has been agreed to, nor will any party to the agreement receive a tangible benefit for entering into the agreement. Generally, a court must have something material to enforce before it can move to enforce an agreement. Thus the impetus to keep this type of agreement comes not from legal coercion but from the moral integrity of the person making the promise, one which has been laden with the necessary legal baggage to show that the promise is soundly sealed.

The canon law offers ways of understanding promises in the poetry of Chaucer and his contemporaries that no other branch of medieval law can offer. It provides evidence that oral contracts cemented by the pledge of "trouthe" carried a considerable amount of legal force in Chaucer's day. This body of law also provides a means for understanding how an audience cognizant of the implications of binding promises with pledges of faith or "trouthe" might have interpreted promises in poetry. Promises were both morally and spiritually binding when based upon a pledge of "trouthe." What bound the promise according to canon law, though, were not just the ritualistic trappings appended to the promise but the promisor's "entente" — the motive lurking beneath the formality of pledging "trouthe." The connection or rift between promises sealed with pledges of "trouthe" and the actual entente in making the promise gives an indication of a person's spiritual condition.

In the Friar's and the Franklin's tales the promises to which the characters are willing to pledge "trouthe" and faith expose their moral shortcomings. Both poems are concerned with a failure to separate reality from appearances or to read beneath appearances to some more profound "trouthe."[32] Characters in both are obsessed with the letter and miss the spirit. The characters of *The Franklin's Tale* perform promises pledged on nothing more than the image of "trouthe." The summoner of *The Friar's Tale* also fails to perceive that more serious consequences lurk beyond what he sees as the end result of his actions, acquisition of money through the misuse of his power. He does not recognize that his words and actions, the letter of his life, can damn

---

[32] Two perceptive essays that explore the consequences of failing to read beyond the letter of experience and apprehend the spirit of things which rests beneath are J. A. Alford, "Scriptural Testament in *The Canterbury Tales*: The Letter Takes Its Revenge," in D. L. Jeffrey, ed., *Chaucer and Scriptural Tradition*, pp. 197–203; and R. A. Shoaf, "*The Franklin's Tale*: Chaucer and Medusa," *ChauR* 21 (1986): 274–90. While Shoaf's essay on *The Franklin's Tale* is more directly pertinent to my consideration of the canon law in the Friar's and Franklin's tales, Alford's essay on *The Summoner's Tale* also deals to some extent with *The Friar's Tale* and is helpful.

him because of his evil will. In both tales, a misunderstanding of the equivocal power of promissory language and the mechanics of making effective promises exposes the spiritual state of the characters and the tenuous relation of language to will and action.

In *The Friar's Tale*, a summoner entraps himself by the deals he makes and his ignorance of the spirit of the law he claims to enforce by virtue of his office.[33] As he rides with the demonic yeoman, he uses promissory language simply as a tool to attain his greedy goals. In so doing, he ignores what any good ecclesiast should not, that the letter of a promise ought to signify the intent with which it was made. He binds himself in brotherhood to a demon and ultimately damns himself in his delusion that his meager power to summon is greater than the power that can see the intention of the heart.

The summoner's chief, and perhaps only, virtue is that he is quite adept at manipulating legal formulas. In binding himself to brotherhood with the demon yeoman, he makes quite certain that correct contractual formalities are followed. The summoner and the yeoman swear to become brothers upon their "trouthe." Notably the ritualistic swearing of faith in each other's hands is observed (lines 1404–1405):

> Everych in ootheres hand his trouthe leith,
> For to be sworne bretheren til they deye.[34]

The bond becomes more substantial when the summoner further stipulates that they share with one another the winnings each gains from his particular mode of extortion (lines 1526–35):

> "For though thou were the devel Sathanas,
> My trouthe wol I holde to my brother,
> As I am sworn, and ech of us til oother,
> For to be trewe brother in this cas;
> And bothe we goon abouten our purchas.
> Taak thou thy part, what that men wol thee yive,
> And I shal myn; thus may we bothe lyve.
> And if that any of us have moore than oother,

---

[33] For contemporary attitudes toward summoners, their function, and its abuse, see T. Hahn and R. W. Kaeuper, "Text and Context."

[34] The entire transaction is of interest, for Chaucer's use of legal terminology suggests that pledges of faith and "trouthe" were synonymous in his day. The yeoman proposes to the summoner: "'I am unknowen as in this contree; / Of thyn aqueyntance I wolde praye thee, / And eek of bretherhede, if that yow leste. / I have gold and silver in my cheste; / If that thee happe to comen to oure shire, / Al shal be thyn, right as thou wolt desire.' / 'Grantmercy,' quod this somonour, 'by my feith!' / Everych in ootheres hand his trouthe leith, / For to be sworne bretheren til they deye" (*The Friar's Tale* 1397–1405).

> Lat hym be trewe, and parte it with his brother."
> "I graunte," quod the devel, "by my fey."

It is ironic that the devil agrees to this stipulation, "'by my fey.'" He has placed in the summoner's hands as symbolic security not his hopes of salvation but a demon's "fey" — faith that he is eternally damned and his hopes of securing the summoner's damnation.

Though invested with the proper formalities to make it appear legal, canon law would consider the summoner's and yeoman's agreement to be illegal. Certain types of promises were deemed invalid even if they were supported by the requisite oath or pledge of faith. Among promises that fell into this category were those which placed one's soul in jeopardy, those which called for the performance of an illegal act, those which contravened customary law or those which were impossible to perform.[35] A similar list of invalid promises is given in *The Tale of Melibee* (lines 1228–29):

> "For the lawes seyn that 'al bihestes that been dishoneste been of no value'; / and eek if so be that it be inpossible, or may nat goodly be parfourned or kept."

Obviously, the object of the summoner's promise, sharing extorted money, is illegal, and the agreement places the health of the summoner's already sickly soul in jeopardy.

Here Chaucer establishes a situation in which a legally binding agreement exists prima facie. But he has manipulated the circumstances surrounding the making of the agreement so that the legal force of the bond is negated. Thus he places the summoner in a position where he must act on the promise according to his own moral proclivity. The rest of the tale centers on his futile attempts to entrap and extort money from an old widow; in the process, he damns himself. To show fully the extent of the summoner's spiritual depravity, Chaucer plays with a fundamental tenet of the law of agreements: no one is bound by his word unless he intended a binding promise.

Because God could ferret out the intention of the heart, canonists, when formulating a law of agreements, asserted that subjective intention was what determined whether or not a promise was binding.[36] Of course, subjective intention could be considered a factor in determining the validity of a promise only on a spiritual plane. In *The Friar's Tale*, Chaucer constructs a fiction which allows him to examine what

---

[35] See Henrici de Segusio, Cardinalis Hostiensis, *De pactis*, "Quis sit effectus," in *Summa aurea*, col. 372; Spies, *De l'Observation des simples conventions*, p. 58.

[36] Spies, *De l'observation des simples conventions*, p. 41.

happens when words and thought unite to become actionable, and
what befalls someone who fails to explore the often deceptive appearances of words for any hint of the true intention of the speaker.
These issues are first examined in the scene where the yeoman and
summoner come upon the "cartere" whose haycart has become mired
in a ditch. As he unsuccessfully attempts to extricate his cart, he curses
his horse (lines 1544–47):

> "The feend," quod he, "yow fecche, body and bones,
> As ferforthly as evere were ye foled,
> So muche wo as I have with yow tholed!
> The devel have al, bothe hors and cart and hey!"

Upon hearing these words, the opportunistic summoner urges his
companion to take what has been granted him. The devil informs the
summoner that he is unable to do so and then explains the legal
distinction which makes it impossible for him to take what seemed to
have been granted him outright (lines 1556, 1567–68):[37]

> "It is nat his entente, trust me weel."

> "Heere may ye se, myn owene deere brother,
> The carl spak oo thing, but he thoghte another."

This devil proves to be something of a canon lawyer. He has expressed in simple terms what Johannes Teutonicus implied (in his gloss
to *Decretum* C. 22, q. 5, c. 12): an action could arise from a nude pact;
that is, a simple promise is binding as long as it reflects the speaker's
serious intention. This concept is expressed in obverse fashion (in
C. 22, q. 2, c. 3) by the phrase "ream linguam non facit nisi rea mens"
("nothing makes the tongue guilty but a guilty mind").[38] Raymond of
Pennaforte also incorporates the phrase into his treatment of oaths and
perjury in his *Summa*.[39] In both works, the context indicates that one
is not guilty of perjury when he swears to something false that he

---

[37] Two articles deal in part with the idea of "entente" as the motivating factor for the
summoner's fate in the latter portion of this tale: R. H. Passon, " 'Entente in Chaucer's *Friar's Tale*,"
*ChauR* 2 (1968): 166–71, sees "entente" in line 1556 and as it occurs elsewhere throughout the
poem as a term which defines the moral culpability of a character; R. T. Lenaghan, "The Irony of
the *Friar's Tale*," *ChauR* 7 (1973): 281–94, is in agreement. Neither article suggests that "entente"
is used in a contractual sense here; cf. *MED*, s.v. *entente* n., 1 and 7(a).

[38] E. Friedberg, ed., *Corpus juris canonici*, vol. 1, col. 867; the same idea is expressed in C.22,
q. 5, c. 11, entitled "Apud Deum verba nostra non ex ore, sed ex corde procedunt" ("Our words
proceed to God not from the mouth, but from the heart"), in ibid., col. 885.

[39] Raymond de Pennaforte, *Summa Sancti Raymundi de Peniafort de poenitentia, et matrimonio cum glossis Joannis de Friburgo*, bk. 1, "De Iuramento et periurio," p. 96.

actually believes to be true. Perjury is committed only when one swears an oath either to seal a promise which he has no intention of performing or to support the truthfulness of an assertion which he knows is false. Concomitantly, intention determines whether or not a promise is binding. This is where the summoner's obsession with forms of power and profit becomes his undoing. He is snared in the yeoman's trap by the very technicality of law that the yeoman has just explicated: promissory language must correspond to the intention of the speaker, the letter of the utterance must match the spirit in which it is uttered, before it can be acted upon.

In his lust for profit, the summoner fails to comprehend the full import of the reasons precluding the yeoman's acquisition of the carter's possessions. As the two companions continue on their adventure in creative profiteering, they come upon an old "rebekke" from whom the summoner tries to extort an inconsequential sum of money. In his attempt to steal her money, the summoner charges her with several fabricated offenses and then offers to exonerate her for a price.[40] When she claims inability to pay, the summoner sets in motion the legal machinery that will bind him over to the devil: " 'Nay thanne,' quod he, 'the foule feend me fecche / If I th'excuse, though thou shul be spilt' " (lines 1610–11). In response to the greedy summoner's escalating demands, most notably for her pan, the widow commits him and her pan to the devil: " 'Unto the devel blak and rough of hewe / Yeve I thy body and my panne also!' " (lines 1622–23). Before acting on this grant, the devil makes sure his claim is valid by asking, " 'Is this youre wyl in ernest that ye seye?' " (line 1627). The widow affirms her intention to grant him both summoner and pan if the summoner continues with his demands (lines 1628–29). "Ernest," as used by the devil, has particular legal connotations. It is a term which, when used in the context of a mercantile agreement, applies to the giving of a token amount of money, the God's penny or God's *borh*, to indicate one's

---

[40] This exchange is found at lines 1585–1638. See P. Ruggiers, *The Art of the Canterbury Tales*, p. 95; and H. L. Hennedy, "The Friar's Summoner's Dilemma," *ChauR* 5 (1971); 213–17, for two different but equally sensible readings of the event which precipitates the summoner's downfall. Ruggiers argues that it is the widow's grant "in ernest" of the summoner and her pan; Hennedy, p. 214, argues that the summoner's statement (lines 1610–11) that the fiend fetch him if he excuses the widow from his demands places him in a no-win situation once the widow grants him to the devil. He is damned either by his own curse or by the widow's, and his only choice is by which curse he will be sent to hell. Neither reading, however, deals with Chaucer's use of legal terminology in this scene and how it may affect an interpretation.

intention to be bound by an agreement.[41] R. L. Henry notes that "earnest" used as an expression of serious intention to be bound by a bargain was very early on associated with earnest money given to bind an agreement.[42] He suggests that "earnest" used in the context of binding an agreement meant seriousness of intention to be bound whether or not money was actually given. Here "ernest" seems to carry a similar significance, for it indicates the widow's intention to make a binding grant to the devil.

Upon hearing that the widow is "in ernest," the summoner reaffirms his intention to continue with his attempts at extortion. His statement of intention reveals not only his depravity but also his blindness to the "entente" of the widow's words and that of his own rashly made threat (lines 1630–32):

> "Nay, olde stot, that is nat myn entente,"
> Quod this somonour, "for to repente me
> For any thyng that I have had of thee."

When the demon is satisfied that the widow is "in ernest" and that the summoner is unwilling to relax his demands, he feels secure in asserting his claim to the summoner and informs him: " 'Thy body and this panne been myne by right' " (line 1635).[43] The demon bases his claim of right, legal claim or title, to both the summoner and the pan, in part, on the widow's grant "in ernest."

In a strictly legal sense the widow has no right to grant the summoner to the devil. But according to the philosophy of law on which the summoner has based his professional career — that legal technicalities are tools to be used to acquire wealth at the expense of the ignorant and innocent — the demon is justified in taking the summoner on the basis of the widow's bequest. In effect, the summoner has placed himself in the devil's power, and acquiesced to the widow's grant, by refusing to " 'repente me / For any thyng that I have had of thee.' " The summoner's

---

[41] See *MED*, s.v. *ernest* n., 1a and 3a, for examples of "ernest" meaning seriousness of intention; but 3b defines "in ernest" in *The Friar's Tale* (line 1627) as "in fact" or "in reality." Since "in ernest" here refers to the seriousness of a grant, a legal meaning of the phrase seems more appropriate. Henry, *Contracts in the Local Courts of Medieval England*, pp. 227–46, presents an extensive discussion of the function of earnest in contractual transactions in medieval England.

[42] Henry, *Contracts in the Local Courts of Medieval England*, p. 229 n. 3.

[43] *OED*, s.v. *right* sb.¹, II 8, records examples of "right" used to mean legal claim or title dating from *Beowulf* and includes examples contemporaneous with Chaucer. F. A. Themblay, ed., "The Latin-Middle English Glossary 'Medulla Grammatice'" (Ph.D. dissertation, Catholic University of America, 1968), p. 329, records *ius*, meaning "legal claim" or "title," as the Latin equivalent of the Middle English "ryth."

blind determination to extort from the widow regardless of cost and his failure to understand the spirit of the technicalities of law which he so often had manipulated for his own profit are both factors which allow the devil to claim him.

In *The Friar's Tale*, the canon law forms the philosophical and legal basis for the way promises work and are acted upon. Words are binding only when they reflect the will of the speaker. Contractual formalities alone carry no true force. The summoner's failure to comprehend this underscores his sour spirit and makes the poetic justice of the tale's conclusion all the more satisfying.

Dorigen's plights of troth in *The Franklin's Tale* exemplify the complex relation of promise and intention. Dorigen is placed in a position where she must choose between conflicting bonds: the bond of marriage and an agreement to violate that marriage bond by committing adultery. Both bonds are sealed by her pledges of "trouthe." Arveragus counsels Dorigen to keep her "trouthe," her agreement to become Aurelius's lover, giving it preeminence over the sanctity of another agreement, that of their marriage vows.[44] For the Franklin's reading of his own tale, "trouthe" is a central virtue, and Arveragus's actions are eminently virtuous. Yet there is something disturbing about the quality of troth that Arveragus insists Dorigen adhere to — especially since it manifests itself in the betrayal of another pledge of troth. Looking at the two agreements made by Dorigen in light of the canon law and the value canon law places on plights of troth can inform a reading of the poem.

The marriage bond Dorigen and Arveragus form seems to result from a perfect meeting of minds with respect to the kind of relationship they are creating (lines 741–52):

> ...prively she fil of his accord
> To take hym for hir housbonde and hir lord,
> Of swich lordshipe as men han over hir wyves.
> And for to lede the moore in blisse hir lyves,
> Of his free wyl he swoor hire as a knyght

---

[44] The issues raised by this conflict are also examined perceptively by A. T. Gaylord and A. David; see Gaylord, "The Promises in the *Franklin's Tale*," which has a thorough discussion of the canonical sources for the invalidity of Dorigen's "rash" promise. Gaylord also notes (p. 335) that when Aurelius demands that Dorigen keep her promise to him he bases that demand on the fact that she has pledged her troth, not on a legal right to performance of her agreement. Gaylord, however, equates Dorigen's trothplight with the solemnity of the trothplight given when couples are entering into a marriage contract; he does not seem to be aware that the pledge of troth is also used to seal regular covenants; see also A. David, *The Strumpet Muse*, pp. 187–92.

> That nevere in al his lyf he, day ne nyght,
> Ne sholde upon hym take no maistrie
> Agayn hir wyl, ne kithe hire jalousie,
> But hire obeye and folwe hir wyl in al,
> As any lovere to his lady shal,
> Save that the name of soveraynetee,
> That wolde he have for shame of his degree.

Arveragus assents to the terms of the marriage "Of his free wyl."
Dorigen pledges her "trouthe" that she will be his wife (lines 758–59):

> "Sire, I wol be youre humble trewe wyf;
> Have heer my trouthe, til that myn herte breste."

The marriage, such as it is, is made, and "trouthe" is pledged, arguably
with full intention that it will be maintained. The terms of the marriage are agreed to unconditionally and with free will by both Arveragus and Dorigen. She has agreed to be Arveragus's "humble trewe
wyf" (line 758). He has agreed, according to the Franklin's interpretation, to be "Servant in love, and lord in mariage" (line 793), though
lord only in name for the sake of appearances (lines 751–52).

"Trouthe" generally has to do with the quality of honesty or
faithfulness. Here "trouthe" is used in a specific, legal sense for the
security which seals the marriage agreement and manifests the intention to be seriously bound by that agreement. From this specific usage
of the term emanate larger connotations. By consciously placing the
term in a precise legal context, Chaucer can more graphically render
the conflict between the ideal and its application, as well as the
contradictions that emerge when "trouthe" as sign becomes manifested
in various forms of signification.

The "trouthe" that binds Dorigen's marriage to Arveragus is threatened when it comes in conflict with the "trouthe" she swears to Aurelius
when she agrees to become his lover on the condition that he remove
the rocks she fears from the harbor. Once Dorigen knows Aurelius's
"entente" (line 982), his desire for her, she discloses her "entente": "'Ne
shal I nevere been untrewe wyf / In word ne werk'" (lines 984–85).
Then in "pley" she contradicts that statement of "entente" (lines
988–98):

> But after that in pley thus seyde she:
>     "Aurelie," quod she, "by heighe God above,
> Yet wolde I graunte yow to been youre love,
> Syn I yow se so pitously complayne.
> Looke what day that endelong Britayne

> Ye remoeve alle the rokkes, stoon by stoon,
> That they ne lette ship ne boot to goon, —
> I seye, whan ye han maad the coost so clene
> Of rokkes that ther nys no stoon ysene,
> Thanne wol I love yow best of any man,
> Have heer my trouthe, in al that evere I kan."

The distinction between this bond sealed by "trouthe" and the marriage bond is crucial. The first pledge of "trouthe" was a true sign carrying legal force, conveying Dorigen's "entente" to be bound by the terms of her marriage agreement. The second "trouthe" is a false sign rendered legally impotent as a means to secure a promise. According to the contractual ideas we have explored thus far, in making her agreement with Aurelius, Dorigen has given objective manifestation of her intention to adhere to her promise by her pledged "trouthe." But that pledge of "trouthe" is grounded only in the appearance of intention to be bound. She has deprived the sign of value because she made the pledge in jest, not earnest. Not only is the "trouthe" functionally void because pledged in jest, but also it is rendered legally invalid. As in *The Friar's Tale*, agreements made to effect immoral purposes, adultery, for instance, were not binding. For a variety of reasons, then, Dorigen's "trouthe" is a dead letter/sign.

Although Dorigen's bond of "trouthe" is made meaningless by her lack of intention, it is this "trouthe" that Aurelius relies on when he seemingly fulfills his side of the bargain and demands reciprocal performance of the agreement (lines 1319–30):

> "But of my deeth thogh that ye have no routhe,
> Avyseth yow er that ye breke youre trouthe.
> Repenteth yow, for thilke God above,
> Er ye me sleen by cause that I yow love.
> For, madame, wel ye woot what ye han hight —
> Nat that I chalange any thyng of right
> Of yow, my sovereyn lady, but youre grace —
> But in a gardyn yond, at swich a place,
> Ye woot right wel what ye bihighten me;
> And in myn hand youre trouthe plighten ye
> To love me best — God woot, ye seyde so,
> Al be that I unworthy am therto."

While Aurelius has in effect fulfilled an illusory agreement with the illusory performance of that agreement, he seems to expect real performance on the part of Dorigen. He requests that performance not by claiming legal right to it but instead by appealing to the "trouthe" she

placed on her promise to be his lover. Aurelius insists on fulfillment of
Dorigen's promise while underscoring the very element that made the
promise ineffectual—a playful trothplight. In so insisting, he renders
"trouthe" as a sign just as equivocal as the promise she made and his
performance of it. Moreover, it is this false "trouthe" securing Dorigen's
agreement with Aurelius that Arveragus counsels his wife to uphold,
instead of the "trouthe" that knits them together as man and wife.

It is understandable that Aurelius would focus on Dorigen's
"trouthe" as the virtue in jeopardy if she reneges on her bargain. Only
through illusion does he have a chance to win Dorigen. Just as both her
conditional agreement and his fulfillment of that condition were illusory, so, finally, must he rely on an illusory standard of conduct as the
basis for exacting her performance of that agreement. Arveragus's
response is more problematic and is based on a literalist's reading of the
significance of "trouthe." In terms of the two types of "trouthe" in *The
Franklin's Tale*, Arveragus seems concerned with being faithful to the
false one, the impotent sign, rather than to the true one, the fecund
"trouthe" of matrimony. If we look at Arveragus's decision with a cold
legal eye and disregard the ethos of Romance which obviously colors
how we should regard it, then Arveragus's valuation of "trouthe"
appears as confused as that of the other characters. With every agreement in this poem the link between promise and performance is
somehow ruptured. No one's performance matches the quality of
"trouthe" pledged. At the beginning of the poem, Arveragus promises
to be a servant in love but a lord in their marriage. Then he immediately abandons Dorigen, and arguably his service to her and his
lordship over her "To seke in armes worshipe and honour" (line 811).
Consequently, he can provide no guidance for her. The "up so doun"
condition of this pre-Christian world is such that true bonds are treated
lightly while false bonds are granted undue significance. As we have
already seen, Dorigen feels constrained to fulfill a clearly invalid
agreement, one conditioned on the performance of an act that can not
be humanly accomplished. When Aurelius insists that Dorigen uphold
the semblance of her "trouthe," because of the semblance of his
performance of their agreement, Arveragus seizes on that false sign of
"trouthe" and insists that it be honored.

In the end everything works out, but not because of the choice of
"trouthe." Ironically, the outcome is the result of the reliance of all of
the main characters on a false value. Even Aurelius's generous response
to Arveragus's insistence that Dorigen uphold her "trouthe" (his release

of her from her bond) is misdirected. It too embraces a false valuation of "trouthe" — one that further supports the notion that he is blind to the difference between a true and a false sign of "trouthe." Like the summoner, these characters fail to look beneath the letter of the signs they rely upon.

The Franklin seems to view "trouthe" as a central virtue of his tale.[45] Chaucer's tale is more complex, and only on a limited and superficial level can it be taken as dramatizing virtuous codes of behavior like "gentilesse," "trouthe," or equality in marriage. Indeed, Chaucer's point seems to be the opposite of that made by those who see *The Franklin's Tale* as endorsing a standard of conduct: codes of value are ambivalent; signs can deceive one, can seem rich with significance when in fact they are empty. The conflict between true and false "trouthe" in *The Franklin's Tale* suggests how easily man can be led to rely on false distinctions when attempting moral judgments and how dangerous it is to take the literal level as absolute; there is always a chance of a rift between signifier and signified that renders any meaning one wants to extract from them indeterminate.

The canon law of agreements provides an important perspective for determining the significance of promises and formalities used to seal promises in the Friar's and the Franklin's tales. Promises were taken quite seriously by church courts, and breached promises carried serious consequences. The promises in Chaucer's poetry do more than merely carry forward the plot. Because the canon law of agreements invested promises with a considerable amount of spiritual significance, Chaucer could use promissory language validated by that law to explore a crucial concern of his poetry — the power of language and how it can both mirror and mask the soul. In both *The Friar's Tale* and *The Franklin's Tale*, the promises that characters make expose the condition of their souls. In *The Friar's Tale*, a summoner fails to realize that an evil heart and wicked intention may lead to damnation. In *The Franklin's Tale*, characters consider only the most superficial level of language and neglect to look beyond the surface of their words for signs that their promises and the "trouthe" sealing them may be based upon something substantial. The use of language as problematized by the prom-

---

[45] See Burrow, *A Reading of* Sir Gawain and the Green Knight, p. 25; M. R. Golding "The Importance of Keeping 'Trouthe' in the *Franklin's Tale*," *MÆ* 39 (1970): 306–12; Golding's article takes Burrow's suggestion regarding the importance of "trouthe" in the tale and expands and modifies Burrow's conclusions, arguing that Burrow is too rigid in advocating that the entire tale exemplifies the ideal of "trouthe."

ises in these tales becomes a crucial moral issue. Language for Chaucer is a powerful and dangerous tool, one that must be used with care because the consequences extend beyond any earthly hardship to those ultimately affecting the soul.

## MARRIAGE AGREEMENTS AND CLANDESTINE MARRIAGE IN *TROILUS AND CRISEYDE*

In the fourteenth and fifteenth centuries, English ecclesiastical courts dealt with agreements far more significant than those sealed simply by pledges of faith: agreements giving rise to espousals or marriages. By far the most controversial disputes regarding marriage agreements for church courts, as well as for Chaucerians, were those concerning a special species of the agreement: disputes over the question of the validity of an existent but secretly formed marriage. Marriages of this sort were commonly referred to as clandestine. An examination of the canonical theory and practice concerning marriage agreements and especially those forming clandestine marriages is a natural extension of any examination of contractual principles observed by church courts in England.

Unlike *fidei laesionis seu perjurii* cases, where church court jurisdiction was based on the presence of an oath sworn to seal an agreement, jurisdiction over marriage agreements was based on the sacramental nature of the agreement. In other words, the jurisdiction was founded on the agreement itself: the fact that promises to marry now or in the future had been exchanged, rather than just that pledges of faith or oaths had been given to secure the promises. At its most basic level the theory behind the church's jurisdiction over both forms of agreement was probably the same: a person is morally bound by the promises made. In marriage agreements, however, the church could base jurisdiction on the exchange of promises rather than a subsidiary element of the agreement, the security that was pledged.

Whether Troilus and Criseyde form a clandestine marriage — that is, a legally binding marriage entered into without benefit of priest and sacrament — is a vexed question in Chaucer criticism.[46] Critics who

---

[46] At least three writers have argued in favor of the possibility that Chaucer may have intended to suggest that a clandestine marriage had taken place between Troilus and Criseyde in book 3: J. Maguire, "The Clandestine Marriage of Troilus and Criseyde," *ChauR* 8 (1974): 262–78; H. A. Kelly, "Clandestine Marriage and Chaucer's 'Troilus,'" in J. Leyerle, ed., *Marriage in the Middle Ages, Viator* 4 (1973); 435–57 (the substance of this article is contained in Kelly, *Love and*

argue that the lovers' relationship is not adulterous rely on the fact that canon law made it relatively easy to enter into a legitimate marriage without resorting to church-administered ritual.[47] To create an indissoluble marriage, the man and the woman simply had to exchange vows indicating their intention to become husband and wife.[48]

Of proponents of the clandestine marriage theory in *Troilus and Criseyde*, H. A. Kelly most persuasively shows how knowledge of canon law of marriage might help critics. Through extensive analysis of the essential decretals defining canon law for marriage, he carefully argues for the possibility that Troilus and Criseyde's words and actions satisfy canon law requirements for a clandestine marriage. Kelly's findings help resolve a troubling crux: while the love between Troilus and Criseyde is apparently adulterous, the poem hints that there is something noble and refined to it.[49] But where others have merely detected hints of a higher love, Kelly argues from the canon law authority for a legitimate marriage and Chaucer's elevation of the dishonorable love of Boccaccio's lovers to one both honorable and virtuous. For Kelly, book 3 of *Troilus and Criseyde* celebrates matrimonial, not adulterous, love. But would Chaucer's audience have recognized that a clandestine

---

*Marriage in the Age of Chaucer*, pp. 163–244); K. P. Wentersdorf, "Some Observations on the Concept of Clandestine Marriage in *Troilus and Criseyde*," *ChauR* 15 (1980): 101–26. Some reviewers of Kelly's book found his argument about clandestine marriage in *Troilus and Criseyde* either unconvincing or overstated; see the reviews by L. K. Shook in *Speculum* 52 (1977), 701–702; D. Brewer in *RES* 28 (1977): 194–97; and R. T. Davies in *MLR* 73 (1978): 871–74. C. Wood has also taken issue with this reading of Troilus and Criseyde's relationship; see his *The Elements of Chaucer's* Troilus, p. 172 n. 7, p. 190 n. 37.

[47] My study of the canon law of marriage and the arguments I make about the question of the plausibility of a clandestine marriage between Troilus and Criseyde are based on several studies of the law dealing with marriage contracts in medieval England: M. M. Sheehan, "The Formation and Stability of Marriage in Fourteenth-Century England: Evidence of an Ely Register," *MS* 33 (1971); 228–63; R. H. Helmholz, *Marriage Litigation in Medieval England*; Adams and Donahue, eds., Introduction, *Select Cases from the Ecclesiastical Courts of the Province of Canterbury c. 1200–1301*, pp. 81–84; C. Donahue, "The Policy of Alexander the Third's Consent Theory of Marriage," in S. Kuttner, ed., *Proceedings of the Fourth International Congress of Medieval Canon Law*, pp. 251–81; M. Ingram, "Spousals Litigation in the English Ecclesiastical Courts c. 1350–1640," in R. B. Outhwaite, ed., *Marriage and Society: Studies in the Social History of Marriage*, pp. 35–57. I have also used the older but still valuable A. Esmein, *Le Mariage in droit canonique*, 2d ed., rev. R. Génestal, 1:151–226.

[48] The general form of the marriage contract is described in *Consuetudines diversarum curiarum* in H. G. Richardson and G. O. Sayles, eds., *Select Cases of Procedure Without Writ Under Henry III*, pp. cxcvii–cxcviii; this brief Latin tract summarizes the procedural steps to be followed for several types of cases in ecclesiastical courts; among the cases considered is one dealing with the marriage contract. To form a valid marriage, commonly the man stated that he took the woman as his wife and pledged his faith to seal the promise. Likewise the woman stated that she took the man as her husband and also pledged her faith.

[49] Kelly, *Love and Marriage in the Age of Chaucer*, pp. 218–19, 225.

marriage had been formed by the words and actions of the two lovers?[50] Would the church courts of Chaucer's day have considered their vows sufficient to create a clandestine marriage?[51]

To make a marriage absolutely licit in the eyes of the church, a public ceremony conducted by a priest and preceded by publication of banns was required.[52] But marriages formed without adhering to any of these requirements were also recognized by the church as binding and valid.[53] [These were termed clandestine marriages—a designation which applied whether or not the marriages were contracted in secret.] Although they were considered legitimate, clandestine marriages were not encouraged by the Church. In fact, those who chose to disregard the proper procedure by marrying in this fashion were assigned penance and threatened with excommunication if the marriage was not sanctified by church ritual. The church recognized two ways of forming a clandestine marriage. The first was by exchanging vows of present consent (*verba de presenti*): "I take you for my husband/wife and pledge my faith thereto." The second was through the exchange of words of future consent (*verba de futuro*), generally words of affiance, such as, "I will take you for my husband/wife." If promises to marry in

---

[50] Kelly and others who argue for Troilus's clandestine marriage to Criseyde think that Chaucer's audience would have known the rules governing clandestine marriages and recognized the formation of one in the poem; see ibid., p. 230; Maguire, "The Clandestine Marriage of Troilus and Criseyde," pp. 275–76; Wentersdorf, "Some Observations on the Concept of Clandestine Marriage in *Troilus and Criseyde*," pp. 102, 122.

[51] Kelly's focus is on the law as expressed by the canon law texts, not on its application by the church courts. But see Kelly's chapter "Ecclesiastical Precept and Lay Observance" in *Love and Marriage in the Age of Chaucer*, pp. 163–76; see also Wentersdorf, "Some Observations on the Concept of Clandestine Marriage in *Troilus and Criseyde*," pp. 103–11. Kelly has made a study of the records of the consistory court in Rochester printed in C. Johnson, ed., *Registrum Hamonis Hethe, Diocesis Roffensis*, 2:911–1043; see Kelly, *Love and Marriage in the Age of Chaucer*, pp. 169–70. These records are from the Act Book of Bishop Sheppy. But because they contain merely summaries of the facts and outcome of cases brought before the court, the cases dealing with clandestine marriage therein are of little use in determining what sort of promissory language was alleged to have been exchanged between parties to a disputed marriage. For the actual language of the marriage vows, one must consult records containing depositions of witnesses to putative marriages like those found in the Selden Society edition of thirteenth-century records from Canterbury ecclesiastical courts. These records give evidence about what words were exchanged between the man and woman.

[52] See X.4, 3, c. 3 in Friedburg, ed., *Corpus juris canonici*, vol. 2, col. 679–80; church rules in England concerning clandestine marriage were published in Archbishop Stratford's Provincial Constitution, *Humana concupiscentia*, text and gloss in Lyndwood, *Provinciale*, pp. 274–77.

[53] Sheehan, "The Formation and Stability of Marriage in Fourteenth-Century England," pp. 234–56; Helmholz, *Marriage Litigation in Medieval England*, p. 27.

the future were followed by sexual intercourse, then a valid marriage resulted.[54]

Kelly and others argue that the various vows and plights of troth exchanged between Troilus and Criseyde constitute at the very least an exchange of future consent to marry, and consent coupled with the consummation of their love in book 3 makes them validly married. But, as I indicate in my earlier discussion of the legal weight of the troth-plight, more is required to bind an agreement than the mere existence of a plight of troth. For a valid marriage between Troilus and Criseyde to have occurred, they must have intended to become married and not just to engage in sexual activity.

Once Troilus has gained access to Criseyde's chamber, they exchange a number of oaths. Are those oaths and the promises which they seal sufficient to convey to the lovers, and to Chaucer's audience for that matter, an intention to marry? Early in the scene, Troilus swoons. Criseyde attempts to revive him with assurances that she is no longer angry with him for his unfounded jealousy about her rumored liaison with Horaste, a rumor created by Pandarus as part of his machinations to bring Troilus and Criseyde together (3.1109–11):

> And therwithal she swor hym in his ere,
> "Iwys, my deere herte, I am nought wroth,
> Have here my trouthe!" and many an other oth; . . . .

Her "trouthe" and the many other oaths are simply sworn on the proposition that she is no longer angry at Troilus for his jealousy. At this point, her oaths are not attached to any words of matrimony. Later she extracts several oaths from Troilus (3.1142–45):

> Soone after this, though it no nede were,
> Whan she swiche othes as hire leste devyse
> Hadde of hym take, hire thoughte tho no fere,
> Ne cause ek non, to bidde hym thennes rise.

The text offers no clue to the terms of the promises that these oaths secure. Criseyde seems to be simply toying with Troilus by having him swear to whatever promise she whimsically devises. Since those promises are ambiguous, and she apparently feels no pressing reason to require them of Troilus, they probably do not carry serious consequences.

---

[54] For the rationale behind the development of these rules, see Helmholz, *Marriage Litigation in Medieval England*, pp. 26–31; Donahue, "The Policy of Alexander the Third's Consent Theory of Marriage," pp. 251–81, and the sources cited therein.

Not all of their vows are so obscure, though. In fact, Troilus's next vow is quite precise (3.1296–99):

> "For certes, fresshe wommanliche wif,
> This dar I seye, that trouth and diligence,
> That shal ye fynden in me al my life;
> N'y wol nat, certein, breken youre defence;...."

Troilus promises to be a true and faithful lover for the rest of his life and also assures her that he will not violate the terms she sets for their relationship. Criseyde responds by accepting him as her knight: "'Welcome, my knyght, my pees, my suffisaunce!'" (3.1309). Following the literal language of their vows, he has promised to be faithful, and she claims him for her knight. On their face, these do not appear to be words of matrimony.

The oaths exchanged before the consummation of their love are fairly vague about the nature of the relationship Troilus and Criseyde are creating. The parting promises are also frustrating in their ambiguity. When they must separate at dawn, Criseyde reconfirms that she is Troilus's with these words (3.1510–12):

> "But herte myn, withouten more speche,
> Beth to me trewe, or ellis were it routhe;
> For I am thyn, by God and by my trouthe!"

How is she Troilus's? The words of the vows provide little in the way of answer. The oaths Troilus and Criseyde exchange are vague and unspecific. At best they seem to amount to promises to be faithful.

By predicating his arguments on the authority of Pope Alexander III's decree on the indissolubility of unconsummated marriages, *licet praeter solitum*, Kelly is able to interpret Troilus and Criseyde's vows as promises to marry.[55] According to that decree, the recitation of special

---

[55] Kelly, *Love and Marriage in the Age of Chaucer*, pp. 199, 229–30; Kelly cites Alexander III's decree, found at X.4, 4, c. 3, in Friedburg, ed., *Corpus juris canonici*, vol. 2, col. 680–81, which essentially states that words as simple and ambiguous as "Ego te accipio in meum" spoken by the woman and "Ego te accipio in meam" spoken by the man are sufficient to form an indissoluble marriage. Esmein, *Le Mariage en droit canonique*, pp. 187–88, commenting on the vagueness of such language, argues that various communities did use specific formulaic expressions which made clear the matrimonial intent of the parties. This is borne out by the evidence provided by extant depositions of witnesses to putative marriages printed in the selection of documents in Adams and Donahue, eds., *Select Cases from the Ecclesiastical Courts of the Province of Canterbury, c. 1200–1301*; and in the depositions from trials in the Bishop's Court in Chester in F. J. Furnivall, ed., *Child-Marriages, Divorces, and Ratifications*. While most of the documents that Furnivall edits date from after the Reformation, Donahue, "The Policy of Alexander the Third's Consent Theory of Marriage," p. 260, considers them useful and much neglected sources for study of medieval English church law on marriage litigation.

formulas was not required to form a marriage. Words as vague as "I take you as mine" exchanged between parties could conceivably create a valid marriage if the requisite consent was embodied in them by the parties making the vows. Kelly illustrates this point of law, however, with a rather problematic example. He proposes that, when the clerk Aleyn bids farewell to Malyne after their night of fornication in *The Reeve's Tale*, "'But everemo, wher so I go or ryde, / I is thyn awen clerk, swa have I seel!'" (lines 4238–39), if she had replied in kind, a clandestine marriage would have resulted. This line of argument implies that Aleyn's words do indeed reflect his intention to marry Malyne and ignores the fact that Aleyn "swived" her throughout the previous night, not out of some affection for her but simply to satisfy his blind lust and desire to exact revenge on her father for tricking him. If we take seriously Kelly's conclusions about Aleyn's remarks, Aleyn's feelings must have changed radically for him to dare utter words that would place him so precariously close to spending the rest of his life with her as his wife. But no evidence exists to support such a change of heart.

A similar analysis of the application of the law prompts Kelly to view Criseyde's "Welcome my knyght" in response to Troilus's kiss as the equivalent of "I take you as mine."[56] According to Kelly, these words reflect the requisite intention to form a clandestine marriage when coupled with Troilus's thanks to Cupid, Venus, and Hymen for his good fortune in love before he pledges eternal devotion to Criseyde.[57] For Kelly, this reference to Hymen is sufficient to show Troilus's marital intention. Would canon law courts have applied the law the same way that Kelly has and found marital intention when that intention was only vaguely hinted at in the words of the couple's promises? It may be useful to consider an actual case involving a much more explicit suggestion of marital intention in which the court nonetheless ruled no clandestine marriage existed. *Cursted* v. *Tournour*, a 1421 Canterbury case, suggests that mere talk about marriage plus sexual relations was not enough to create a clandestine marriage at law.[58] Robert Cursted had proposed to Alice Tournour that if she would give him her lands he

---

[56] Kelly, *Love and Marriage in the Age of Chaucer*, p. 230.

[57] "Than seyde he thus, 'O Love, O Charite! / Thi moder ek, Citherea the swete, / After thiself next heried be she, / Venus mene I, the wel-willy planete! / And next that, Imeneus, I the grete; / For nevere man was to yow goddes holde / As I, which ye han brought fro cares colde'" (3.1254–60). See Kelly, pp. 229, 239.

[58] Helmholz, *Marriage Litigation in Medieval England*, p. 196; the case is at p. 198.

wished to marry her.[59] She replied that she was not willing to give him her lands, but afterward they engaged in sexual intercourse. The court held that no marriage had been created between the two. While Robert's words mentioned marriage, they only stated a condition under which he would be willing to marry Alice. This condition was not fulfilled despite their sexual congress. Troilus's apostrophe to "Imeneus" follows one to Cupid and Venus; the god of marriage is mentioned as an afterthought in a speech praising two gods of sexual love for the success they have given him in love. One invocation of Hymen seems slim evidence of an intention to marry. That the god is praised along with Venus and Cupid may suggest, however, Troilus's confusion about the nature of the love that defines his relationship with Criseyde.

The closest either Troilus or Criseyde comes to pronouncing words similar to "I take you as mine" is when they are about to leave one another after their first night together. Before Troilus goes, Criseyde begs, "'Beth to me trewe,'" and claims, "'For I am thyn, by God and by my trouthe!'" (3.1511-12). Whether these words disclose her understanding that they became married during the previous night, and are a retroactive expression of marital intention, is difficult to determine. Just a few moments earlier she also attested (3.1495-98)

> "That first shal Phebus fallen fro his spere,
> And everich egle ben the dowves feere,
> And everi roche out of his place sterte,
> Er Troilus out of Criseydes herte."

It certainly takes something much less than the world turning "up so doun" for Troilus to lose to Diomede his place in Criseyde's heart. Her words seem nothing more than a strong expression of undying love and do not indicate that she considered herself bound to Troilus in matrimony.

One problem with Kelly's interpretation of canon law is that it permits a case for clandestine marriage to be made out of almost any illicit sexual relationship. Thus had Malyne shouted out "and I is thy awen lady" to the departing Aleyn's "I is thy awen clerk," Symkyn could have been cursed with a clerk for a son-in-law. Were the law as broad as Kelly posits it, then words blurted out during the heated moments of

---

[59] The salient details in the record are as follows: Robert asked Alice, "'Alicia es tu in voluntate dandi mihi terras tuas et ego volo facere sicut vir faceret uxori sue?' Que respondebat quod nollet alienare terras suas. Tamen carnaliter cognovit eandem, et postea idem Robertus contraxit cum Leticia Bett' de eadem per verba de presenti."

virtually any youthful indiscretion would have resulted in the instantaneous marriage of young couples throughout Chaucer's England. Yet, as examinations of ecclesiastical court records reveal, this was hardly the case. In their studies of matrimonial disputes in English church courts, Sheehan and Helmholz found that clear matrimonial intent had to be expressed in the words exchanged between parties for a contested clandestine marriage to be held valid.[60] Generally, this had to be corroborated by the testimony of two witnesses.[61] The depositions of witnesses in clandestine marriage causes support Sheehan's and Helmholz's findings.[62]

Much was at stake in a disputed clandestine marriage proceeding: rights to property hung in balance, and the outcome of the case often determined whether subsequent marriage contracts or marriages were valid. Therefore, witnesses to a purported clandestine marriage had to be quite explicit in their description of the clandestine marriage ceremony.[63] They not only had to recall the terms of the agreement made between the couple but often gave detailed descriptions of setting. Trial records regarding the disputed clandestine marriage of William Smith and Alice Dolling illustrate the specificity of the testimony given in causes supporting or disputing the existence of a clandestine marriage.[64] The records also show the degree of proof that courts required before they would decide that an actual marriage existed.

On July 10, 1271, Alice Dolling, of Winterbourne Stoke, appeared before the consistory court of the bishop of Salisbury claiming that William Smith had married her and asking the court to adjudge him to be her husband. William denied the claim. Alice then produced three female witnesses who testified that they were present at the marriage which took place on the Feast Day of Saint Stephen at Christmas two years before (December 26, 1268). They also described the words of the marriage agreement and the clothes both Alice and William wore. One of the ladies, Cecilia, swore that William pledged his faith into Alice's

---

[60] Sheehan, "The Formation and Stability of Marriage in Fourteenth-Century England," pp. 237–39; Helmholz, *Marriage Litigation in Medieval England*, pp. 40–47, 195–99; see also Donahue, "The Policy of Alexander the Third's Consent Theory of Marriage," pp. 260–70.

[61] Adams and Donahue, eds., Introduction, *Select Cases from the Ecclesiastical Court of the Province of Canterbury, c. 1200–1301*, p. 82.

[62] See the cases edited by Adams and Donahue in ibid. and those edited by Furnivall in *Child-Marriages, Divorces, and Ratifications*.

[63] Adams and Donahue, eds., Introduction, *Select Cases from the Ecclesiastical Court of the Province of Canterbury, c. 1200–1301*, p. 83.

[64] Ibid., pp. 127–37.

hands and said, "I William will have you Alice as wife for as long as we both shall live and to this I give you my faith."[65] Alice responded in kind: "I Alice will have you as husband and to this I give you my faith." Cecilia then went on to detail the circumstances surrounding the exchange of promises. When asked whether she had actually seen them consummating (*commiscentes*) the marriage after the exchange of words of future consent, Cecilia said that she had not but that she had seen them naked in bed. The account by Cecilia is typical of the depositions of the witnesses in this cause. While some may not have been as specific as Cecilia in the description of the clothing worn, or perhaps left out details in describing some of the other physical circumstances of the marriage, all accounts were quite specific about the terms of the vows exchanged between the couple. That specificity proved unfortunate to Alice's cause.

On October 26, William again appeared before the court and admitted having sexual intercourse with Alice but denied that they had exchanged vows to marry. Instead he claimed that he was out of town on the day of the alleged marriage. Alice brought four witnesses to testify otherwise. William countered by calling in ten men to testify that he was nowhere near the house on the day Alice claimed the marriage took place. From the ninth hour of that day until noon of the next, William was four miles away in Bulford serving as butler at a feast of the parish guild conveniently held at his mother's house. But because William could not produce those ten men for reexamination on February 11, 1272, when it came time for the court to decide the case on May 11, William was adjudged Alice's husband.

On appeal to the court of Canterbury, William was more successful. The examiners of the court reviewed the depositions of the case and annulled the Salisbury court's ruling. The reasons for annulling the prior decision suggest precisely how difficult it was to prove a clandestine marriage and how carefully formed it had to be to hold up under the scrutiny of a court. The examiners of the court found discrepancies in the testimony of Alice's witnesses concerning the wording of the marriage vows. Two witnesses—Cecilia was one—testified about a contract *per verba de futuro*. The third witness testified that the man spoke *per verba de presenti*, while Alice's words were *de*

---

[65] Cecilia's deposition is in ibid., pp. 129–30. The actual language of the records is, of course, in Latin. William vowed: "Ego Willelmus habebo te Aliciam in uxorem quamdiu ambo vixerimus et ad hoc do tibi fidem meum." Alice responded: "Et ego Alicia habebo te in virum et ad hoc do tibi fidem meam." See p. 129.

*futuro*. Thus, at least according to the third witness, there was no marriage agreement at all; the vows the two exchanged did not match.[66]

The depositions in Alice's case and those studied by Helmholz, Sheehan, and Adams and Donahue show the importance of the wording of vows exchanged between the couple; witnesses were asked to recite, as precisely as memory would allow, those words because the language of the vows determined whether or not a marriage had been formed. Courts were reluctant to find clandestine marriages unless clear matrimonial intent had been expressed in the promises of both parties to the putative marriage.

Proponents of the clandestine marriage theory suggest that the trothplights exchanged by Troilus and Criseyde on the night they consummate their love convey matrimonial intent.[67] That intent, they argue, is reinforced by the playful exchange of rings before the lovers separate the next morning (3.1366–69):

> Soone after this they spake of sondry thynges,
> As fel to purpos of this aventure,
> And pleyinge entrechaungeden hire rynges,
> Of whiche I kan nought tellen no scripture; . . . .

After an extensive consideration of the functional role of the ring exchange in medieval marriages in law and literature, Kelly finds a number of examples where an exchange of rings signifies matrimonial intent.[68] He suggests that the context in which the exchange of rings occurs in *Troilus* warrants a similar interpretation:

> The exchange of rings is postponed until after Troilus's initial pledge of fidelity and after they have spoken "of sondry thynges / As fel to purpos of this aventure," and it is described not as part of a solemn covenant but as a game. . . . We may ascribe this to Chaucer's effort to keep the presumption of their marriage from becoming too obvious. But we can hardly forget Troilus's invocation of the God of Marriage and his promise of eternal fidelity; nor can we suppose that they are not in deadly earnest about the love and loyalty normally signified by such exchanges.[69]

Perhaps the exchange of rings signified the lovers' intention to be faithful to one another, but as lovers, not as husband and wife. Neither the trothplights nor the exchange of rings is enough to show marital

---

[66] The findings of the examiners appear in ibid., pp. 134–36.
[67] Maguire, "The Clandestine Marriage of Troilus and Criseyde," p. 272; Kelly, *Love and Marriage in the Age of Chaucer*, pp. 225–29, 238–39.
[68] Kelly, *Love and Marriage in the Age of Chaucer*, pp. 234–42.
[69] Ibid., pp. 238–29.

intention, since the trothplight is an element in the exchange of marriage vows subordinate to the actual promises to marry. It is the security which assures the fulfillment of the vows and seals them. The parties pledge their faith that the terms of the promises will be kept. What defines the kind of bargain entered into are the words indicating marital intent ("I take you as my wife/husband"), not the trothplights. As ecclesiastical court records indicate, the words the courts looked to in determining whether or not a marriage had been made were the functional terms defining the relationship, not the subsidiary terms securing the promises. These were the only words that could possibly define the nature of the contract for the court. Only the words of promise could generate and explicitly publish a licit marriage agreement, rather than an invalid agreement to cohabitate outside the bond of matrimony. As for the exchange of rings, that act performed in play, in "game" and not in "ernest," argues against, not for, the possibility that Troilus and Criseyde intended anything as serious as a marriage to result from their words and actions.

Laymen who wanted to marry were well aware of what was necessary to form a valid marriage outside the church. In view of the evidence presented by court records, it is inaccurate to assert that clandestine marriages were formed without resorting to formalities. Many such marriages were public acts performed to satisfy the couple that they had formed a valid marriage, assure them of witnesses, and make it possible for the marriage to be generally known in the neighborhood.[70] Accordingly, if Chaucer's audience knew anything about clandestine marriages, they also were aware of the care which had to be taken in the wording of the exchange of vows. Nothing suggests that the trothplights and playful exchanges of rings in *Troilus and Criseyde* are more than teasing suggestions of marital intent. While Troilus and Criseyde are, of course, pagans, Chaucer's audience would surely have considered them married or unmarried in light of fourteenth-century views on what words and rituals created a marriage in the eyes of church courts. No church court would have declared Troilus and Criseyde married on the evidence presented in the poem.

Elsewhere Chaucer distinguishes between situations where the man and woman are married and those where they enter into an affair with no intention of becoming married. For example, in *The Legend of*

---

[70] Sheehan, "The Formation and Stability of Marriage in Fourteenth-Century England," pp. 244–47; Helmholz, *Marriage Litigation in Medieval England*, pp. 27–31; Ingram, "Spousals Litigation in the English Ecclesiastical Courts c. 1350–1640," p. 46.

*Good Women*, Chaucer clearly specifies when a marriage has taken place; his pagans swear vows to one another like those exchanged when a clandestine marriage is created. In the legend of Dido, promises of future consent exchanged between Dido and Aeneas are followed by coitus, thus effecting what would have looked like a clandestine marriage to Chaucer's audience. There is evidence in the text of the poem that Chaucer considered that a valid marriage had been formed (lines 1232–39):

> For there hath Eneas ykneled so,
> And told hire al his herte and al his wo,
> And swore so depe to hire to be trewe,
> For wel or wo, and chaunge hire for no newe,
> And as a fals lovere so wel can pleyne,
> That sely Dido rewede on his peyne,
> And toke hym for husbonde, and becom his wyf
> For everemo, whil that hem laste lyf.[71]

In the legends of Medea, Ariadne, and Phyllis, future promises of marriage are exchanged. In the legends of Medea and Phyllis, coitus follows.[72] In these two legends, as well as in *The Parliament of Fowls*, *The Knight's Tale*, and *The Franklin's Tale*, marriage is often the result of diligent service to a lady, but it does not necessarily follow that Chaucer considered the mere exchange of simple vows of fidelity equivalent to marriage vows in situations where sexual activity followed.

Instead, it seems that Chaucer carefully differentiated between married and unmarried relationships and that he used terminology associated with canonically valid marriage contracts to indicate when a marriage agreement had been formed. Furthermore, Chaucer's use of the pledge of faith or plight of troth to bind agreements suggests that he was aware that, although this ritual was essential for the creation of a legally binding agreement, it was merely a subsidiary component to the agreement, one subordinate to the main element of any legal

---

[71] Kelly's consideration of the marriage contract in *The Legend of Good Women* seems much more convincing than that of *Troilus and Criseyde*. In the *Legend*, the contractual language is much clearer; see Kelly, *Love and Marriage in the Age of Chaucer*, pp. 202–16. Cf. the following lines in *The Legend of Dido*: "'And, so ye wole me now to wive take, / As ye han sworn, thanne wol I yeve yow leve / To slen me with youre swerd now sone at eve! / For thanne yit shal I deyen as youre wif'" (lines 1319–22). Cf. *The House of Fame* 1.243–324.

[72] *The Legend of Medea* 1635–44, *The Legend of Phyllis* 2465–69, *The Legend of Ariadne* 2089–2108.

agreement, the promises. Considering that promises in Chaucer's work are almost always bound by some form of pledge of faith, it seems logical to conclude that Chaucer used that formality fully intending its various levels of meaning to be understood even in situations where neither the legal nor the moral level is explicitly mentioned.

# 3

## Chaucer and
## the Secular Law
## of Agreements

### Introduction to the Law

As we have seen, the fundamental idea behind the canon law and the secular law of agreements was the same: "Biheste is dette." According to available evidence, ecclesiastical, manor, borough, and city courts enforced oral agreements made in good faith on the condition that certain legal formalities were observed. Generally the local courts required only what ecclesiastical courts required — a promise supported by an oath or pledge of faith. Often the pledge of faith or oath would be coupled with another ritual like the exchange of a handshake, drink, or wed. The *Liber albus* and other sources indicate that oral agreements were taken as binding in the city courts of London during the fourteenth century.

The major difference between the ecclesiastical and secular courts' policy toward oral agreements was not in enforcement but in philosophy. Ecclesiastical courts based their jurisdiction on violation of a pledge of faith or sworn oath. Their concern was to mend the breach and save the soul of the violator by coercing enforcement of the agreement. Secular courts were more pragmatic in enforcing oral agreements. They made sure that an injured party was compensated for injury incurred by virtue of a violated promise or that the promise was fulfilled. Their concern was to maintain the economic status quo and civil order by ensuring that citizens were honest in their dealings with one another.

With the exception of the king's courts then, "Biheste is dette" seems to have been a fundamental rule of the law of agreements. This exception, though, is important to note because those who have set about to attempt the reconstruction of the history of the development of the English law of contracts have focused predominantly on the practice of the king's courts regarding agreements and contracts.[1]

The royal courts had more rigid requirements of proof than local courts in matters involving agreements. Like local courts, royal courts would hear actions on debt agreements without requiring written proof. In debt cases that came before the king's courts, however, where the plaintiff presented no documentary proof of the transaction, he had to satisfy two other evidentiary requirements: proof that the debt consisted of a "sum certain" and proof that the defendant had received a material benefit, a quid pro quo, from the plaintiff without compensating him for it. With regard to actions on covenants, those agreements that were not based on a debt transaction, standards of proof were stricter. Royal courts refused to hear actions on breached covenants unless the plaintiff could produce a written document affixed with the defendant's seal as record of the agreement.[2] Late in the fourteenth century, lawyers began to devise means of circumventing the requirement for documentary proof of covenants by basing their client's claim on an alternative cause of action: assumpsit. By this means, the royal courts eventually began to hear actions based on violation of oral agreements having nothing to do with debts. It is not certain, however, whether this practice was sufficiently known in Chaucer's day for

[1] The basic outlines of the practice of the royal courts regarding contracts are dealt with in chapter 2. Among the most recent and most comprehensive treatments of the common law of agreements are Simpson, *A History of the Common Law of Contract*; Milsom, *Historical Foundations of the Common Law*, pp. 243–82, 314–60; McGovern, "The Enforcement of Informal Contracts in the Later Middle Ages," pp. 1145–93; McGovern, "Contract in Medieval England, pp. 173–201; Arnold, "Fourteenth-Century Promises," pp. 321–34.

[2] But see McGovern, "The Enforcement of Oral Covenants Prior to Assumpsit," pp. 576–614, for examples of special types of oral covenants which were enforced in the king's courts.

laymen to have been aware of it. In any event, during the fifteenth and sixteenth centuries royal courts began hearing a significant number of contractual cases based on assumpsit, thus allowing certain types of claims based on breach of oral agreements to be heard.

Considering that one would turn to local courts rather than royal courts to have a breached oral agreement enforced, it is interesting that Chaucer's Man of Law, ostensibly a sergeant of the king's courts, should proclaim, "Biheste is dette," when, according to the rules of the courts in which he would have practiced, that was not the case. Perhaps Chaucer modeled his lawyer after those who practiced in local courts. He knew lawyers of both species. As justice of the peace, he served on a commission with several of the king's sergeants. Ralph Strode, on the other hand, was common pleader for the city of London. Records show that Strode's title was *communis narrator* or *communis serviens*, that is, common pleader or sergeant.[3] The portrait of the Man of Law in *The General Prologue* offers evidence which could place him as either kind of sergeant.[4] If his statement about the law of agreements has any evidentiary weight, then there is a chance that Chaucer used a *communis serviens* as the model for his lawyer.

Because the principles governing the law of agreements were much simpler in Chaucer's time, the major difficulty in analyzing fourteenth-century agreements is determining which type of agreement would have come under the rules of which forum. If based on an oath or pledge of faith, an action for breach of promise could conceivably be brought in either an ecclesiastical court or a secular court. In fact, there

[3] A. H. Thomas, ed., *Calendar of Select Pleas and Memoranda of the City of London, 1381–1412*, 3:16, n. 1.

[4] Although it is commonly assumed that Chaucer's Man of Law was a king's sergeant, the evidence to support this is not as unambiguous as supposed. King's sergeants were often appointed to serve as justices in assize, as is Chaucer's lawyer (*General Prologue* 314–15). J. P. Dawson, *The Oracles of the Law*, pp. 24, 509, thinks that between 1340 and 1380 lawyers who were not of the rank of king's sergeant were often appointed to aid central court justices conducting local trials by serving as justices in assize. He suggests that some of the lawyers appointed to serve as "serjeants" on these trial commissions served in the capacity as sergeant only for the duration of the trial term. In his opinion, during Richard II's reign, sergeants at law were not necessarily the upper-echelon lawyers that they became later. Dawson argues that during the last half of the fourteenth century "serjeant" was a generic name for lawyer. But see G. O. Sayles's arguments in support of the establishment of a formal rank of lawyers known as sergeants by 1340; G. O. Sayles, ed., *Select Cases in the Court of King's Bench Under Richard II, Henry IV and Henry V*, 7:xxviii–xli. Jill Mann, in *Chaucer and Medieval Estates Satire*, pp. 86–87, thinks that the credentials given to Chaucer's lawyer are mostly exaggerated; he is given the qualifications of both lawyer and judge to make him representative of both professions. In other words, his qualifications do not particularly reflect those of a real sergeant at law.

is evidence to suggest that many enterprising litigants covered all contingencies by bringing actions on the same agreement simultaneously in both forums.[5] Ultimately any attempt to divide the agreements in Chaucer's works into spiritual and secular piles is an arbitrary process. Yet it seems necessary if one is to comprehend the different implications attached to agreements in Chaucer's day.

The issues dealt with when considering the canon law of agreements are still relevant when discussing the secular law governing the same topic. Even though an action for a breached promise is brought in a secular court, the spiritual welfare of the breacher's soul is still in a precarious position where faith has been pledged on the promise. Therefore, it is important to remember that what has been discussed with respect to breach of promise according to canon law is equally relevant to agreements actionable in secular courts.[6] In the pages that follow "secular agreements" will be used as an abbreviated way of referring to agreements that would be actionable in the various secular courts of medieval England.

## CONTRACTUAL TERMINOLOGY USED BY CHAUCER

Before proceeding to discuss secular agreements in Chaucer's works, it would be best to consider specific terms in Chaucer which refer to elements of agreements. These terms are "contract," "dette," "accord," "composicioun," "covenant," and "foreward."

Chaucer uses the term *contract* only once. In *The Friar's Tale*, disputes involving "contractes" are listed among the matters over which the archdeacon's court has jurisdiction. H. A. Kelly thinks that this is a reference to marriage contracts, and he is probably correct.[7] But, as I indicated earlier, "contract" usually referred to real contracts, those involving debt transactions. As Helmholz has shown, ecclesiastical courts often claimed jurisdiction over actions involving debts where the obligation was also based on the exchange of an oath or pledge of faith.

---

[5] See Guth, "Enforcing Late-Medieval Law," p. 82; Adams and Donahue, eds., Introduction, *Select Cases from the Ecclesiastical Courts of the Province of Canterbury, c. 1200–1301*, p. 96.

[6] Milsom, *Historical Foundations of the Common Law*, pp. 23–25, underscores the difficulty in determining jurisdiction over lay agreements in cases where a pledge of faith had been interposed to seal the agreement. The action could be brought in a secular or an ecclesiastical forum; ecclesiastical courts would even try cases dealing with lay debts as long as the defendant did not obtain a writ of prohibition from the royal courts.

[7] See Kelly, *Love and Marriage in the Age of Chaucer*, p. 170; see also *MED*, s.v. *contract* n., 1.

So "contract," as used in *The Friar's Tale*, may refer to more than just the marriage contract.

A more common contractual term used by Chaucer is "dette." The term usually denotes the obligation incurred by virtue of an agreement rather than the agreement itself.[8] It often refers to an obligation to do something, to repay a loan or return goods. "Dette" is used several times to signify a monetary obligation. For example, the merchant in *The Shipman's Tale* rejoices because he is "riche and cleerly out of dette" (line 376) after he redeems his bond. At other times, however, the term is used in a general fashion to denote an obligation founded on a promise or agreement. "Dette" may merely signify a moral obligation like the duty to one's God mentioned in *The Parson's Tale* (line 251):

> Wel may he be sory thanne, that oweth al his lif to God as longe as he hath lyved, . . . that no goodnesse ne hath to paye with his dette to God to whom he oweth al his lyf.[9]

Finally, "dette" can refer to the duty of sexual performance, incurred by virtue of the marriage vows, which spouses owe to each other.[10]

Other contractual terms that appear in Chaucer's works refer to the agreement which creates the obligation rather than to the obligation itself. "Accord" denotes a formal agreement to settle a lawsuit.[11] In *The House of Fame*, the Eagle mentions that "love-dayes and acordes" (line 695) are to be among the things "Geffrey" will hear about at Fame's house. There "acordes" are agreements to settle a lawsuit out of court. For the most part, however, Chaucer uses the term simply to signify an agreement. In *The Physician's Tale*, the word is used to refer to a nonpromissory agreement in the phrase " 'My lord and I been ful of oon accord' " (line 25). Yet in other places it is used to signify an agreement based on an exchange of promises. For instance, the marriage promises between Dorigen and Arveragus in *The Franklin's Tale* are a "humble, wys accord" (line 791).

"Composicioun" is another term which describes a reconciliation or agreement to settle a dispute.[12] It often means "treaty" or "truce," but,

---

[8] *MED*, s.v. *dette* n., 1; see Milsom, *Historical Foundations of the Common Law*, pp. 259–62.

[9] *MED*, s.v. *dette* n., 3 a(a).

[10] *MED*, s.v. *dette* n., 4b; see, for example, *The Parson's Tale* 374–80, 940; *The Wife of Bath's Tale* 130; *The Merchant's Tale* 2048.

[11] *MED*, s.v. *accord* n., 4 and 5; see also J. Rastell, *An Exposition of Certaine Difficult and Obscure Wordes and Termes of the Lawes of this Realme*, pp. 8–9, s.v. *accorde*.

[12] See *OED*, s.v. *composition*, I, 12; III, 24.

like "accord," it can also mean simply "agreement."[13] In Chaucer, however, the word appears to refer more particularly to the specific rights and duties defined by the terms of an agreement. In *The General Prologue*, "composicioun" refers to the terms of the tale-telling agreement. The reader learns that the Knight "telle he moste his tale, as was resoun, / By foreward and by composicioun" (lines 847–48). In *The Knight's Tale*, the word refers to the rules of the tournament in which Palamon and Arcite fight for Emelye. When a participant is caught by a member of the opposing team, he must cease fighting "By force and eek by composicioun" (line 2651).

Chaucer uses two other words which seem to function as generic terms for "agreement": "covenaunt" and "foreward." A more detailed examination of these terms will be made when the focus of this chapter turns to specific agreements in Chaucer's work; at this point I shall note their general significance. In *The Legend of Good Women*, both terms refer to simple, nonlegal agreements.[14] Elsewhere in Chaucer they denote legal agreements. Since "covenant" seems to have been the generic term for "agreement" in Chaucer's day, the term refers to both written and oral agreements. "Foreward" is a synonymous term, at least in Middle English poetry.[15] The *Promptorium parvulorum* considers

---

[13] *MED*, s.v. *composicioun* n., 2.

[14] In *The Legend of Thisbe*, the promise exchanged by the lovers to meet outside the walls of the city is termed a "covenant" and is sealed with a trothplight (lines 778–90). In *The Legend of Cleopatra*, Cleopatra's promise to Antonious is termed a "covenaunt": "'And in myself this covenaunt made I tho, / That ryght swich as ye felten, wel or wo, / As fer forth as it in my power lay, / Unreprovable unto my wyfhod ay, / The same wolde I fele, lyf or deth, — / And thilke covenant, whil me lasteth breth, / I wol fulfille; and that shal ben wel sene, / Was nevere unto hire love a trewer quene'" (lines 688–95). In *The Legend of Ariadne*, the promise to help Theseus defeat the Minotaur is a covenant: "And shortly of this mater for to make, / This Theseus of hire hath leve take, / And every poynt was performed in dede, / As ye han in this covenaunt herd me rede" (lines 2136–39). In *The Legend of Phyllis*, "forward" is the term denoting the agreement Demophon made to return and marry her on a certain date: "'Thyn hostesse,' quod she, 'O Demophon, / Thy Phillis, which that is so wo begon, / Of Rodopeye, upon yow mot compleyene / Over the terme set bytwixe us tweyne, / That ye ne holde forward, as ye seyde'" (lines 2496–2500).

[15] *MED*, s.v. *covenaunt* n.; s.v. *foreward* n.; see, for example, *Sir Gawain and the Green Knight*, ed. J. R. R. Tolkien and E. V. Gordon, rev. N. Davis, for synonymous use of "covenaunt" and "foreward" to describe the beheading agreement between the Green Knight and Gawain and the exchange-of-winnings agreement between Bercilak and Gawain. The beheading agreement (the Green Knight to Gawain): "'And þou hatz redily rehersed, bi resoun ful trwe, / Clanly al þe couenaunt þat I þe kynge asked...'" (lines 392–93); "'3if I þe telle trwly, quen I þe tape haue / And þou me smoþely hatz smyten, smartly I þe teche / Of my hous and my home and myn owen nome, / Þen may þou frayst my fare and forwardez holde...'" (lines 406–409). The exchange-of-winnings agreement: "And efte in her bourdyng þay bayþen in þe morn / To fylle þe same forwardez þat þay byfore maden: / Wat chaunce so bytydez hor cheuysaunce to chaunge, / What

the Middle English terms synonymous and gives *conventio* and *pactum* as their Latin equivalents.[16] Both the *conventio* and the *pactum* were simple agreements at Roman law.[17] It seems reasonable to consider "foreward" and "covenaunt" both as interchangeable terms and as denoting similar types of legally valid agreements.

Apart from the promises which make up agreements and define their terms, other important features of the law of agreements were the ritualistic vestments whose absence or presence in an agreement most often determined the legal validity of the agreement. The sworn oath and the pledge of faith were among the forms of vestments used to bind an agreement or "covenantz assuren" (*The Knight's Tale* 1924). As mentioned earlier, these formulas were often accompanied by a handshake, wed, or drink. Sometimes, however, an agreement was sealed with something more substantial than formulaic phrases and ritualistic gestures. A debtor would assure his creditor of his intention to repay a loan by finding sureties or pledges who would stand for the debt in the event the debtor defaulted on the loan. At other times, a piece of valuable property served to secure a promise. Before I treat specific agreements in Chaucer's works, I will illustrate the function of these contractual formalities.[18] "Security" will be used to refer to the thing given to bind a bargain: "surety," for the person who stood as pledge to enforce an agreement.

In very early English law, there was a distinction between terminology used to describe the security given to seal a bargain and that describing the surety who was found to hold a person to his promise. The object was a "wed," while the person was termed a "borh."[19] By the fourteenth century the distinction seems to have become blurred because "borwe," from the Old English "borh," comes to be use not only to denote a surety but also the security.[20] "Wed," however, remains

---

nwez so þay nome, at naȝt quen þay metten. / Þay acorded of þe couenauntez byfore þe court alle..." (lines 1404–1408). The various agreements in the poem are interpreted by Blanch and Wasserman in "Medieval Contracts and Covenants; pp. 598–610. See also R. A. Shoaf's discussion in *The Poem as Green Girdle: "Commercium" in "Sir Gawain and the Green Knight,"* pp. 46–65.

[16] Way, ed., *Promptorium parvulorum*, s.v. *forwarde*, p. 173.

[17] See Simpson, *A History of the Common Law of Contract*, p. 382.

[18] The basic sources for the following discussion of terminology dealing with medieval security devices are Henry, *Contracts in the Local Courts of Medieval England*, pp. 202–204, 230–31; Holdsworth, *A History of English Law*, 2:83–87; Plucknett, *A Concise History of the Common Law*, pp. 629–31; Pollock and Maitland, *The History of English Law Before the Time of Edward I*, 2:185–98.

[19] Pollock and Maitland, *The History of English Law Before the Time of Edward I*, 2:185 n. 2.

[20] See *MED*, s.v. *borgh* n. I have found that a similar confusion exists with regard to a synonymous term in Chaucer, "seureté"; it can mean either security or surety depending on the context. See N. Davis et al., eds., *A Chaucer Glossary*, s.v. *seureté / suretee* n.

associated with the physical or, in certain cases, symbolic object given as security.[21]

The use of "wed" occurs twice in Chaucer. In *The Knight's Tale*, it is used in a figurative sense to describe the security which binds Arcite's promise to Theseus never to return to Athens. Theseus advises him that "his nekke lith to wedde" (line 1218) as the security for the promise. In effect, Arcite's life is the security which will be forfeited if he violates his promise to the duke. In *The Shipman's Tale*, "wed" is used in a similarly figurative manner. The merchant's wife informs her husband that "'Ye shal my joly body have to wedde'" (line 423) for any debt, monetary or marital, that she might owe him.

In Chaucer's work, a "borwe" can be a real or a symbolic thing deposited with the person receiving a promise as security to solidify the bond; it can also be a person who serves as a surety. The use of "borwe" to mean the symbolic object serving to secure a promise is illustrated in *The Franklin's Tale*. The clerk pledges his faith to secure his promise to Aurelius to perform properly his part of their agreement. He gives Aurelius his "feith to borwe" (line 1234).[22] Another occurrence of the term denoting the security binding a promise is found in the Legend of Ariadne where Theseus pledges his heart's blood, his life, as "borwe" to secure his promise to marry Ariadne.[23]

A "borwe" as surety could refer to a person who functioned in one of two ways, either as surety for the undertaking of an obligation or as mainpernor who ensured a defendant's appearance in court. The function of a surety as security for a debt is very ancient and harks back to the time when hostages were taken by the injured person's kin to ensure the payment of wergild.[24] When an object was given as security for the

[21] *OED*, s.v. *wed* sb., Obs., 1.

[22] As noted earlier, Maitland viewed the pledge of faith as a form of symbolic security which bound a promise and which was metaphysically passed into the possession of the promisee until the promise was fulfilled; see Pollock and Maitland, *The History of English Law Before the Time of Edward I*, 2:190–91. If the promise to which that faith was pledged was broken, the breacher was said to forfeit his hopes of salvation into the hands of the person to whom he had made the pledge. For an example of the pledge of faith used as security to seal a promise, see *The Knight's Tale* 1622; the pledge of faith made between Palamon and Arcite to battle for the right to Emelye is a "borwe": "Whan ech of hem had leyd his feith to borwe."

[23] *The Legend of Ariadne*: "'And haveth hereof myn herte blod to borwe'" (line 2105).

[24] For the function of sureties in early English law, see H. D. Hazeltine, "The Formal Contract of Early English Law," *Columbia Law Review* 10 (1910): 608–17; for the legal liability of a surety in Chaucer's day and a discussion of the general liability of a surety for a debt and how certain statutory changes modified this liability, see H. Hall, ed., *Select Cases Concerning the Law Merchant*, 3:xxix–xxx; for London law regarding sureties for debts, see *The Liber Albus*, pp. 199–201.

repayment of a debt, it was forfeited upon default of the debtor. Sureties also functioned in this manner according to Anglo-Saxon law. That is, they were hostages of the creditor and became his slaves if the obligation was not paid. In the fourteenth century, though, their function was either to force the debtor to pay his debt or, in a situation where the debtor had insufficient assets, to undertake to fulfill the obligation themselves. "Borwe" is used figuratively to signify surety in *Troilus and Criseyde* when Pandarus uses the term in reply to statements made to him by both lovers.[25] "Borwe" also denotes someone who serves as a mainpernor to ensure the court appearance of a party to a lawsuit. In *The Tale of Melibee*, those who have injured Melibee's family must find "borwes" to ensure their presence at trial (lines 1805–08) and must promise to appear by swearing on their "borwes" and "plegges," a synonym for "borwe" (lines 1826–29).[26]

Another term used by Chaucer for the security binding an agreement is "seuretee." Like "borwe," this term refers either to the surety or security that binds a person to his agreements. While the context of the use of "borwe" usually indicates whether that term means surety or security in Chaucer, "seuretee" is a more ambiguous term. For example, in *The Franklin's Tale*, Aurelius promises to find "seuretee" for his debt to the clerk if the clerk will allow him to repay the debt in installments (lines 1581–82):

> "But wolde ye vouche sauf, upon seuretee,
> Two yeer or thre for to respiten me, . . . ."

Here "seuretee" could mean either surety or security, though sureties often were required to stand for debts. The term is equally ambiguous in *The Wife of Bath's Tale*. The queen seems to demand some sort of "suretee" (line 911), security or surety, to ensure that the knight will

---

[25] At Troilus's insistence that he means only the best for Criseyde, Pandarus exclaims: "'And I thi borugh? fy! no wight doth but so" (1.1038). To Criseyde's plea that he reveal the secret he is keeping from her, Pandarus replies: "'And I youre borugh, ne nevere shal, for me / This thyng be told to yow, as mote I thryve!'" (2.134–35).

[26] "And right anon they tooken hire wey to the court of Melibee, / and tooken with hem somme of hire trewe freendes to maken feith for hem and for to been hire borwes" (lines 1806–1807). "Thanne Melibee took hem up fro the ground ful benignely, / and receyved hire obligaciouns and hire boondes by hire othes upon hire plegges and borwes, / and assigned hem a certeyn day to retourne unto his court, / for to accepte and receyve the sentence and juggement that Melibee wolde comande to be doon on hem by the causes aforeseyd" (lines 1826–29). See *Promptorium parvulorum sive clericorum*, s.v. *borowe*, pp. 44–45, for synonymous use of *borowe* and *plegge*.

return within a year and a day to tell her court what thing women desire most.[27]

A final method used in Chaucer's day to secure the performance of an agreement was the bond or obligation, technically known as a conditional bond. Generally the term "bond" refers to a promise. Legally, however, a bond was an instrument, in some cases an oral agreement, obligating a person to pay a specified amount of money upon failure to perform an agreement.[28] Chaucer often uses "bond" in its general sense as a promise in conjunction with other quasilegal terms. For example, in *The Knight's Tale*, when Arcite revokes his pledge of brotherhood to Palamon, he states (lines 1604–1605):

> "For I defye the seurete and the bond
> Which that thou seist that I have maad to thee."

The *MED* considers the "bond" referred to here to be merely their agreement of brotherhood.[29] Thus Arcite defies his promise and the security or surety that bound it. The ambiguous terms "seurete" and "bond" simply heighten the sense that this bond of brotherhood was strong and not a casually made promise. In *The Franklin's Tale*, Aurelius's release of Dorigen from her vow to him contains similar terminology (lines 1533–35):

> "I yow relesse, madame, into youre hond
> Quyt every serement and every bond
> That ye han maad to me. . . ."

The bond is no doubt Dorigen's conditional promise to be Aurelius's lover, while the "serement" probably refers to the oath that sealed it. As I show later, the language of this release is based on formulaic phrases used in legal releases of Chaucer's day. "Serement" and "bond" are part of the legal jargon of which such releases are composed. Finally, in *The Merchant's Tale*, January conveys a certain amount of land to May by means of "scrit" and "bond" (line 1697). The narrator describes the transaction as follows (lines 1696–98):

---

[27] "'And if thou kanst nat tellen it anon, / Yet wol I yeve thee leve for to gon / A twelf-month and a day, to seche and leere / An answere suffisant in this mateere; / And suretee wol I han, er that thou pace, / Thy body for to yelden in this place'" (lines 907–12).

[28] For a discussion of the function of the conditional bond in medieval England, see Simpson, *A History of the Common Law of Contract*, pp. 250–53. For "bond" meaning simply "agreement," see *MED*, s.v. *bond* n., 3; examples of "bond" used in this fashion are found in *The Book of the Duchess* 935 and *The House of Fame* 321.

[29] *MED*, s.v. *bond* n., 3a.

I trowe it were to longe yow to tarie,
If I yow tolde of every scrit and bond
By which that she was feffed in his lond, . . . .

The *MED* defines "bond" as it occurs in this passage as a document witnessing the grant of a feudal tenure.[30] Yet given Chaucer's ambiguous use of the term in combination with "seurete" and "serement" and its convenient position as a rhyme word in all three passages, such a specific identification of "bond" as meaning something more than agreement is unwarranted. Interestingly, conditional bonds were often secured by oaths and sureties[31] and were also used in the Middle Ages to secure conveyances of land.[32] Thus the meaning of "bond" in the three passages considered here carries both its general meaning as a formal agreement and its more specific meaning as conditional bond. In all likelihood, though, Chaucer was merely using "bond" with "seurete," "serement," and "scrit" as jargon to suggest that some sort of legal transaction had taken place without intending the usage to evoke a specific type of transaction.

As various examples of bonds in the *Calendar of Select Pleas and Memoranda of the City of London* indicate, however, conditional bonds were popular means of securing various types of transactions in Chaucer's day.[33] Accordingly, Chaucer also makes more specific references to bonds which are unquestionably of the type that required the obligor, the person executing the bond, to forfeit a sum of money to the obligee, the recipient of the bond, upon breach of an agreement. For instance, in *The Tale of Melibee*, when Melibee's enemies promise to appear before him and be tried for their crimes against him, they execute a bond. They promise Prudence (lines 1764–66):

" . . . we putten us and oure goodes al fully in youre wil and disposicioun, / and been redy to comen, what day that it like unto youre noblesse to lymyte us or assigne us, / for to maken oure obligacioun and boond as strong as it liketh unto youre goodnesse, . . . "

---

[30] *MED*, s.v. *bond* n., 4. There is no evidence anywhere in *The Merchant's Tale* that January transfers a feudal tenure to May by means of his "scrit" and "bond." Instead he seems to be making an outright grant of a real proprietary interest in the land.

[31] For example, see the Middle English translations of the Latin bonds in L. T. Smith, ed., *The Boke of Brome: A Common-Place Book of the Fifteenth Century*, pp. 147–49.

[32] For examples of bonds used to secure conveyances of land, see Milsom, *Historical Foundations of the Common Law*, p. 251; Simpson, *A History of the Common Law of Contract*, pp. 90–92.

[33] A. D. Thomas, ed., *Calendar of Select Pleas and Memoranda of the City of London, A.D. 1381–1412*; see vol. 3, index, s.v. *bonds*, for page numbers.

Later Melibee takes their "obligaciouns and hir boondes" (line 1827) and assigns them a day to appear in court.[34] Since their exact nature is not specified in the tale, the bonds executed by Melibee's enemies could have been either oral or written. Oral bonds, recited before an officer of the court and recorded by him, were legally binding; but written instruments executed by both parties to the bond always made the best record of the existence of an obligation.[35] There are a few examples of written bonds in Chaucer. In *The Shipman's Tale*, the merchant executes a bond of indebtedness with certain Lombard businessmen. The bond is canceled once he (lines 366–68)

> . . . payd eek in Parys
> To certeyn Lumbardes, redy in hir hond,
> The somme of gold, and gat of hem his bond; . . . .

This bond is referred to earlier in the tale as a "reconyssaunce" (line 330), a written acknowledgment of indebtedness allowing the creditor to distrain the debtor's goods upon failure to meet the terms of the instrument.[36]

## VARIETIES OF SECULAR AGREEMENTS IN CHAUCER

Having examined the different elements of secular agreements and the terminology used by Chaucer to describe those elements, I now focus on a number of places where these elements play a substantial narrative role. First I concentrate on agreements for the performance of particular acts and contractual transactions creating debts of a nonmercantile nature. Next I consider specialized agreements for the conveyance of land and mercantile agreements. Finally I analyze Chaucerian legal

---

[34] "Obligacioun" and "boond" appear to be synonyms and are a translation of *obligation* (lines 1068, 1126) in Chaucer's source; see *Livre de Mellibee et Prudence* in Bryan and Dempster, eds., *Sources and Analogues of Chaucer's* Canterbury Tales, pp. 609, 612. In his discussion of Chaucer's translation of *The Tale of Melibee* from this source, Severs notes that Chaucer often translated a word from his French text with a pair of synonyms (see p. 565). Chaucer translated the French *pleges* (line 1127) as "plegges and borwes" (line 1827).

[35] For the legal status of oral bonds in medieval England, see Milsom, *Historical Foundations of the Common Law*, pp. 258–59; for a more extensive examination, see Henry, *Contracts in the Local Courts of Medieval England*, pp. 111–30. Both studies indicate that oral bonds were valid in local courts as long as they were witnessed before the authorities of the court.

[36] For detailed examinations of the function of recognizances, see Fifoot, *History and Sources of the Common Law*, pp. 221–22; Simpson, *A History of the Common Law of Contract*, pp. 126–35.

theory associated with two distinctive types of debts, the monetary
debt and the marriage debt.


## PERFORMANCE AND DEBT AGREEMENTS


Probably the best-known agreement in Chaucer's works is the tale-
telling agreement proposed by the Host in *The General Prologue*.[37] It
is made up of a number of clauses that make it rather more than a
simple agreement to tell stories. Harry Bailly first proposes that the
pilgrims " 'stonden at my juggement, / And for to werken as I shal yow
seye' " (lines 778–79). After he secures their assent to this stipulation,
the Host proposes the tale-telling contest and its prize, supper for the
winner at his establishment paid for by the other participants in the
contest (lines 790–801):

> "This is the poynt, to speken short and pleyn,
> That ech of yow, to shorte with oure weye,
> In this viage shal telle tales tweye
> To Caunterbury-ward, I mene it so,
> And homward he shal tellen othere two,
> Of aventures that whilom han bifalle.
> And which of yow that bereth hym best of alle,
> That is to seyn, that telleth in this caas
> Tales of best sentence and moost solaas,
> Shal have a soper at oure aller cost
> Heere in this place, sittynge by this post,
> Whan that we come agayn fro Caunterbury."

In effect, Harry Bailly uses the tale-telling contest to lure the pilgrims
into contracting to give him more business at the end of the journey.
The pilgrims swallow the bait and accept the terms of Bailly's proposition. In describing the terms of the agreement and its ratification,
Chaucer incorporates a number of legally significant formalities which
give the agreement the illusion of being legally binding. First the Host
proposes an agreement that would impose a material obligation on
those who accept its terms, that is, to contract to buy supper at his
tavern. The terms of the agreement are emphasized by being reiterated
many times in the remaining lines of *The General Prologue*. For
example, when the narrator describes the pilgrims' acceptance of the
terms of the agreement, the Host's stipulations are repeated word for
word (lines 810–20). Repetition of the terms of an agreement is an

---

[37] The following focuses on *The General Prologue* 769–858.

important part of the formation of any oral contract. It ensures that both parties to the proposal are aware of and agree to its precise terms. *Sir Gawain and the Green Knight* affords an excellent example of the observation of this formality in the making of an agreement.[38] Before allowing Gawain to hack at his head, the Green Knight makes sure that Gawain can recite the terms of the beheading agreement so that Gawain agrees to the exact terms that the Green Knight proposed.

Not only do the pilgrims repeat the terms of the agreement, but other contractual rituals are also observed. Oaths are sworn, and wine is drunk (*The General Prologue* 810–21):

> This thyng was graunted, and oure othes swore
> With ful glad herte, and preyden hym also
> That he wolde vouche sauf for to do so,
> And that he wolde been oure governour,
> And of oure tales juge and reportour,
> And sette a soper at a certeyn pris,
> And we wol reuled been at his devys
> In heigh and lough; and thus by oon assent
> We been acorded to his juggement.
> And therupon the wyn was fet anon;
> We dronken, and to reste wente echon,
> Withouten any lenger taryynge.

Although the drink could be interpreted merely as a gesture of fellowship observed by the travelers, since the gesture is made in the context of the acceptance of this agreement, it also has legal significance. F. W. Maitland discovered evidence in records from thirteenth-century fair courts indicating that drinking was a ritual practiced in mercantile circles upon the closing of a bargain. The drink was shared among parties to the agreement and sealed the agreement by serving as evidence of each party's intention to observe and perform the agreed-upon terms in good faith.[39] In literature, we have to look no further

---

[38] "Þen carppez to Sir Gawan þe knyȝt in þe grene, / 'Refourme we oure forwardes, er we fyrre passe. / Fyrst I eþe þe, haþel, how þat þou hattes / Þat þou me telle truly, as I tryst may.' / 'In god fayth,' quoþ þe goode knyȝt, 'Gawan I hatte, / Þat bede þe þis buffet, quat-so bifallez after / And at þis tyme twelmonyth take at þe an oþer / Wyth what weppen so þou wylt, and wyth no wyȝ ellez on lyue.' / Þat oþer onswarez agayn, / 'Sir Gawan, so mot I þryue / As I am ferly fayn / Þis dint þat þou schal dryue.' / 'Bigog,' quoþ þe grene knyȝt, 'Sir Gawan, me lykes / Þat I schal fange at þy fust þat I haf frayst here. / And þou hatz redily rehersed, bi resoun ful trwe, / Clanly al þe couenaunt þat I þe kynge asked, / Saf þat þou schal siker me, segge, bi þi trawþe, / Þat þou schal seche me þiself'" (lines 377–95).

[39] See Maitland, ed., *Select Pleas in Manorial and Other Seignorial Courts*, pp. 138–39, for an example of a drink being used to bind a bargain. It is clear from the language of the plea that the drink is not superfluous to the facts averred in the plea because it is mentioned together with

than *Sir Gawain and the Green Knight* for an example of this practice. In the poem, Sir Gawain and Bercilak bind their agreement to exchange winnings with a drink: "Who bryngez vus þis beuerage, þis bargayn is maked" (line 1112).[40] It seems reasonable to assume, given the context of the act in *The General Prologue* and corroborative legal and literary evidence, that the pilgrims' communal drink after the reiteration of the terms of the agreement is an example of their observation of a specific type of contractual formality to bind the agreement.

On the morning the pilgrims begin their journey, the agreement is mentioned twice more. Before they are to begin, the Host reminds them of their agreement and terms it a "foreward."[41] When the Knight draws the lot to become the first tale-teller, the narrator again mentions the agreement and describes the Knight's obligation under the terms of the "foreward" (lines 847–49):

> ...telle he moste his tale, as was resoun,
> By foreward and by composicioun,
> As ye han herd; ....

Mindful of the obligation he has incurred by virtue of his agreement, the Knight determines "To kepe his foreward by his free assent" (line 852) and begins his tale as the pilgrims go on their way.

In a matter of sixty-six lines, Chaucer has compiled enough legal detail to give the impression that a serious, binding agreement has been created. The terms of the agreement are repeated by the parties to the agreement, the formalities for securing the agreement are observed, and the type of agreement is specified. Although the agreement is simple, only Harry Bailly seems to be aware of its full significance. He stands to make a good deal of money from the pilgrims by virtue of the contract they have made with him. The inclusion of legal

---

the giving of earnest as evidence that a valid agreement had been entered into. Maitland notes (p. 139 n. 1) that "according to common custom the bargain is bound by a drink. In French, if not in English, law, this solemnity seems to have had a legal force." The term used in this plea to denote drink is "beverech"; in other Latin records the term is *beveragium*, see C. Gross, ed., *Select Cases Concerning the Law Merchant*, 1:47, 52, for use of *beveragium* to bind agreements. Plucknett, *A Concise History of the Common Law*, p. 630, notes that the use of a drink to bind an agreement was a formality associated with mercantile transactions.

[40] See also *Sir Gawain and the Green Knight* 1409 for another example of a beverage used to seal an agreement; see *MED*, s.v. *beverage* n., (b), which suggests that the term can refer to the drink binding the bargain or to the bargain itself.

[41] "... 'Lordynges, herkneth, if yow leste. / Yet woot youre foreward, and I it yow recorde' " (lines 828–29).

details in Chaucer's description of the ratification of the agreement makes it look as if the Host has bound his guests to a quasi-legal obligation to spend their money with him when they return home.

In contrast to the tale-telling agreement in *The General Prologue*, the agreement that Aurelius makes with the clerk in *The Franklin's Tale* is more straightforward. Aurelius is cognizant of the implications of his covenant.[42] He agrees to pay the clerk one thousand pounds if he will remove the rocks that terrify Dorigen.[43] Aurelius swears upon his "trouthe" (line 1231) that he will pay the agreed-upon sum, and the clerk gives his faith as pledge, "have heer my feith to borwe" (line 1234), that he will not be slow to perform his end of the bargain. One interesting aspect of the agreement is not only that Chaucer has imbued it with all the necessary formalities for a binding agreement but also that upon the clerk's performance of his side of the bargain the legal basis for actionability changes. This change is reflected in Chaucer's subsequent handling of the agreement in the tale. Had the clerk broken the agreement before performance, a cause of action would have been based on the promise, and a lawsuit could have been brought to compel performance of that promise or impose damages for violation of the agreement.[44] Once the clerk performs his part of the agreement, however, Aurelius becomes indebted to him for the agreed-upon sum, and the clerk could bring an action on the debt to compel payment. It is noteworthy that the debt in *The Franklin's Tale* is such that it satisfies all the requirements necessary to bring an action of debt in the royal courts.[45] Although the agreement is oral, the debt is for a "sum certain," one thousand pounds, and the debtor has received something from the creditor without compensating him for it. The *Life-Records* indicate that Chaucer was well acquainted with debt litigation in the royal courts; on several occasions actions in debt were

[42] On line 1587, the clerk refers to the bargain as a "covenant."

[43] The complete contractual transaction is worth noting in full: "At after-soper fille they in tretee / What somme sholde this maistres gerdon be, / To remoeven alle the rokkes of Britayne, / And eek from Gerounde to the mouth of Sayne. / He made it straunge, and swoor, so God hym save, / Lasse than a thousand pound he wolde nat have, / Ne gladly for that somme he wolde nat goon. / Aurelius, with blisful herte anoon, / Answerde thus: 'Fy on a thousand pound! / This wyde world, which that men seye is round, / I wolde it yeve, if I were lord of it. / This bargayn is ful dryve, for we been knyt. / Ye shal be payed trewely, by my trouthe! / But looketh now, for no negligence or slouthe / Ye tarie us heere no lenger than to-morwe.' / 'Nay,' quod this clerk, 'have heer my feith to borwe'" (lines 1219–34).

[44] Milsom, *Historical Foundations of the Common Law*, p. 247, discusses the legal theory supporting a cause of action on a covenant.

[45] See generally W. M. McGovern, "Contract in Medieval England: The Necessity for Quid pro Quo and a Sum Certain," *American Journal of Legal History* 13 (1969): 173–201.

brought against him in the court of common pleas.[46] It is possible that Chaucer knew of the requirements for bringing an action in debt in those courts from his experience with that very type of litigation.

For the resolution of the indebtedness that occurs in the last lines of the tale, Chaucer makes use of specific legal devices associated with abrogating a debtor's liability for a debt. First Aurelius begs for an extension of the time period to pay the money owed. He refers to his obligation as a "dette" to be "quyt" and offers some form of security as assurance that he will pay the debt (lines 1581–82):

> "But wolde ye vouche sauf, upon seuretee,
> Two yeer or thre for to respiten me, . . . ."[47]

Once the clerk learns of Aurelius's charity to Dorigen with regard to the special debt she owed him, the clerk executes an oral release, one similar to that which Aurelius granted to Dorigen, which forgives him of his obligation. A release, or quitclaim, was the safest way one could become released from a legal obligation. It vitiated any legal claim by relinquishing any further legally enforceable right to it.[48] The terms of both releases in *The Franklin's Tale* are significant because they mimic the formulaic language of legally valid quitclaims. The plea rolls for the City of London are filled with examples of quitclaims whose terms are similar to those granted in *The Franklin's Tale*.[49] Commonly one party

[46] *LR*, pp. 384–401.

[47] The complete passage reads: "With herte soor he gooth unto his cofre, / And broghte gold unto this philosophre, / The value of fyve hundred pound, I gesse, / And hym bischeth, of his gentillesse, / To graunte hym dayes of the remenaunt; / And seyde, 'Maister, I dar wel make avaunt, / I failled nevere of my trouthe as yit. / For sikerly my dette shal be quyt / Towardes yow, howevere that I fare / To goon a-begged in my kirtle bare. / But wolde ye vouche sauf, upon seuretee, / Two yeer or thre for to respiten me, / Thanne were I wel; for elles moot I selle / Myn heritage; ther is namoore to telle'" (lines 1571–84).

[48] For the function of releases, also referred to as quitclaims and acquittances, in English law, see Pollock and Maitland, *The History of English Law Before the Time of Edward I*, 2:91. The releases in *The Franklin's Tale* are discussed by Roland Blenner-Hassett in "Autobiographical Aspects of Chaucer's Franklin," *Speculum* 28 (1953): 791–800; he compares these releases to the release executed in Chaucer's favor by Cecily Champaign and considers that release a real-life counterpart to those in *The Franklin's Tale* (pp. 797–98).

[49] See Thomas, ed., *Calendar of Select Pleas and Memoranda of the City of London, 1381–1412*, vol. 3, index, s.v. *quitclaims*, for page references. Although the texts recorded in this edition are often only summaries of the Latin and Anglo-Norman documents found in the actual plea rolls, Thomas generally records the salient terms of the documents. For the releases executed by Cecily Champaign, see *LR*, pp. 343–47. As the releases in *The Franklin's Tale* suggest, Chaucer was quite familiar with the formulaic language of those particular types of legal instruments. The *Life-Records* show that he dealt with releases at several times during his life; see *LR*, pp. 1–2 (deed of release executed in 1381 by Chaucer quitclaiming his right to the house and land formerly possessed by his father); 420, 423–24, 428 (acquaintances executed between 1390 and 1391 in

releases the other from any claim based on any cause of action he might have against him. If the claim is based upon a contract, then, he is released from claims based on any contract.[50] Some quitclaims, however, are not as limited in their terms and contain blanket statements of release such as the one executed by Peter the goldsmith in favor of John the parson which released John from "all actions, real and personal, suits, plaints and demands from the beginning of the world to the present day."[51]

Aurelius's release to Dorigen, though less specific than Peter's to John, follows the formulaic pattern of the quitclaims recorded in the London records (lines 1533–38):

> "I yow relesse, madame, into youre hond
> Quyt every serement and every bond
> That ye han maad to me as heerbiforn,
> Sith thilke tyme which that ye were born.
> My trouthe I plighte, I shal yow never repreve
> Of no biheste, . . . ."

The clerk's release of Aurelius from his debt is a shorthand version of Aurelius's to Dorigen. Still it contains all the essential terms for a legal release (lines 1613–15):

> "Sire, I releesse thee thy thousand pound,
> As thou right now were cropen out of the ground,
> Ne nevere er now ne haddest knowen me."

Chaucer's use of specific legal formulas to give the illusion of legally binding agreements in *The General Prologue* and *The Franklin's Tale* and legally valid releases in *The Franklin's Tale* demonstrates his grasp of the fundamental principles governing valid agreements. He is careful to indicate the terms of an agreement and the formalities observed to secure the agreement. In *The Wife of Bath's Tale*, he exercises the same care in setting up the agreement between the knight and the hag and presents evidence that he knew the legal procedure practiced in bringing an action on a covenant in a local court.

Although the agreement in *The Wife of Bath's Tale* is rather inno-

---

Chaucer's favor by various workers for wages paid to them by Chaucer as clerk of the king's works); 504–505 (charter of release witnessed by Chaucer in 1393).

50 For example, Thomas, ed., *Calendar of Select Pleas and Memoranda of the City of London*, 3:83, records the following quitclaim: "Quitclaim from Peter Garcyan, merchant of Lucea, to Francis dil Masse of Siena and Sanctus, . . . of all actions arising from any debt, contract etc. between 8 March 1382 and the present day."

51 Ibid., p. 138.

cent on its surface, the ultimate result of making it proves almost disastrous for the knight. According to the agreement, the knight promises that " 'I wolde wel quite youre hire' " (line 1008) if she can tell him what it is that women most desire.[52] She in turn agrees to give him the answer on the condition that he agree to a counterproposal (lines 1009–12):

> "Plight me thy trouthe heere in myn hand," quod she,
> "The nexte thyng that I requere thee,
> Thou shalt it do, if it lye in thy myght,
> And I wol telle it yow er it be nyght."

Like the promise Dorigen made to Aurelius, the promise made by the knight to the hag is based on troth plighted into the hands of another, a specific form of binding an agreement recognized by courts as sufficient to generate a legally valid agreement. The knight accepts the hag's stipulation by pledging his troth: " 'Have heer my trouthe,' quod the knyght, 'I grante' " (line 1013).

C. A. Breslin, in a dissertation on law and justice in *The Canterbury Tales*, quite properly analyzes this agreement as a covenant for a debt.[53] The debt in this case is the knight's obligation to perform whatever the hag requires of him once she correctly reveals what women most desire. The quid pro quo here is obvious, since the knight receives a valuable benefit, the preservation of his life, and consequently owes the hag performance of his promise. Though Breslin has identified the type of agreement created by the knight and hag, she barely touches upon the fact that the scene in which the hag demands performance of the covenant follows the typical pattern of a lawsuit to recover a debt brought in local courts. In this scene, the hag claims performance from the knight after he exonerates himself before the queen's court by correctly identifying the thing that women desire most. She demands that the debt be fulfilled and that the court " 'do me right' " (line 1049) and see to it that he performs what she requires of him.[54] In demanding her "right," like the demon in *The Friar's Tale*, the hag is demand-

---

[52] " 'My leeve mooder,' quod this knyght, 'certeyn / I nam but deed, but if that I kan seyn / What thyng it is that wommen moost desire. / Koude ye me wisse, I wolde wel quite youre hire' " (lines 1005–1008). R. J. Blanch touches on the legal nuances of the agreement between the hag and the knight in " 'Al Was This Land Fulfiled of Fayerye': The Thematic Employment of Force, Willfulness, and Legal Conventions in Chaucer's *Wife of Bath's Tale*," *SN* 57 (1985): 45–47.

[53] C. A. Breslin, "Justice and Law in Chaucer's *Canterbury Tales*" (Ph.D. dissertation, Temple University, 1978), pp. 118–19.

[54] " 'Mercy,' quod she, 'my sovereyn lady queene! / Er that youre court departe, do me right' " (lines 1048–49).

ing that her legal claim to the performance of her contract be vindicated. The procedure for bringing a plea in debt followed a similar pattern.[55] The plaintiff first narrates his claim before the court in some detail. In the tale, the hag delineates the basis of her claim, specifying the details pertinent to it (lines 1050–57):

> "I taughte this answere unto the knyght;
> For which he plighte me his trouthe there,
> The firste thyng that I wolde hym requere,
> He wolde it do, if it lay in his myghte.
> Bifore the court thanne preye I thee, sir knyght,"
> Quod she, "that thou me take unto thy wyf;
> For wel thou woost that I have kept thy lyf.
> If I seye fals, sey nay, upon thy fey!"

After the plaintiff presents his plea, the defendant is given the opportunity to deny it word for word and wage his law, that is, swear to the truth of his counterassertions about the facts of the case.[56] If the defendant could produce the required number of compurgators to vouch for the truth of his statements, then, he defeated the plaintiff's claim. The hag alludes to the wager of law when she challenges the knight to deny her assertions upon his pledge of faith: "'If I seye fals, sey nay, upon thy fey!'" (line 1057).

The knight does not deny the hag's claim but instead begs for a variance of the terms of performance of his "biheste." His pleas, however, are "al for noght; . . . / Constreyned was, he nedes most hire wedde" (lines 1070–71). In essence, the knight is forced to fulfill his promise because both he and the hag entered into their agreement in good faith. The hag performed her part of the bargain so he must do the same.

In *The Wife of Bath's Tale*, as in *The General Prologue* and *The Franklin's Tale*, Chaucer adds specific details that emphasize the legality of the situation in which the characters find themselves. Agreements are vested with the essential formalities necessary to give them the semblance of legality. With *The Wife of Bath's Tale*, Chaucer goes further by incorporating elements from courtroom procedure and showing not only the formation but also the enforcement of the agreement by a law court.

[55] This procedure is outlined in E. Shanks, ed., *Novae narrationes*, pp. xxv-xxvi; see also Milsom, *Historical Foundations of the Common Law*, pp. 247–48.

[56] Henry, *Contracts in the Local Courts of Medieval England*, pp. 11–47, examines the pleading practices in local courts in some detail.

In *The Summoner's Tale*, Chaucer uses a promise based on a pledge of faith as catalyst for the humorous outcome of the plot and also incorporates into the tale a type of courtroom scene where the performance of the pledge of faith is outrageously enforced. All three poems of fragment D of *The Canterbury Tales* (*The Wife of Bath's Tale*, *The Friar's Tale*, and *The Summoner's Tale*) center on pledges of faith and deal with the consequences of pledging one's faith on promises to perform unspecified acts. In *The Summoner's Tale*, the friar promises to divide Thomas's unspecified bequest equally among his brethren. The friar pledges his faith on the promise (lines 2137–39):

> "I swere it," quod this frere, "by my feith!"
> And therwithal his hand in his he leith,
> "Lo, heer my feith; in me shal be no lak."

In his rage at discovering the insubstantial, yet pungent, nature of the gift, the friar goes to the lord of the manor to seek redress against Thomas. It comes to light, however, that the friar's problem is not just that he has been tricked by Thomas but that he has pledged his faith to perform something that is impossible to perform: divide a fart. Responding to the lord's wife's opprobrious opinion of Thomas's ingenuity, the friar implies that he is concerned with the impossibility of performing the duty that he has pledged his faith to perform. Obviously, his true concern is with revenge (lines 2210–15):

> "Madame," quod he, "by God, I shal nat lye,
> But I on oother wyse may be wreke,
> I shal disclaundre hym over al ther I speke,
> This false blasphemour, that charged me
> To parte that wol nat departed be,
> To every man yliche, with meschaunce!"

The lord pretends to be concerned with the dilemma of the friar keeping his faith, for he puzzles over the problem of the division of the fart (lines 2216–42). Thanks to the perspicacity of the lord's squire, the friar's dilemma of division is deftly dispensed with. Employing imagination equal to that used by Thomas in conceiving the nature of his bequest to the friar and his brethren, the squire devises a means for distributing Thomas's fart and allowing the friar to keep his promise.

In *The Summoner's Tale*, the friar's pledge of faith to Thomas serves as the catalyst precipitating the humorous ending of the tale. Although the pledge of faith is a minor element in the tale, Chaucer's use of it here to bind the friar's promise to execute Thomas's bequest and divide it equally among his brothers does show that such pledges were common means of securing promises in Chaucer's day. Here, however, the friar's voiced concern with his initial inability to keep the pledge is merely a manifestation of his desire to get even with Thomas for making him look so foolish.

## CONVEYANCING AND COMMERCIAL CONTRACTS

Thus far I have dealt with relatively simple agreements which call for the performance of some act in exchange for some sort of compensation from the person receiving the benefit of that act. From here onward I am concerned with Chaucer's use of agreements which effect transfers of a more commercial nature: those executing conveyances of land or effecting loans of money. My examination of Chaucer's use of terminology associated with real property conveyances focuses on book 3 of *Troilus and Criseyde* and on *The Merchant's Tale*. In dealing with loan agreements, I focus on *The Shipman's Tale*. Finally, in winding up this discussion of Chaucerian agreements and obligations, I examine the correlation Chaucer seems to be drawing between the exchange for value, the economic basis for the underlying transaction in any agreement dealing with loans or the conveyance of property, and sexual love. The characters in *The Merchant's Tale*, *The Shipman's Tale*, and the *Prologue* to *The Wife of Bath's Tale* exhibit a certain confusion in their attitude toward sexual love, specifically sex in marriage as characterized by the canonical theory of the marriage debt. They tend to confuse the theory associated with the marriage debt with notions connected with monetary debts. Issues raised by the examination of conveyancing and commercial instruments in Chaucer find their logical culmination in Chaucer's handling of the marriage debt in his poetry.

Sanford Meech notes that Pandarus often acts as if he were negotiating a contract between Troilus and Criseyde.[57] In book 3 of the poem, Chaucer employs conveyancing terminology to describe the consummation of their love and imply that a contract conveying property is being negotiated. The terms are the noun "chartre" and the verbs "sese" and "feffe." Pandarus uses the first term to describe the consummation of Troilus and Criseyde's affair. After Criseyde accepts Troilus into her service at Deiphebus's house, Pandarus lectures Troilus on the importance of keeping faith in love (3.337–40):

---

[57] S. Meech, *Design in Chaucer's Troilus*, pp. 281–84.

"For wel I woot, thow menest wel, parde;
Therfore I dar this fully undertake.
Thow woost ek what thi lady graunted the,
And day is set, the chartres up to make."

The verb "graunted" used in context with "chartre" metaphorically associated Criseyde's grant of her love to Troilus with a property conveyance and, consequently, suggests that once the charters are drawn up the property will vest in Troilus. While a "chartre" could be any formal document which is signed and sealed, the term most specifically refers to a deed conveying title to a tract of land.[58] According to A. W. B. Simpson, the usual procedure was to deliver a charter or deed upon conveying land even though the presence or absence of such documents had no legal effect on the conveyance.[59] Instead the charter served as evidence that the conveyance had been made.

Later Troilus lies in bed awake, disturbed by his unassuaged passion for Criseyde. His insomnia is described by the narrator as follows (3.442–45):

Nil I naught swere, although he lay full softe,
That in his thought he nas somwhat disesed,
Ne that he torned on his pilwes ofte,
And wold of that hym missed han been sesed.

"Sesed" is derived from the Old French verb *saisir*, meaning "to put in possession of" or "take possession of" something. According to the *OED*, the Middle English word is a legal term associated with the conveyance of property. In its passive sense, as used in the preceding passage, to be "sesed" means to be put in legal possession of a tract of land.[60] Possession, in medieval England, if created by seisin, was the equivalent of legal ownership of property. Strictly speaking, however, seisin was not ownership but rather legal possession. Lawful possession of a tenement of land gave the person in seisin the power to convey the property.[61] The act that conveyed possession of land was the act of placing the feoffee in seisin of property. This act was ritualistic in nature and known as "livery of seisin." The ritual was performed by the feoffor, the grantor of the land, by passing to the feoffee an object representing

---

[58] *MED*, s.v. *chartre* n., 2(b).

[59] A. W. B. Simpson, *A History of the Land Law*, 2d ed., pp. 120–21.

[60] *OED*, s.v. *seize* v., I.1.b. For a discussion of the legal use of this term in other Middle English poems, see J. A. Alford, "Literature and Law in Medieval England," pp. 944–46.

[61] For the feudal connotations of seisin, see Milsom, *Historical Foundations of the Common Law*, pp. 119–22; Simpson, *History of the Land Law*, pp. 36–44, 119–20.

the tract of land, usually a clump of sod from the tract itself, in an act of symbolic relinquishment of possessory rights to the land. Generally, livery of seisin was performed while the parties were standing on the tract of land being transferred. At the time of livery, charters were read confirming the transfer.[62]

The metaphor of conveyance is reasserted before Troilus's arrival in Criseyde's chamber at Pandarus's house when Pandarus admonishes her that to "'feffe hym with a fewe wordes white'" (3.901) will not subdue an ostensibly jealous Troilus. Pandarus is perhaps suggesting that she should "feffe" him with more than words. The verb "feffen," like "seisen," is predominantly legal in denotatioh and means to put someone in possession of a tract of land or to endow a person with something by way of gift.[63] To be seised of an estate in land is to be enfeoffed of that land. Given Chaucer's use of other terms associated with conveyancing in connection with Troilus's ultimate possession of Criseyde, it seems likely that Pandarus's use of "feffe" is to be regarded in that context as well. The legal metaphor playfully implies that Criseyde should place Troilus in "seisen" of a very personal piece of her own property.

A conveyance is also found in *The Merchant's Tale*. Here, however, the language is used literally. Feoffment is part of the terms of a marriage agreement, or "tretee," arranged by January's counselors (lines 1691–1702):

> For whan they saughe that it moste nedes be,
> They wroghten so, by sly and wys tretee,
> That she, this mayden, which that Mayus highte,
> As hastily as evere that she myghte,
> Shal wedded be unto this Januarie.
> I trowe it were to longe yow to tarie,
> If I yow tolde of every scrit and bond
> By which that she was feffed in his lond,
> Or for to herknen of hir riche array.
> But finally ycomen is the day

---

[62] For a detailed examination of the concept of seisin and the ceremony of livery of seisin, see F. W. Maitland, "The Mystery of Seisin" and "The Beatitude of Seisin," in *The Collected Papers of Frederic William Maitland*, 1:358–84, 407–57; for a medieval English account of this ritual, see the late-thirteenth-century legal treatise *Britton*, ed. and trans. F. M. Nichols, pp. 212–14 (see chapter 4, note 10 below).

[63] *MED*, s.v. *feffen* v., 1, 2; cf. the use of "feffen" in *Piers Plowman: The B Version*, passus 2, line 79. Passus 2, lines 69–114, deals with the charter of Meed and is filled with language associated with conveyances of property.

That to the chirche bothe be they went
For to receyve the hooly sacrement.

The "bond," as previously mentioned, is probably the agreement to make the conveyance (or possibly the instument that secures the promise to convey) which is witnessed by the "scrit," the charter or deed documenting the conveyance.[64] Here, though, the conveyance is not an ordinary transaction but one made in anticipation of marriage, an inducement for May to wed old January.

Although the tale is silent on the precise quality of the legal interest in the land that is granted by January's prenuptial gift, there is a suggestion that the grant is one fixing the size of her dower interest in his land, rather than a grant of a fee simple estate. The dower interest was the wife's right to a life estate in a portion of her husband's lands at his death.[65] Often, prenuptial grants of property conveyed a future interest in the land, a dower interest, rather than a present interest. Maitland notes that the amount of dower granted by the husband could be determined by agreement between the prospective husband and the prospective bride's family. May's dower rights were perhaps one of the matters determined by the "sly and wys tretee" negotiated by January's counselors. Given January's age, a grant of a sizable dower interest in his land would have been sufficient incentive for May to marry him. She probably would have had only a short while to wait before he died and her inchoate rights to the land became vested.

Although the size of a wife's dower interest in her husband's lands could be determined before the wedding, unless both the solemnization of the marriage and the endowment of the property occurred at the church door, any prior grant of dower rights was invalid. The endowment at the church door of May's dower rights may be implied by the reference to the church service immediately after the reference to the grant of land. The type of dower endowed at the church door, known as dower *ad ostium ecclesiae*, is not to be confused with common law dower, which was a woman's legal right to a dower interest in a proportion of her husband's land, in the event that no dower interest was granted her by her husband, as long as her marriage was solem-

---

[64] *OED*, s.v. *scrite*, Obs.

[65] For an extensive examination of the law of dower in medieval England, see Pollock and Maitland, *The History of English Law Before the Time of Edward I*, 2:374–75, 420–26; Holdsworth, *A History of English Law*, 5th ed., 3:189–97; Nichols, ed., *Britton*, pp. 518–22.

nized at the church door.[66] As a sidenote, it is significant that Chaucer twice mentions that the Wife of Bath married all of her husbands at the church door, an allusion to her financial acumen in assuring that her dower rights would not be vitiated by improper observation of the requisite ritual.[67]

As *The Merchant's Tale* turns out, January eventually must resort to bribing his young wife with a promised conveyance of all of his lands in an attempt to purchase her fidelity. In a sense, January is promising to override his gift of dower by executing a conveyance that would vest his property in her immediately rather than upon his death. He begs her (lines 2168–77):

> "... though that I be oold, and may nat see,
> Beth to me trewe, and I wol telle yow why.
> Thre thynges, certes, shal ye wynne therby:
> First, love of Crist, and to youreself honour,
> And al myn heritage, toun and tour;
> I yeve it yow, maketh chartres as yow lest;
> This shal be doon to-morwe er sonne reste,
> So wisly God my soule brynge in blisse.
> I prey yow first, in covenant ye me kisse;
> And though that I be jalous, wyte me noght."

Like the "scrit" documenting his earlier conveyance to May, the "chartres" referred to here are, no doubt, charters of feoffment. Interestingly, January terms his promise to convey the lands to her a "covenant," and he wants May to seal that covenant with a kiss.

In both *Troilus and Criseyde* and *The Merchant's Tale*, Chaucer uses conveyancing terminology to describe some aspect of the acquisition of sexual love. In *Troilus and Criseyde*, the terms of feoffment are used metaphorically to describe Troilus's attempt to gain possession of

---

[66] See Nichols's note on the issue of the availability of common law dower for women in the thirteenth and fourteenth centuries as evidenced by changes in manuscripts of *Britton*; see Nichols, ed., *Britton*, pp. 519–20 n. 1.

[67] See *The General Prologue*, "Housbondes at chirche dore she hadde fyve" (line 460); *The Wife of Bath's Prologue*, "Housbondes at chirche dore I have had fyve" (line 6). T. A. Reisner, "The Wife of Bath's Dower: A Legal Interpretation," *MP* 71 (1974): 301–302, comes to the conclusion that these lines refer to the Wife of Bath's ensuring that her dower rights will vest legally. Although he has probably reached the correct conclusion, Reisner's evidence is a bit strange. He bases his information about medieval dower on the definition of dower given in a judge's opinion in a twentieth-century Tennessee case and on that found in a number of modern legal dictionaries. Despite the fact that the southern states continue to maintain constant communion with their heritage, legal and otherwise, even in Tennessee legal theory has advanced sufficiently to allow today's judges to refer to a more contemporary definition of dower than that understood by medieval jurists.

Criseyde's love. The terminology implicitly equates the objects of the conveyance, Criseyde and her love, with real property. The connection is more overt in *The Merchant's Tale*, where January turns his land into the currency which he uses to buy from May first their marriage and later promises of affection and fidelity. Chaucer's use of conveyancing terminology in *The Merchant's Tale* suggests that love is a commodity that can be acquired in exchange for material goods.

This undercurrent of meaning is especially apparent in Chaucer's use of language associated with commercial instruments and transactions in *The Shipman's Tale*. In this tale, several different methods of evidencing or creating debts are dealt with: the informal unsecured loan, the recognizance, and the tally. Because the various transactions in the tale are mercantile in nature, their validity in a court of law would have been determined by the rules of a body of law known as the "law merchant," which dealt exclusively with mercantile transactions. Before proceeding with an analysis of these transactions, I mention some of the essential features of the law merchant in Chaucer's day.

Because many medieval merchants were itinerant, a special set of legal principles known as the "law merchant" was formulated to ensure uniformity in business transactions. These rules were said to be known by all European merchants and were thus international in character.[68] Concerned chiefly with evidentiary matters, law merchant rules provided methods of proof of the validity of contracts and the legal worth of the tally and God's penny. These special rules were administered in the courts of fairs, markets, towns, and boroughs. Common law courts also referred to the law merchant in determining the outcome of mercantile disputes involving merchants from different parts of the country or different nations.

In the thirteenth and fourteenth centuries, statutes such as the Statute of the Staple of 1353 gave formal recognition to many law merchant customs by creating a special forum, the court of the staple at Westminster, to settle disputes involving commercial transactions.[69]

---

[68] For studies on the law merchant in medieval England, see Pollock and Maitland, *The History of English Law Before the Time of Edward I*, 1:467; F. R. Sanborn, *Origins of the Early English Maritime and Commercial Law*, pp. 346–54; W. Mitchell, *An Essay on the Early History of the Law Merchant*. See also J. H. Baker, "The Law Merchant and the Common Law Before 1700," *Cambridge Law Journal* 38 (1979): 295–322; rpt. in J. H. Baker, *The Legal Profession and the Common Law*, pp. 341–68.

[69] For the effects of statute law on law merchant procedure in England and for the practice of local courts regarding the law merchant, see Gross, ed., Introduction and cases, *Select Cases Concerning the Law Merchant*, vol. 1; Hall, ed., *Select Cases Concerning the Law Merchant*, vols. 2, 3; Bateson, ed., *Borough Customs*, 2:lxxxiv–lxxxv, 183–93; Thomas, ed., *Calendar of Select Pleas and Memoranda of the City of London*, 3:vii–xli.

Local custom gave the city courts of London, the sheriff's and mayor's courts, jurisdiction over mercantile disputes by reference to law merchant as well. The jurisdiction of the staple court did not necessarily abrogate that of the city courts over commercial litigation but rather created a royally sanctioned forum to protect the interests of merchants of the staple. Since Chaucer was controller of customs for the wool staple, it seems likely that he would have had ample opportunity to become acquainted with law merchant rules.

While the courts observing law merchant custom were competent to hear a wide range of mercantile disputes, most often they were asked to resolve litigation involving agreements between merchants. Many of these disputes concerned debts, especially debts incurred in credit transactions. Law merchant rules were designed to enforce all good-faith transactions between merchants; thus, in theory, all forms of loan agreements made in good faith were enforceable. Since, however, good faith could be a slippery means of ensuring payment by itself, creditors encouraged the good faith of their debtors by using a variety of commercial instruments to prove the existence of debts and secure their repayment. Among these instruments were the tally and recognizance. Both devices were effective to varying degrees as legal proof of the existence of a debt.

In *The Shipman's Tale*, these two instruments are mentioned as means of securing the repayment of a loan of money.[70] The primary credit transactions of the tale, though, are two informal loans.[71] The tale's main plot concerns a merchant's informal, unsecured loan of one

[70] K. S. Cahn, "Chaucer's Merchants and the Foreign Exchange: An Introduction to Medieval Finance," *SAC* 2 (1980): 81–119, discusses certain aspects of the merchant's lending ventures in *The Shipman's Tale*, mostly matters dealing with his ventures in monetary exchanges; these aspects of the tale are not within the purview of my discussion. A number of critics have observed that Chaucer uses the loan, tally, and wed in *The Shipman's Tale* to suggest the commercialization of sex; none, however, have looked at the legal significance of these devices to determine how that affects interpretation. See A. H. Silverman, "Sex and Money in Chaucer's *Shipman's Tale*," *PQ* 32 (1953): 329–36; P. S. Schneider, "'Taillynge Ynough': The Function of Money in the *Shipman's Tale*," *ChauR* 11 (1977): 201–209; V. J. Scattergood, "The Originality of the *Shipman's Tale*," *ChauR* 11 (1977): 210–31; G. R. Keiser, "Language and Meaning in Chaucer's *Shipman's Tale*," *ChauR* 12 (1978): 147–61. Theological ideas associated with the notion of debt and their relation to *The Shipman's Tale* are explored by R. Adams, "The Concept of Debt in *The Shipman's Tale*," *SAC* 6 (1984): 85–102.

[71] Simpson, *A History of the Common Law of Contract*, pp. 146–48, considers the informal loan the most common form of credit transaction in medieval England. He thinks that the reason the yearbooks fail to deal with such cases was that they were too simple to be of any interest to the reporters, whose main interest was in recording cases dealing with difficult or unique rules of proof or pleading.

hundred franks to John the monk and John's informal, yet in a sense secured, loan of the same sum of money to the merchant's wife. The monk acts as a broker who, for a fee, finds the funds to refinance the wife's debts. He makes sure, however, that she is ultimately liable for the loan. With regard to the first transaction, John the monk asks for a loan of one hundred franks ostensibly to purchase livestock for his monastery. Letting his affection for the monk obscure his business instincts, the merchant gives him the money, assuming that he will be repaid in due time (lines 284–92):

> "My gold is youres, whan that it yow leste,
> And nat oonly my gold, but my chaffare.
> Take what yow list, God shilde that ye spare.
>   But o thyng is, ye knowe it wel ynogh,
> Of chapmen, that hir moneie is hir plogh.
> We may creaunce whil we have a name;
> But goldlees for to be, it is no game.
> Paye it agayn whan it lith in youre ese;
> After my myght ful fayn wolde I yow plese."

Notably, the monk takes every precaution to ensure that the transaction is kept secret (lines 295–96):

> No wight in al this world wiste of this loone,
> Savynge this marchant and daun John allone.

As indicated earlier in the tale, the monk has obtained the loan for the merchant's wife, who seems to have overextended her financial liabilities and is being hounded by creditors cognizant that she has become an unsound credit risk. She has promised John prompt repayment if he can provide the capital necessary to fend off the hungry creditors (lines 190–92):

> "...at a certeyn day I wol yow paye,
> And doon to yow what plesance and service
> That I may doon, right as yow list devise."[72]

Once he loans her the money, the monk demands payment in service, not in kind. The wife (lines 314–17)

[72] The passage leading to these lines is as follows: "'A Sonday next I moste nedes paye / An hundred frankes, or ellis I am lorn. / Yet were me levere that I were unborn / Than me were doon a sclaundre or vileynye; / And if myn housbonde eek it myghte espye, / I nere but lost; and therfore I yow preye, / Lene me this somme, or ellis moot I deye. / Daun John, I seye, lene me thise hundred frankes. / Pardee, I wol nat faille yow my thankes, / If that yow list to doon that I yow praye'" (lines 180–89).

> . . . acorded with daun John
> That for thise hundred frankes he sholde al nyght
> Have hire in his armes bolt upright;
> And this acord parfourned was in dede.

The wife soon learns that she must repay the loan twice, because John, thinking the merchant was asking for repayment, claims that he left the sum lent him with the merchant's wife. In a sense, then, her payment to the monk was simply a broker's fee; her actual indebtedness for the money given her by the monk is to her principal creditor, her husband. Upon being queried by her husband about the whereabouts of the money, the wife realizes and slyly acknowledges that she owes him the money, even though she protests that she innocently thought the money was a gift from the monk (lines 411–17):

> "But sith I se I stonde in this disjoynt,
> I wol answere yow shortly to the poynt.
> Ye han mo slakkere dettours than am I!
> For I wol paye yow wel and redily
> Fro day to day, and if so be I faille,
> I am youre wyf; score it upon my taille,
> And I shal paye as soone as ever I may."

By suggesting that the debt be scored upon her "taille," besides making the obvious sexual pun, the credit-conscious wife alludes to a traditional device used to record indebtedness, the tally. Although royal courts did not consider a tally sufficient proof of an indebtedness to support an action of debt, the rules of the law merchant did.[73] A debt was recorded in this fashion by first cutting a notch in a piece of wood, the tally stick, to indicate the amount of the debt. The tally was then split down the center, one half going to the creditor and the other half to the debtor as record of the debt. In the tale, the tally serves as a record of the wife's debt to her husband, which she will only repay sexually.

She affirms the sexual dimensions of the monetary obligation to her husband by restating to him that he can expect physical repayment of the fiscal debits she incurs from him: "'Ye shal my joly body have to wedde'" (line 423). That is, her body will serve as the security for any debt she creates, and it will be delivered up to him upon her failure to

---

[73] The royal court's treatment of the tally is examined in M. S. Arnold, ed., *Year Books of Richard II, 2 R II, 1378–79*, pp. xxiii–xxv; local courts were less rigid in their requirements for proof of a debt and, therefore, considered a tally legitimate evidence of a debt; see Thomas, ed., *Calendar of Select Pleas and Memoranda of the City of London*, 3:xxvi.

repay him. In this line Chaucer may have been playing with an expression found in many legal records of debt litigation in his day; that is, upon being found guilty of owing money to a creditor, the debtor offers his body as pledge to satisfy the debt.[74] Also, Chaucer makes explicit what was implied by the wife's command to score the debt "'upon my taille.'" The tally was a form of wed passed to the creditor to serve as record of and symbolic security for the debt.[75] Her body, the "wedde" and "taille," is her means of satisfying her creditor.

The unbusinesslike manner in which the merchant handled these transactions dealing with sexual credit and debt is contrasted sharply with his practice in matters of business.[76] Although he is negligent in the conduct of his personal affairs, with respect to mercantile matters (lines 304–306)

> He neither pleyeth at the dees ne daunceth,
> But as a marchaunt, shortly for to telle,
> He let hys lyf. . . .

This is illustrated in the way he handles his business debts, specifically an obligation to pay twenty thousand shields to Lombard money-lenders. This obligation is based on a particular type of bond, a recognizance, which was in effect a contract of record executed by the debtor. The terms of the document acknowledged the debt and allowed the creditor to seize the debtor's goods to satisfy the debt in the event he failed to pay it on the date it became due.[77] Thus it was extremely important to pay the loan by the due date if the merchant wanted to retain possession of his goods. The merchant's relief at extricating himself from this bond is genuine.[78]

[74] See Gross, ed., *Select Cases Concerning the Law Merchant*, 1:15, for an example of the court allowing a debtor's body to serve as surety for his debt.

[75] Henry, *Contracts in the Local Courts of Medieval England*, pp. 202–204. See J. P. Hermann, "Dismemberment, Dissemination, Discourse: Sign and Symbol in the *Shipman's Tale*," *ChauR* 19 (1985): 302–37, for the view that the wife's body is not security for the loan but the principal itself.

[76] Keiser, "Language and Meaning in Chaucer's *Shipman's Tale*," p. 155, notes the discrepancy in the merchant's management of business and personal affairs.

[77] "For he was bounden in a reconyssaunce / To paye twenty thousand sheeld anon" (lines 330–31). See Thomas, ed., *Calendar of Select Pleas and Memoranda of the City of London*, 3:xxxiii–xxxiv, for discussion of the handling of recognizances in London courts; see also Simpson, *A History of the Common Law of Contract*, pp. 126–30; both sources deal with the distinction between civic and statutory recognizances.

[78] "This marchant, which that was ful war and wys, / Creanced hath, and payd eek in Parys / To certeyn Lumbardes, redy in hir hond, / The somme of gold, and gat of hem his bond; / And hoom he gooth, murie as a papejay, / For wel he knew he stood in swich array / That nedes moste he wynne in that viage / A thousand frankes aboven al his costage" (lines 365–72).

The careful manner in which this merchant conducts his business is also illustrated by the fact that upon payment of the loan to the Lombards, he "gat of hem his bond" (line 368). That is, he took the document with him. In Chaucer's day, unless one received a written release for a debt or the canceled instrument at payment, unscrupulous creditors might use the uncanceled instrument evidencing the debt in a lawsuit as proof that the debt remained outstanding. If the debtor could tender no stronger evidence contradicting the proof of the bond, he would lose his case and have to pay again.[79]

## COMMERCIAL AND MARITAL DEBTS

In *The Shipman's Tale*, Chaucer contrasts the merchant's personal dealings with his business dealings by showing the different types of credit arrangements he enters into in each sphere and the varying degrees of care he takes with them. By so doing, Chaucer suggests that, while commerce flourishes because of the attention paid to it, human relationships disintegrate out of neglect. In *The Shipman's Tale*, as in *The Merchant's Tale* and *Troilus and Criseyde*, Chaucer uses legal terminology to draw a correlation between the sex act and commercial transactions: a conveyance of property in *Troilus and Criseyde*, an exchange of property for sex in *The Merchant's Tale*, and payment of a debt in *The Shipman's Tale*. This correlation is also made explicit by the Wife of Bath. Although *Troilus and Criseyde* deals with love outside marriage, in *The Wife of Bath's Prologue* and the Merchant's and Shipman's tales, sex in marriage is viewed as a commodity to be bartered with; it is to be given up in repayment for the receipt of something of value from the other spouse. In these tales the marriage debt is seen in terms of a monetary debt. This attitude is in direct opposition to the canonical notion of the marriage debt. It seems a fitting finish to this examination of Chaucerian agreements to consider how Chaucer uses this confusion of ideas, association of a monetary debt with the marriage debt, to suggest that the marriage bond, in his day, was being undermined by the rising emphasis on commercialization in his culture.[80]

---

[79] See Milsom, *Historical Foundations of the Common Law*, p. 250; Hall, ed., *Select Cases Concerning the Law Merchant*, 3:xxx–xxxi.

[80] Although critics have been quick to note the correlation between sex in marriage and in commerce in these poems, none seem to have looked either at the way this conception of the marital debt is similar to legal theory regarding lay debts (though Silverman, "Sex and Money in

As mentioned previously, the theory supporting a legal action on a debt was that one person had given some sort of benefit, a quid pro quo, to another, for which he has not been compensated. In other words, the action was based upon the fact that the debtor had yet to pay for what he had received. Like a monetary debt, the marriage debt was something that was owed by one person to another. But, according to canon law, unlike a monetary debt, the marriage debt was a mutual obligation owed by spouses to one another by virtue of the sacrament of marriage and not by virtue of some exchange for value.[81] The marriage debt was the mutual duty shared by husband and wife to perform sexually at each other's request. It was to be granted freely by one spouse upon the need of the other. This conjugal obligation served to keep the marriage bond solidified through the sexual union of husband and wife. The wife had as equal a right as the husband to exact payment of the debt. Neither spouse had the right to withhold its payment.

The canonist position is best reflected by *The Parson's Tale*. Among the three things for which "a man and his wyf flesshly mowen assemble" (line 938) is (line 939)

> to yelden everich of hem to oother the dette of hire bodies; for neither of hem hath power of his owene body.

It is further noted that (line 940)

> she hath merite of chastitee that yeldeth to hire housbonde the dette of hir body, ye, though it be agayn hir likynge and the lust of hire herte.

Implicit in this conception of sexuality in marriage is the notion that one should accede freely to the sexual needs of one's spouse. This obligation stems from the sacrament of marriage and is paid only

---

Chaucer's *Shipman's Tale*," p. 333, and Scattergood, "The Originality of the *Shipman's Tale*," p. 225, observe similarities without concerning themselves with legal theory) or at how that theory diverges from the canonical notion of the marriage debt. But see J. F. Cotter, "The Wife of Bath and the Conjugal Debt," *ELN* 6 (1969): 169–72, who examines two patristic sources, Jerome and Thomas Aquinas, for the concept but neglects the canon law sources; S. Delany, "Sexual Economics, Chaucer's Wife of Bath, and *The Book of Margery Kempe*," *MinnR*, n.s., 5 (1975): 104–15, who uses a Marxist-feminist approach to conclude that the Wife of Bath's "sexuality is as capitalistic as her trade" but thinks that the Wife developed her sexual attitude in retaliation against the social repression of women in the Dark Ages.

[81] A thorough and concise study of the concept of the marriage debt in the Middle Ages and its canonical sources is that of E. M. Makowski, "The Conjugal Debt and Medieval Canon Law," *Journal of Medieval History* 3 (1977): 99–114; my account of the canon law doctrine regarding the marriage debt is based on this article and the citations therein.

within the context of the marital union. Neither spouse should have to resort to material enticements to obtain what is his or her due.

In *The Wife of Bath's Prologue*, *The Merchant's Tale*, and *The Shipman's Tale*, payment of the marriage debt occurs only when a wife has acquired some form of compensation from her husband. For instance, although the Wife of Bath expounds a muddled version of the doctrinal line of thought regarding the marriage debt, her account of her first three marriages indicates that she considers the marriage debt analogous to a monetary debt: something owed for a material benefit received. She declares (lines 149–61):

> "In wyfhod I wol use myn instrument
> As frely as my Makere hath it sent.
> If I be daungerous, God yeve me sorwe!
> Myn housbonde shal it have bothe eve and morwe,
> Whan that hym list come forth and paye his dette.
> An housbonde I wol have, I wol nat lette,
> Which shal be bothe my dettour and my thral,
> And have his tribulacion withal
> Upon his flessh, whil that I am his wyf.
> I have the power durynge al my lyf
> Upon his propre body, and noght he.
> Right thus the Apostel tolde it unto me;
> And bad oure housbondes for to love us weel."

Her true understanding of the nature of the marriage debt, though, is reflected in the following lines (lines 201–14):

> "As help me God, I laughe whan I thynke
> How pitously a-nyght I made hem swynke!
> And, by my fey, I tolde of it no stoor.
> They had me yeven hir lond and hir tresoor;
> Me neded nat do lenger diligence
> To wynne hir love, or doon hem reverence.
> They loved me so wel, by God above,
> That I ne tolde no deyntee of hir love!
> A wys womman wol bisye hire evere in oon
> To gete hire love, ye, ther as she hath noon.
> But sith I hadde hem hoolly in myn hond,
> And sith they hadde me yeven al hir lond,
> What sholde I taken keep hem for to plese,
> But it were for my profit and myn ese?"

As soon as she gets what she wants from her husbands, she no longer considers it necessary to fulfill her marital duties. To her way of thinking, the marriage debt has been paid, the quid granted pro quo.

Similarly, in *The Merchant's Tale*, January propounds the party position regarding the marriage debt, but his actions reveal that he conceives of it in commercial terms. When arguing in favor of marriage, he mouths the canonically accepted stance regarding the marriage debt. He observes (lines 1446–55) that if a man

> "...may nat lyven chaast his lyf,
> Take hym a wyf with greet devocioun,
> By cause of leveful procreacioun
> Of children, to th'onour of God above,
> And nat oonly for paramour or love;
> And for they sholde leccherye eschue,
> And yelde hir dette whan that it is due;
> Or for that ech of hem sholde helpen oother
> In meschief, as a suster shal the brother;
> And lyve in chastitee ful holily."

Despite his speeches, however, he must resort to promising to grant May all of his land to win her promise of fidelity. By means of a commercial exchange, January thinks that he can acquire the exclusive rights to his wife's sexual favors.

The same attitude toward the marriage debt is evident in *The Shipman's Tale* through the merchant's wife's reference to the marriage debt in terms associated with commercial debts. Her debts to her husband are scored on her "taille" and are to be collected in bed. Following a philosophy similar to that expounded by the Wife of Bath and January, this merchant's wife thinks of the marriage debt as something to be granted in exchange for some material benefit. In all three instances the canonical conception of the marriage debt as something owed by one spouse to the other and yet to be freely rendered seems to have become confused with a credit transaction. By drawing a connection between commerical and canonical debt, Chaucer illustrates how the growth of commercial and mercantile institutions in the fourteenth century had begun to influence and distort the conception of sacred interpersonal bonds like the marriage bond.

## CONCLUSION

Chaucer spent much of his life associating with merchants and observing how they went about their business. No doubt he observed that an important asset for a merchant was his reputation both for good faith in business dealings and, more important, for keeping his end of the bargain in contractual transactions. For commerce to continue, contracts had to be reliable. Chaucer's understanding of this simple fact is shown not only by the use he makes of agreements and contracts in his works but also by the particular care he takes to describe the formulas and ritual that make agreements binding. This attention to detail is symptomatic of a concern beyond the plane of commerce to that of human relationships. That concern is manifested in the virtue of "trouthe" and the emphasis underlying all contractual transactions in his works, regardless of how heavily laden they are with legal formulas, on the notion that the fundamental force binding any agreement, moral or legal, is the bond of "trouthe." Through the keeping of "trouthe," one honors and fulfills the expectation that motivates anyone entering into any sort of relationship with another; that is, that the terms which both parties to the relationship have agreed will govern their conduct in that relationship will be adhered to in good faith. These are the elements that bind every type of bargain at its lowest level, and these are the values which must be honored and maintained not only if commerce is to function properly but also if individuals are to deal with their fellows in any civilized or humane fashion.

# 4

# Chaucer and Medieval
# English Criminal Law
# and Criminal Procedure

As the studies of L. O. Pike and J. Bellamy demonstrate, criminal activity ran rampant and was virtually uncontrollable in Chaucer's day.[1] This state of affairs persisted despite the existence of a system of customary and statutory criminal law that attempted to maintain a modicum of social order by both defining criminal acts and prescribing punishments for those acts. The problem lay in the enforcement of those laws. There was no real police force to speak of in medieval England. Much of what we consider today the job of the police, the capture of criminals, for instance, was the duty of local citizenry. Also, once a known criminal had been captured and brought to trial, there was no guarantee that he would be convicted, even if his activities were notorious.

Among Chaucer's works, *The Canterbury Tales* reflects the general

---

[1] L. O. Pike, *A History of Crime in England*; an account of crime and criminal law in thirteenth- and fourteenth-century England is given in vol. 1, pp. 170–422; J. Bellamy, *Crime and Public Order in England in the Later Middle Ages.*

disregard in which the law was held in Chaucer's time. Indeed, much work has been done to point out the criminal traits of certain pilgrims like the Miller and the Shipman and certain of the ecclesiastical figures described in *The General Prologue*.[2] Work focusing on crime and punishment in Chaucer has also been done on *The Reeve's Tale*, with its quasi-legal handling of the clerks' revenge against the larcenous miller,[3] and on *The Friar's Tale*'s litany of the criminal abuse of legal process by officers of church courts.[4] Although Chaucer is quick to reveal the criminal traits of many of the characters in his works and the abuse of the legal system by scoundrels like the summoner and his archdeacon, he is also interested in the particular legal elements that define certain categories of crimes and the different modes of legal procedure designed to control criminal activity. Because the more obvious examples of secular and ecclesiastical crimes in *The General Prologue*, *The Reeve's Tale*, and *The Friar's Tale* have been examined extensively, I shall not deal with those works in this chapter. Instead I concentrate on Chaucer's use of secular criminal law and procedure in his other works. First I focus on Chaucer's use of the English law on felony. Then I consider the various modes of legal procedure, the rules for arresting and determining guilt of those suspected of criminal behavior, that occur in his works.

FELONY

THE FELONIES IN MEDIEVAL ENGLISH LAW

Among the allegorical figures painted on the walls of the Temple of Mars in *The Knight's Tale* are Felony and his retinue. Although the

---

[2] Breslin, "Justice and Law in Chaucer's *Canterbury Tales*," recapitulates much of the scholarship on this subject in her discussions of law in *The General Prologue* (pp. 1–83), *The Reeve's Tale* (pp. 193–202), and *The Friar's Tale* (pp. 228–45). For a discussion of the criminal traits of various pilgrims, see M. Bowden, *A Commentary on the* General Prologue *to the* Canterbury Tales.

[3] This aspect of *The Reeve's Tale* has received extensive treatment. The focus of several studies has been on the Reeve's citation of the proverb "'For leveful is with force force of-showve'" (line 3912) as justification for telling a tale in retaliation for *The Miller's Tale*; see F. Montgomery, "A Note on the Reeve's Prologue," *PQ* 10 (1931): 404–405; L. M. Myers, "A Line in the Reeve's Prologue," *MLN* 49 (1934): 222–26; J. L. Baird, "Law and the *Reeve's Tale*," *NM* 70 (1969): 679–83. For a discussion of this maxim and the clerk's justification for taking revenge on the miller later in the tale, "'. . . gif a man in a point be agreved, / That in another he sal be releved'" (lines 4181–82), see P. Olson, "The *Reeve's Tale*: Chaucer's *Measure for Measure*," *SP* 59 (1962): 1–17.

[4] See Hahn and R. W. Kaeuper, "Text and Context," pp. 67–102.

description of these figures is derived primarily from Chaucer's source for *The Knight's Tale*, Boccaccio's *Teseida*,[5] it is a graphic rendering of the types of acts that were recognized as felonies by English law (lines 1995–2008):

> Ther saugh I first the derke ymaginyng
> Of Felonye, and al the compassyng;
> The crueel Ire, reed as any gleede;
> The pykepurs, and eek the pale Drede;
> The smylere with the knyf under the cloke;
> The shepne brennynge with the blake smoke;
> The tresoun of the mordrynge in the bedde;
> The open werre, with woundes al bibledde;
> Contek, with blody knyf and sharp manace.
> Al ful of chirkyng was that sory place.
> The sleere of hymself yet saugh I ther, —
> His herte-blood hath bathed al his heer;
> The nayl ydryven in the shode a-nyght;
> The colde deeth, with mouth gapyng upright.

Among the crimes recognized as felonies in medieval England were homicide, rape, arson, larceny, robbery, and treason. Originally a felony was a feudal crime; it was any act which constituted a breach of the fealty or faith the vassal has pledged to his lord under the terms of the feudal contract. This offense was so serious that the feudal relationship ended immediately, and the lord was entitled to reclaim possession of the vassal's feudal tenement. The vassal's land was said to escheat to the lord, while his goods, his chattels, were forfeited to the crown. By Chaucer's day, however, most felonies were not the result of breach of a feudal bond. As will be considered later, treason alone among the felonies retained its affiliation with the old feudal felony. Treason in Chaucer's time was an act that breached the bond of faith or trust between lord and man or between king and subject.

Even though most felonies were no longer crimes against lordship, the consequences associated with those crimes continued to reflect the feudal origins of the offense. The lands of a felon still escheated to his

---

[5] For the source of these lines, see Robinson's Explanatory Notes to *The Knight's Tale* 1967–2050, *The Works of Geoffrey Chaucer*, ed. Robinson. For the history of the term "felony" and the development of the various types of felonies, see Holdsworth, *A History of English Law*, 2:357–60, 3:55–56; Pollock and Maitland, *The History of English Law Before the Time of Edward I*, 1:303–305, 2:464–70; Milsom, *Historical Foundations of the Common Law*, pp. 403–406. For a study of the various felonies in thirteenth- and fourteenth-century England, see H. N. Schneebeck, "The Law of Felony in Medieval England from the Accession of Edward I Until the Mid-Fourteenth Century," Ph.D. dissertation, University of Iowa, 1973, and sources cited therein.

lord, and his chattels still were forfeited to the king. The king also was allowed to waste the felon's lands for a year and a day before they reverted to his lord; that is, the king could strip them of valuable resources or fixtures before the lord retained possession of them. Also, the term "felony" and terms like *"felon"* derived from it carried some association with early notions of the crime as a breach of faith or trust.[6]

In the following I examine first those felonies like homicide and rape that by Chaucer's day were no longer considered simply feudal crimes. Then I consider Chaucer's use of treason, the one crime that did retain elements of the feudal felony.

### CHAUCER'S USE OF VARIOUS FELONIES

*The law of homicide and* The Parson's Tale. *The Parson's Tale* contains a discussion of spiritual and corporal homicide. Spiritual homicide was the killing of another's soul, while, logically, corporal homicide was the killing of another person. Both forms of homicide were considered sins engendered by Ire.[7] The Parson's discussion of them is based on Raymond of Pennaforte's account of homicide in his *Summa*.[8] Raymond on homicide, and consequently the discussion of that sin in *The Parson's Tale*, reflects canon law doctrine. Raymond's treatment of the rules relating to corporal or bodily homicide was also borrowed to formulate a statement of the common law regarding the crime homicide in the treatise attributed to Henry de Bracton, *De legibus et consuetudinibus angliae*.[9] This work is a fairly accurate

------

[6] See *MED*, s.vv. *felonie* n., 1; *feloun* n. (1), 1(a) and 4; *felonous* adj., (a).

[7] *The Parson's Tale* 563–78.

[8] Raymond of Pennaforte's *Summa* was identified as the source of Chaucer's passage on homicide in *The Parson's Tale* by D. R. Johnson, "'Homicide' in the *Parson's Tale*," *PMLA* 57 (1942): 51–56. Whether Chaucer actually used Raymond's text or a text based on Raymond's for this passage and for other passages in *The Parson's Tale* said to be derived from his *Summa* has not been resolved. See, for instance, S. Wenzel, "The Source of Chaucer's Seven Deadly Sins," *Traditio* 30 (1974): 351–78. Although the passages on the Seven Deadly Sins in *The Parson's Tale* have been attributed to the *Summa seu tractatus de viciis* of Guilielmus Peraldus by K. O. Petersen, *The Sources of the Parson's Tale*, Wenzel has found manuscripts containing tracts based on that of Peraldus which seem closer to the discussion of the sins in *The Parson's Tale*. He has not, however, found a redaction of Raymond's work that contains the material found in *The Parson's Tale* and is closer to that material than Raymond's text.

[9] Traditionally the authorship of this treatise has been attributed to Henry de Bracton (or de Bratton), a justice of the king's bench from 1248 to 1257. In the introduction to his translation of this work, however, S. E. Thorne has shown that the treatise is a compilation of the work of several writers of whom Bracton was the last; see Henry de Bracton, *Bracton de legibus et consuetudinibus angliae*, ed. G. E. Woodbine, trans. and rev. S. E. Thorne, 3:xiii–lii; hereafter cited

statement of the common law on homicide in Chaucer's day. The account of the sin of bodily homicide in *The Parson's Tale*, therefore, shares affinities with Bracton on homicide because of the mutual appropriation by Chaucer and Bracton of Raymond's discussion of the sin. *The Parson's Tale* on homicide can thus be regarded as reflecting aspects of both canon law conception of the sin and common law formulation of the crime.[10]

Since the Parson's statements about homicide merely paraphrase Raymond, they may be important as facts that present the law of the time, but they can tell us little about the extent of Chaucer's understanding of that law. Nevertheless, the treatment of bodily homicide in *The Parson's Tale* is noteworthy because it illustrates how fundamental elements of the common law and canon law on the subject converged.[11] To elucidate this point, the affinities shared by *The Parson's Tale* and Bracton on homicide will be considered briefly. This examination will also help place the later discussion of Chaucer's use of elements of the crime of murder in a broader legal context.

It is worth noting the differences in Chaucer's and Bracton's borrowings from Raymond. Chaucer borrowed from Raymond's exegesis of the classes of spiritual homicide and bodily homicide and his discussion of infanticide, abortion and contraception as forms of homicide. Bracton borrowed only Raymond's definition of homicide and his examination of bodily homicide and abortion. Appropriately, Bracton omitted

---

as Bracton. For a discussion of Bracton's use of Raymond on homicide, see F. Schulz, "Bracton and Raymond de Peñafort," *Law Quarterly Review* 61 (1945): 286–92; H. G. Richardson, *Bracton: The Problem of His Text*, pp. 27–28, 126–31.

[10] For a thorough analysis of the law of homicide in the late thirteenth and early fourteenth centuries, see Schneebeck, "The Law of Felony in Medieval England from the Accession of Edward I Until the Mid-Fourteenth Century," 1:221–321, which deals with felonious homicide; 2:322–430, which deals with justifiable and excusable homicide. For more concise treatments of the law of homicide in medieval England, see Pollock and Maitland, *The History of English Law Before the Time of Edward I*, 2:478–85; T. A. Green, "Societal Concepts of Criminal Liability for Homicide in Mediaeval England," *Speculum* 47 (1972): 669–94. The three major common law treatises of the thirteenth century also contain statements about the law of homicide which fairly accurately reflect the law in Chaucer's day; see Bracton, 2:340–42; H. G. Richardson and G. O. Sayles, eds. and trans., *Fleta*, 2:60–61; Nichols, ed. and trans., *Britton*, pp. 29–32. *Fleta* and *Britton* are late-thirteenth-century redactions of Bracton. *Fleta*, in Latin and surviving in only one manuscript, paraphrases Bracton and adds to it material from other texts and statutes enacted after Bracton's text was completed. *Britton*, in Anglo-Norman, survives in several manuscripts.

[11] The relationship of this passage in *The Parson's Tale* to the canon law on homicide is examined by J. Shaw, "Corporeal and Spiritual Homicide, the Sin of Wrath, and the 'Parson's Tale,'" *Traditio* 38 (1982): 281–300. Shaw thinks that this passage is closely related to the treatment of homicide as a branch of Ire in the vernacular penitential manuals of Chaucer's day.

Raymond's discussion of spiritual homicide from his treatise on secular law.

*The Parson's Tale* describes bodily homicide as follows (line 569–73):

> Bodily manslaughtre is, whan thow sleest him with thy tonge in oother manere; as whan thou comandest to sleen a man, or elles yevest hym conseil to sleen a man. / Manslaughtre in dede is in foure maneres. That oon is by lawe, right as a justice dampneth hym that is coupable to the deeth. But lat the justice be war that he do it rightfully, and that he do it nat for delit to spille blood, but for kepynge of rightwisnesse. / Another homycide is that is doon for necessitee, as whan o man sleeth another in his defendaunt, and that he ne may noon ootherwise escape from his owene deeth. / But certeinly if he may escape withouten slaughtre of his adversarie, and sleeth hym, he dooth synne and he shal bere penance as for deedly synne. / Eek if a man, by caas or aventure, shete an arwe, or caste a stoon, with which he sleeth a man, he is homycide.

In discussing bodily homicide, Chaucer deals first with homicide by word and then with homicide by deed.[12] His statement of the types of verbal homicide corresponds with the first two types of verbal homicide listed by Bracton: precept (commanding someone to slay another) and counsel (counseling someone to slay another). Chaucer omits the third type of verbal homicide mentioned by Bracton, homicide by denial.[13] Next Chaucer observes that there are four types of homicide by deed and then proceeds to discuss only three.[14] Bracton lists and discusses

---

[12] Bracton's treatment of homicide is similar to that found in *The Parson's Tale* but, of course, more detailed. The translation here is that of Thorne in Bracton, 2:340–42: "Corporal homicide is where a man is slain bodily, and this is committed in two ways: by word or by deed. By word in three ways, that is, by precept, by counsel, and by denial. . . . By deed in four ways, that is, in the administration of justice, of necessity, by chance and by intention. In the administration of justice, as when a judge or officer kills one lawfully found guilty. But it is homicide if done out of malice or from pleasure in the shedding of human blood and though the accused is lawfully slain, he who does the act commits a mortal sin because of his evil purpose. But if it is done from a love of justice, the judge does not sin in condemning him to death, nor in ordering an officer to slay him, nor does the officer sin if when sent by the judge he kills the condemned man. . . . Of necessity, and here we must distinguish whether the necessity was avoidable or not; if avoidable and he could escape without slaying, he will then be guilty of homicide; if unavoidable, since he kills without premeditated hatred but with sorrow of heart, in order to save himself and his family, since he could not otherwise escape danger, he is not liable to the penalty for homicide. By chance, as by misadventure, when one throws a stone at a bird or elsewhere and another passing by unexpectedly is struck and dies. . . . By intention, as where one in anger or hatred or for the sake of gain, deliberately and in premeditated assault, has killed another wickedly and feloniously and in breach of the king's peace."

[13] The Latin term for this type of homicide is *defensio*. Shaw thinks that this was an obscure classification of homicide even for canonists; she suggests, therefore, that Chaucer intentionally omitted that classification; but see Bracton, 2:340, where Thorne translates the term as "denial."

[14] For a theory of the reason that Chaucer omitted intentional homicide from his account of bodily homicide, see Johnson, "'Homicide' in the *Parson's Tale*," pp. 55–56.

four types: homicide committed in the administration of justice, homicide by necessity, homicide by chance or accident, and intentional homicide. Chaucer lists all but intentional homicide.

Up to the point where the discussion turns to infanticide, Chaucer's treatment of corporal homicide is an accurate, though uneven, account of both the canon law and the common law on the subject. Primarily there were three types of homicides recognized by English law: inexcusable, excusable, and justifiable.[15] Execution of criminals by judges properly carrying out a sentence were lawful and therefore justifiable homicides. Other types of justifiable homicides, not mentioned by the Parson, were the slaying of thieves, robbers, or housebreakers caught in the act or the slaying of outlaws resisting arrest. Excusable homicides were homicides committed by necessity or chance — that is those committed in self-defense or unintentionally. In fact, Chaucer's statement of the rules of self-defense (lines 571–72) accurately reflects the law on the subject. One who slays in self-defense must make every possible attempt to escape his adversary and must use only enough force in retaliating to ward off his attacker; deadly force was permitted only when necessary to preserve one's life. If the slayer used more force than reasonably necessary to preserve his life, the homicide was not excusable. This rule is stated in *The Tale of Melibee* (lines 1531–35). Accidental homicides were also excusable except in instances where the death was due to the slayer's willful negligence. Those convicted of excusable homicides were pardoned. Deliberate homicides, those committed willfully, were inexcusable and punishable by death.

Up to line 573 of *The Parson's Tale*, Chaucer's treatment of corporal homicide agrees with Bracton and the salient features of English law on the subject.[16] *The Parson's Tale*'s handling of infanticide, abortion, and contraception as types of homicide diverge from Bracton's account. Bracton and the common law considered only abortion of a living fetus homicide. Chaucer, following Raymond, considered both abortion and contraception as types of homicide punishable by penitential sanctions.[17]

---

[15] This summary of the English law of homicide is based primarily on Green, "Societal Concepts of Criminal Liability for Homicide in Mediaeval England," pp. 669–71; and Pollock and Maitland, *The History of English Law Before the Time of Edward I*, 2:478–85.

[16] For a discussion of Chaucer's use of Raymond for the remainder of his account of homicide, see Johnson, "'Homicide' in the *Parson's Tale*," pp. 55–56.

[17] For a discussion of Chaucer's treatment of contraception and abortion as well as that of Bracton and *Fleta*, see J. T. Noonan, *Contraception*, pp. 215–17. Noonan, however, does not appear to be aware that both Chaucer's treatment of contraception and abortion and a portion of Bracton's are based on Raymond's *Summa*.

"Mordre" *in Chaucer and Popular Notions About the Classification of Homicides in the Fourteenth Century.* From *The Parson's Tale's* uneven yet fairly legalistic definition of homicide, one might assume that Chaucer knew something about the technical nuances of the crime. Yet his use elsewhere of terminology denoting the crime of homicide suggests that his knowledge of the crime was based on popular ideas associated with it rather than an understanding of the legal niceties of homicide. The legal term for all killings, whether they were justifiable, excusable, or inexcusable, was *homicidium*.[18] This term is translated as "manslaughtre" in *The Parson's Tale*: ". . . understonde wel that homycide, that is manslaughtre, is in diverse wise" (line 563). Elsewhere, though, Chaucer uses "homycide" to denote either the sin of spiritual homicide or a person who slays another.[19] "Manslaughtre" is mentioned in *The Pardoner's Tale* (line 593) as a type of spiritual homicide and in *The Former Age* as a type of slaying distinctive from "mordre" (line 63).[20] Chaucer's separation of killings in *The Former Age* into distinct classes, "manslaughtre" and "mordre," hints at an aspect of Chaucer's knowledge of the crime of homicide that an examination of his use of the term "mordre" will bring into sharper focus.

"Mordre" is the term Chaucer uses instead of "homycide" to describe slayings; the term refers to premeditated slayings perpetrated through stealth or in secret. The use of "mordre" instead of "homycide" to refer to particular kinds of killings reflects an interesting dichotomy between the popular separation of slayings into two classes, murder and man-

18 Cf. *MED*, s.v. *homicidi(e* n.: the crime of murder or manslaughter. In the following examination of the history of terminology associated with the crime of homicide, I pay special attention to the legal usage of "murder" as a term denoting a particularly aggravated degree of slaying. I rely heavily on the following studies: Green, "Societal Concepts of Criminal Liability for Homicide in Mediaeval England"; T. A. Green, "The Jury and the English Law of Homicide, 1200–1600," *Michigan Law Review* 74 (1976): 413–99 (this article is a reevaluation of the conclusions reached by Kaye, below); J. M. Kaye, "The Early History of Murder and Manslaughter," *Law Quarterly Review* 83 (1967): 365–95, 569–601; Pollock and Maitland, *The History of English Law Before the Time of Edward I*, 2:485–88; Schneebeck, "The Law of Felony in Medieval England from the Accession of Edward I Until the Mid-Fourteenth Century," 1:229–30. At p. 230 n. 28, Schneebeck notes that "murder" referred both to secret slayings and to premeditated slayings not committed surreptitiously.

19 Cf. *MED*, s.v. *homicide* n., c, which defines a homicide as one who kills another.

20 *The Former Age* ends with a list of crimes and sins: "For in oure dayes nis but covetyse, / Doublenesse, and tresoun, and envye, / Poyson, manslauhtre, and mordre in sondry wyse" (lines 61–63). Although the poem is based on Boethius's *Consolation of Philosophy* 2, m. 5, these lines appear to be Chaucer's addition; see W. W. Skeat's introduction to the poem in *The Complete Works of Geoffrey Chaucer*, 2d ed., 1:78–79. That Chaucer lists both "manslauhtre" and "mordre" seems to support the following argument that he considered them separate offenses.

slaughter, and the legal classification of all killings as homicides.[21] In early English law, only the most vicious killings were deserving of capital punishment; such killings were termed "murders," killings committed by stealth or through ambush. Sometime during the twelfth century all killings became capital offenses, and, gradually, all killings came under the legal heading of *homicidium*. The distinction, however, between those killings which were inexcusable and deserving of punishment by death and those which were either excusable or justified was often expressed in the legal treatises of the thirteenth century by reference to the first type of killing as *murdrum* and the latter types as *homicidium*. For example, although both degrees of killings are listed as homicide by Bracton under his definition of homicide, he also includes a section that presents the older definition of murder as a killing distinguished from homicide because it was a premeditated act perpetrated through some vicious and secretive means.[22] Although by the fourteenth century *homicidium* was the legal "term of art" for both types of slayings, *murdrum* had its significance in another context: it was the term for the fine which the hundred had to pay when a foreigner was killed within the community and no suspect could be produced. The hundred, an administrative subdivision of a shire, was both the area over which the local court — the hundred court — had jurisdiction and, as well, the collective designation for the residents and landowners of that area. Until the abolition of the fine in 1340, this was the only legal significance of *murdrum*.[23] Although *murdrum* appeared in indictments brought before justices

[21] See Milsom, *Historical Foundations of the Common Law*, pp. 422–24; Green, "Societal Concepts of Criminal Liability for Homicide in Mediaeval England," pp. 669–83.

[22] For the definition of "murder" in certain thirteenth-century legal tracts, see Bracton, 2:378–79; Richardson and Sayles, eds. and trans., *Fleta*, 2:78–79.

[23] For a discussion of the effect of the statute of 1340, see Pollock and Maitland, *The History of English Law Before the Time of Edward I*, 2:488. Green, "The Jury and the English Law of Homicide," pp. 427–71, discusses the various uses of "murder" as a quasi-legal term in the fourteenth century. Although a 1390 statute restricting the king's power to pardon in certain types of criminal cases listed murder as one of the crimes under the purview of the statute, this distinction had no permanent effect on the substantive law of homicide. Green also notes that the term was used in indictments by coroners and justices of the peace and that those convicted of crimes termed "murder" in these indictments were sentenced more harshly than those convicted of lesser homicides. He concludes that, although "murder" was not a legal "term of art" during this period, it carried distinctive legal associations in the popular mind. For example, juries would use this extralegal term to distinguish among simple and aggravated homicides. See also Green, "Societal Concepts of Criminal Liability for Homicide in Mediaeval England," pp. 687–88; T. F. T. Plucknett, "A Commentary on the Indictments," in B. H. Putnam, ed., *Proceedings Before the Justices of the Peace in the Fourteenth and Fifteenth Centuries*, pp. cxlvii–cxlix.

of the peace in the fourteenth and fifteenth centuries and was used in a 1390 statute to denote an aggravated type of slaying, it was not considered a technical legal term again until the sixteenth century.[24]

Studies indicate, however, that, despite its exile from the realm of legal respectability, "murder" survived in popular usage as a term which distinguished those slayings perpetrated at night, in secret, by ambush, poison, or through any other devious or clandestine method from excusable or justifiable slayings. Jurors, for instance, continued to maintain the distinction between murder and homicide when considering which slayings should be punished by death, since they deemed only those acts formerly classed as murder capital offenses, even though the law classed all types of slayings as homicides and, technically, considered all but justifiable homicides capital crimes. Those homicides that I have previously referred to as excusable homicides, those committed by accident or necessity, legally were capital crimes as well, but the circumstances surrounding the commission of slayings of that nature warranted that the punishment be voided by a pardon for the crime.

Chaucer's uses of "murder" and the types of slayings he associates with the term thus appear to agree with a popular rather than a legal conception of the crime. For example, the slaying of the little clergeon in *The Prioress's Tale* is a "mordre" (line 630). It is a premeditated slaying committed in secret; members of the Jewish community first plot to kill the child and then refuse to acknowledge that the slaying occurred. The various examples of slayings upon which Chauntecler meditates in *The Nun's Priest's Tale* (lines 3053, 3114) are also called "murders" and fit the definition of the term that has been proposed here. That murder was normally considered a clandestine affair is emphasized by the proverb found in both *The Prioress's Tale* (line 576) and *The Nun's Priest's Tale* (lines 3052, 3057): "Mordre wol out."[25]

Except when it is used to describe spiritual homicide, as in *The Pardoner's Tale* (lines 644, 657, 896) and *The Parson's Tale*, "homycide" is used by Chaucer to describe the person committing the crime rather than the crime itself. Interestingly, Chaucer calls killers both "mordrours" and "homycides" even if the slayings were secret. Perhaps the act of slaying in secret was distinguished in the popular mind by

---

[24] For an extensive analysis of this development, see Green, "The Jury and the English Law of Homicide," pp. 472–97.

[25] For other instances of the use of this maxim, see Whiting, ed., *Proverbs, Sentences, and Proverbial Phrases*, M806.

"murder," while terminology denoting the perpetrator of the crime was not as precise. For example, in *The Pardoner's Tale*, the revelers who kill their fellow upon his return from fetching wine are "homycides" (line 893), as is the hired killer in *The Prioress's Tale* (line 567). The fox who spirits Chauntecler away in *The Nun's Priest's Tale* is called a "mordrour" (line 3226), as is Duke Walter of *The Clerk's Tale* (line 732) when the unexplained disappearances of his children raise suspicions that he may have killed them.

It seems safe to conclude that Chaucer's conception of the crime of murder was based on popular notions about the nature of the crime rather than on a knowledge of the legal theory defining the act. This is supported by his preference for "mordre" over "homycide" to describe killings as well as his use of "mordre" particularly to describe killings perpetrated through stealth and premeditation.

*Rape.* Chaucer's handling of elements of the crime of rape in his works reflects popular notions about the crime as much as legal ones. Today rape has a clear legal definition: sexual assault without consent of the victim. In Chaucer's day, as those who have tried to determine why Chaucer was charged with the *raptus* of Cecily Champaign have discovered, the definition of the crime was less distinct.[26] Then the crime could have been either sexual assault or abduction of a woman. *Raptus*, *rapio*, or, in the vernacular, "ravisshe" referred to either act.[27] Thus when either word appears alone, it is impossible to determine whether the term denotes sexual assault or abduction. Although legal records occasionally distinguish sexual assault from abduction by referring to the former act with *rapuit* and the latter with *abduxit*,[28] often the

[26] See the discussion of the release executed in Chaucer's favor regarding an action of *raptus* against him and the summary of the different theories propounded for the meaning of *raptus* in *LR*, pp. 343–47. Basically the ambiguous language in the release makes it impossible to determine whether Chaucer had been accused of abduction or sexual assault. For a survey of the medieval law of rape, see Pollock and Maitland, *The History of English Law Before the Time of Edward I*, 2:490–91; Schneebeck, "The Law of Felony in Medieval England from the Accession of Edward I Until the Mid-Fourteenth Century," 2:433–505; B. Toner, *The Facts of Rape*, pp. 89–94.

[27] In Latin the verb *rapere* denoted both sexual assault and abduction: see *OED*, s.v. *rape* v.²; the Old French verb for both acts was *raviss*: see *OED*, s.v. *ravish* v. In discussing this crime, I follow the procedure adopted by J. B. Post in "Ravishment of Women and the Statutes of Westminster," in J. H. Baker, ed., *Legal Records and the Historian*, pp. 150–64; he used "rape" to refer solely to sexual assault, while "ravish" functioned as the more ambiguous term that encompassed both sexual assault and abduction.

[28] See G. O. Sayles, ed., *Select Cases in the Court of King's Bench Under Richard II, Henry IV and Henry V*, 7:53, 134 181.

records will use the same verb, *ravir* in the French or *rapere* in the Latin,[29] to describe both acts.[30] It is possible, however, that this failure to distinguish adequately between the two acts in the legal terminology may indicate that rape and abduction were perceived as interrelated and therefore virtually indistinguishable crimes.

The statutes of rape enacted in England in the twelfth and thirteenth centuries are partly responsible for the confusion of terminology dealing with rape and abduction. Before the enactment of these statutes, the law of rape was basically defined by custom and common law. The legal treatises of the late twelfth and early thirteenth centuries considered rape a crime of forcible sexual assault deserving of punishments ranging from blinding and castration to death.[31] The statutes, however, broadened the definition of the crime and changed the nature of the punishment for it.[32] The first Statute of Westminster (1275) made it a crime to ravish (*ravir*) or take away by force (*prendre*) a maiden under age twelve, regardless of consent, or matrons and maidens over twelve without their consent. The crime was to be punished by imprisonment for two years and ransom. These provisions were modified by the second Statute of Westminster (1285), which made it a capital crime to ravish (*ravir*) either a maid or a matron without her consent either before or after the act. The statute also gave the king suit in cases where the woman assented to the act after the fact. In this statute, ravishment appears to refer either to sexual assault or to abduction. The latter part of the statute, however, is less ambiguous and makes certain types of abduction lesser offenses. A third statute, enacted in 1382, reinforced the penalty for ravishment decreed by the

[29] See 6 Richard II, Statute 1, c. 6, in *The Statutes of the Realm*, 2:27. Here *rapere* is used for both sexual assault and abduction; it is often unclear which act is being referred to.

[30] J. B. Post discusses the English law of rape as promulgated by statutes enacted in the thirteenth and fourteenth centuries. He also deals with the ambiguous nature of the crime and how the terminology used to refer to those crimes did little to clarify matters; see Post, "Ravishment of Women and the Statutes of Westminster"; J. B. Post, "Sir Thomas West and the Statute of Rapes, 1382," *Bulletin of the Institute of Historical Research* 53 (1980): 24–30.

[31] For a convenient summary of the prestatutory law of rape in England, see Toner, *The Facts of Rape*, pp. 89–90; for how that law was altered by statute, see the articles by Post cited in n. 30 above. My discussion of the law of rape as propagated by statute law in medieval England is based on Post's studies. For other discussions of the modification of the law of rape by statute in medieval England, see Pollock and Maitland, *The History of English Law Before the Time of Edward I*, 2:491; Schneebeck, "The Law of Felony in Medieval England from the Accession of Edward I Until the Mid-Fourteenth Century," 2:434–44.

[32] For the three statutes of rape, see 3 Edward I (1275), Statute of Westminster 1, c. 13, *The Statutes of the Realm*, 1:29; 13 Edward I (1285), Statute of Westminster 2, c. 34, ibid., 1:87; 6 Richard II (1382), Statute 1, c. 6, ibid., 2:27.

second Statute of Westminster and also gave husbands or fathers of victims of the crime a right of action against ravishers when a wife or a daughter consented to the act. Again the same terminology is employed to describe both sexual assault and abduction.

Although Chaucer always seems to use the Middle English "ravisshe" to mean abduction or seizure rather than sexual assault, permutations of the term's sense as sexual assault can occasionally be detected. In the examples below, the primary meaning of the term is abduction or seizure. For example, in book 4 of *Troilus and Criseyde*, Pandarus suggests that Troilus "ravisshe" (line 530) Criseyde to keep her from leaving Troy. Pandarus is, of course, suggesting that Troilus kidnap Criseyde, not that he rape her. One reason Troilus opposes Pandarus's plan is that abducting Criseyde would compound the offense which precipitated the war with the Greeks: "ravysshyng of wommen so by myght" (4.548), the rape of Helen. Further use of "ravysshe" to mean abduction is found in *The Merchant's Tale* and *The Summoner's Tale*. In *The Merchant's Tale*, Pluto is described as having "ravysshed [Proserpyne] out of Ethna" (line 2230). In the *Prologue* to *The Summoner's Tale*, a friar "ravysshed was to helle" (line 1676) to get a glimpse of the quarters housing friars in the afterlife.

Chaucer also deals with sexual assault, though he usually describes or alludes to the act rather than giving it a name. His descriptions generally contain elements associated with the legal definition of the crime. For example, two of the heroines of *The Legend of Good Women* were forcibly raped. The legal treatises and statutes dealing with the crime indicate that one of its elements was the forcible assault of a woman. It should be noted that, though many of the other women in the legends are duped into relinquishing their virtue, they are not coerced into coitus but consent.

Lucrece and Philomela are the two women who are sexually assaulted in the legends. Lucrece is raped at sword point by Tarquin, who threatens to accuse her falsely of adultery if she refuses to submit to his passions. Chaucer avoids an explicit description of the rape by describing her faint (lines 1812–18):

> These Romeyn wyves lovede so here name
> At thilke tyme, and dredde so the shame,
> That, what for fer of sclaunder and drede of deth,
> She loste bothe at ones wit and breth,
> And in a swogh she lay, and wex so ded,

> Men myghte smyten of hire arm or hed;
> She feleth no thyng, neyther foul ne fayr.

Chaucer is less guarded in his description of the rape of Philomela by Tereus (lines 2324–26):

> By force hath he [Tereus], this traytour, don that dede,
> That he hath reft hire of hire maydenhede,
> Maugre hire hed, by strengthe and by his myght.

As in the rape of Lucrece, here the deed is committed by force. Interestingly, Tarquin's act is called "tresoun" (line 1783), and Tereus is called a "traytour" (line 2324). As my discussion of treason will clarify, although legally no treason was committed by either man, morally a treason of sorts was perpetrated by both. Each of them violated a bond of trust: Tarquin by betraying the trust of his knight Colatyn, whose wife he rapes, and Tereus by betraying the trust of both his wife and her sister, Philomela.

In *The Wife of Bath's Tale*, Chaucer more explicitly deals with the legal aspects of the crime of rape by using elements of the legal definition of the crime and the punishment for the crime. Chaucer also deals with certain elements of the legal procedure used to prosecute rape, but those details will be considered in a later section of this chapter.

Chaucer describes the knight's crime and his punishment, as proposed by King Arthur, in the following manner (lines 882–93):

> And so bifel it that this kyng Arthour
> Hadde in his hous a lusty bacheler,
> That on a day cam ridynge fro ryver;
> And happed that, allone as he was born,
> He saugh a mayde walkynge hym biforn,
> Of which mayde anon, maugree hir heed,
> By verray force, he rafte hire maydenhed;
> For which oppressioun was swich clamour
> And swich pursute unto the kyng Arthour,
> That dampned was this knyght for to be deed,
> By cours of lawe, and sholde han lost his heed—
> Paraventure swich was the statut tho—....

Breslin has noted that the punishment levied by Arthur on the knight, death, accorded with the severity of the punishment for rape set forth in Bracton and other legal treatises.[33] She observes that these works prescribed blinding and castration as the ultimate punishments for the crime. Her discussion, however, fails to consider that statute law had significantly modified both the definition of rape and the degree of punishment for the crime since the compilation of the thirteenth-century lawbooks she relies on. Indeed, the punishment prescribed by English statute law for rape precisely matched that levied upon the knight by Arthur—death.

The existence of these statutes makes Chaucer's lines attributing the nature of the knight's punishment to the possible existence of a statute intriguing (lines 891–93):

> That dampned was this knyght for to be deed,
> By cours of lawe, and sholde han lost his heed—
> Paraventure swich was the statut tho— . . . .

There are several ways Chaucer could have known about a statute on rape without ever having actually read it. For instance, it is common to find in the records of ravishment cases brought before the king's bench a recitation of the alleged facts of the case which included a formulaic statement that the rape and abduction had occurred in violation of the statute (*contra formam statuti*).[34] Usually the name and substance of the statute were not included in the record. Possibly as justice of the peace, justice *ad inquirendum* in the case of Isabella Hall's abduction, or in the terms of the charge of *raptus* made against him, Chaucer heard accusations presented in a formula similar to that in the king's bench records which alleged that the abduction had occurred *contra formam statuti*. Since the same punishment was levied whether the matter involved sexual assault or abduction, it would have made no difference whether Chaucer heard the formula recited in a case involving rape or one dealing with abduction.

In all probability, Chaucer did not consider abduction and sexual assault as different crimes. The law usually did not distinguish between them, and there is a good possibility that they were not distinguished

---

[33] See Breslin, "Justice and Law in Chaucer's *Canterbury Tales*," pp. 115–18. A more recent study of the law of rape in *The Wife of Bath's Tale*, one that covers some of the same areas I cover here, is R. J. Blanch, "'Al Was This Land Fulfild of Fayerye': The Thematic Employment of Force, Willfulness, and Legal Conventions in Chaucer's *Wife of Bath's Tale*," *SN* 57 (1985): 41–51.

[34] The formula was stated generally as follows: "Rapuit et abduxit contra pacem domini regis et contra formam statuti etc."; see Sayles, ed., *Select Cases in the Court of King's Bench Under Richard II, Henry IV and Henry V*, 7:53, 134, 181.

in the popular imagination. Studies indicate that a large percentage of those appealed for rape were either found not guilty or were merely fined rather than subjected to the full force of the punishment decreed by statute.[35] The knight's eventual pardon for his crime in *The Wife of Bath's Tale* is more in line with the actual treatment of convicted rapists in Chaucer's day than is the sentence of death imposed by Arthur. Women rarely won appeals of rape. In fact, most appeals of that sort failed on technical grounds, such as misstatement of the appeal or failure to raise hue and cry. The general attitude regarding the crime was that rape and abduction were offenses against property and not against the person.

J. B. Post's studies of the development of the three statutes of rape suggest that each successive statute was designed to favor those who had an economic interest in the woman: either the husband or the father. The statutes made it easier for these parties to seek and receive redress for the injury done to their property when a wife or daughter was raped or ravished. Post argues that, while the statutes provided a cause of action for the victim's husband or father, they made it more difficult for the victim herself to bring a successful appeal, and he implies that a rape victim in medieval England was treated by English law as no more than damaged goods.

An attitude similar to that of equating rape victims with damaged goods is suggested by the miller's despair upon learning of his daughter's nocturnal alliance with Aleyn the clerk in *The Reeve's Tale*. When the miller learns that Malyne has given up her virtue to the clerk, his first concern is that she has become "disparaged" (lines 4271–72):

> "Who dorste be so boold to disparage
> My doghter, that is come of swich lynage?"

When a woman was forced to marry below her social station, she was said to have been "disparaged."[36] The term can also mean "dishonor."

---

[35] The following examination of the realities surrounding criminal procedure and punishment in cases of rape is based on the findings of Post in his articles on the rape statutes (see note 30 above); see also Schneebeck, "The Law of Felony in Medieval England from the Accession of Edward I Until the Mid-Fourteenth Century," 2:443–89; Toner, *The Facts of Rape*, pp. 89–94. Schneebeck found that few juries would inflict capital punishment on a man convicted of rape in the fourteenth century and that after 1385 few of those accused in appeals of rape were convicted. The typical punishment was either a fine or brief imprisonment. The common theme in all three studies is that few appeals of rape were successful and that most successful rape actions were those prosecuting the defendant for commission of a trespass, an action implying a lesser degree of criminal liability and carrying with it a lesser degree of punishment.

[36] See *MED*, s.v. *disparagen*, v., 1–3.

Although Malyne has not married below her social station but has slept with Aleyn, according to the miller's bloated conception of her lineage, she has been "disparaged": her parson's stock has been polluted by that of a lowly clerk. Consequently the miller considers her devalued as a marriageable and marketable product. Malyne's actions have jeopardized her chances both for making a good marriage and for remaining her grandfather's heir. In this light, the miller's despair at her disparagement is like that of a merchant on discovering broken merchandise and reflects a view analogous to that perpetrated by the English statutes of rape: that rape was a crime against property.

## TREASON

### THE MEDIEVAL ENGLISH LAW OF TREASON

While homicide and rape were properly classified as felonies, another crime, treason, began as a felony and only later was classified as a separate offense. Treason was distinguished from other felonies both by the types of acts that constituted the crime and by the severity of the punishment inflicted on those found guilty of the crime.[37] Although commission of any of the crimes labeled as felonies conceivably could constitute treason, treason was a distinctive crime because it alone of the other felonies retained elements associated with the original, feudal conception of felony. The fundamental element of treason was the commission of an act that violated the bond of fealty owed to one's

[37] My discussion of the law of treason in medieval England is based on the following studies: J. G. Bellamy, *The Law of Treason in England in the Later Middle Ages*, ed. D. E. C. Yale; S. H. Cuttler, *The Law of Treason and Treason Trials in Later Medieval France*; Holdsworth, *A History of English Law*, 2:449–50, 3:287–93; Pollock and Maitland, *The History of English Law Before the Time of Edward I*, 2:500–508. Of particular interest are two studies by W. R. J. Barron, "The Penalties for Treason in Medieval Life and Literature," *Journal of Medieval History* 7 (1981): 187–202, and *"Trawthe" and Treason*; see especially pp. 187–91 of his article for a concise summation of the development of the law of treason in medieval England and a discussion of the crime's origins in the offense of breach of the feudal bond of fealty. The article also contains an extensive bibliography of sources dealing with the medieval law of treason. Barron's book, an interpretation of *Sir Gawain and the Green Knight*, is based on the idea that the basic element underlying the crime of treason was breach of a quasi-contractual bond of "trawthe" between two people. He applies this idea to his interpretation of the poem with specific emphasis on the "foreward" between Bercilak and Gawain and Gawain's ultimate violation of that agreement. My arguments regarding the theme of treason in Chaucer's works are similar to those of Barron on that theme in *Gawain*; since the root of treason is bad faith, then, on a moral level, the betrayal of a bond of trust or "trouthe" is a treason.

lord or the bond of allegiance owed to one's king.[38] Although Bracton and *Fleta* (see note 10 above) refer to treason solely in terms of the Roman crime *laesa majestas*, a crime against the crown,[39] *Britton*, another thirteenth-century law tract based in part on Bracton, provides a broader definition of the crime. *Britton's* definition of treason reflects that crime's roots in the feudal law of felony:

> 1. Treason consists of any mischief, which a man knowingly does, or procures to be done, to one to whom he pretends to be a friend. And treasons may be either great or little, of which some require judgment of death, some loss of limb, pillory, or imprisonment, and others lighter punishment, according to the nature of the case.
> 2. Great or high treason is to compass our death or to disinherit us of our kingdom, or to falsify our seal, or to counterfeit our coin, or to clip it. A person may likewise commit great treason against others in several ways, as by procuring the death of any one who trusts him; as for instance those who poison their lords or others, and those who lead persons into such perils, that they lose life and member or chattels.
> 3. The judgment in high treason is to be drawn and to suffer death for the felony. The same judgment is incurred by those, who in appeals of felony are attainted of having counterfeited or otherwise falsified the seal of their lord, of whose dependence or homage they are, or of adultery with the wives of their lords, or of violation of the daughters of their lords or the nurses of their children. And if a woman be attainted of any treason, let her be burnt.[40]

Treason, according to *Britton*, was fundamentally the violation of a bond of trust between two people. The moral reprehensibility of the crime was emphasized by the equation of that bond of trust with the simplest and least legally defined relationship: friendship. Although a breach of the bond of friendship might not have been punishable as treason at law, it was nonetheless the moral equivalent of the crime.

The punishment for treason was designed to emphasize the serious nature of the offense. Bracton, *Fleta*, and *Britton* are in general agree-

[38] See D. E. C. Yale, Editor's Preface, in Bellamy, *The Law of Treason in England in the Later Middle Ages*, pp. vii–viii.

[39] See Bracton, 2:334–37; Richardson and Sayles, eds. and trans., *Fleta*, 2:56–58; for an analysis of the legal theory on treason presented by these and other medieval English legal texts, see Bellamy, *The Law of Treason in England in the Later Middle Ages*, pp. 1–22; for a discussion of the influence of the Roman law dealing with crime of *laesa majestas* on the English law of treason, see ibid., pp. 1–14.

[40] Nichols, ed. and trans., *Britton*, pp. 34–35. *Britton's* formulation of treason as a deliberate injury committed against a friend diverges from the more restricted definitions of the crime found in Bracton and *Fleta*, which are rooted in the Roman law's *laesa majestas*, a crime solely against the crown. Unlike Bracton and *Fleta*, *Britton* takes into account treason's roots in the feudal underpinnings of English law; see Bellamy, *The Law of Treason in the Later Middle Ages*, pp. 15–22, 225–26; Barron, "The Penalties for Treason in Medieval Life and Literature," pp. 188–89.

ment on the proper punishment for the crime. Most felonies were merely punishable by death, but for treason other punishments were included. For instance, a convicted traitor was usually drawn behind a horse to the place where he was to be hanged.[41] Moreover, a conviction for treason against the crown was generally accompanied by additional punishment after the death of the traitor.[42] The corpse of the convict might be quartered or mutilated in some other fashion and the various parts scattered about the country. A popular modification of this method of debasing the corpse of a traitor was to place the lifeless head on display at a prominent place as admonition for others with treasonous impulses.

Along with loss of life and limb, the traitor's property was also confiscated by the crown. As noted earlier, in cases where the crime was treason against lordship, the traitor's chattels went to the king, while his land eventually reverted to his feudal lord. In cases of treason against the crown, however, both the chattels and the land of the traitor were forfeited to the king. Bracton thought not only that a convicted traitor should be totally divested of his lands and chattel but also that his heirs should be disinherited for perpetuity. In certain cases, Bracton deemed it might be appropriate to kill the heirs along with the traitor.[43] Generally, however, even though the traitor's lands were forfeited to the king, the heir was entitled to his inheritance in those lands once he came of age.[44]

In 1352, a statute was enacted to distinguish those crimes which constituted treason against the crown, high treason, from those acts which were treason against lordship, later known as petty treason.

---

[41] Maitland observed that the reason for inflicting further punishment beyond death on one guilty of treason was that mere hanging was too easy a punishment for one who killed his lord. Because of that rationale, drawing the traitor to the place where he was to be hanged was added. Later, in cases of high treason, drawing and hanging were considered too slight punishments for treason against the crown, and more extreme punishments like disemboweling, burning, beheading, and quartering were added to the punishment inflicted on the traitor; see Pollock and Maitland, *The History of English Law Before the Time of Edward I*, 2:500–501; Bellamy, *The Law of Treason in the Later Middle Ages*, pp. 18, 20–21.

[42] For a general discussion of the types of punishment for treason in England, see Bellamy, *The Law of Treason in the Later Middle Ages*, index, s.v. *punishment*; Barron, "The Penalties for Treason in Medieval Life and Literature," pp. 187–202.

[43] Bracton, 2:335: "If he [the one accused of treason] is convicted he shall suffer the extreme penalty with torture, the loss of all his goods, and the perpetual disherison of his heirs, who are admitted neither to their paternal nor maternal inheritance. For this crime is so serious that his heirs are hardly permitted their lives." See also Richardson and Sayles, eds. and trans., *Fleta*, 2:56.

[44] See C. D. Ross, "Forfeiture for Treason in the Reign of Richard II," *English Historical Review* 71 (1956): 560–75; Bellamy, *The Law of Treason in the Later Middle Ages*, pp. 21–22.

There was an economic as well as legal reason for this statute.[45] By enacting a statute that delineated those crimes that would be considered high treason, the crown's claim to the land of those who committed crimes enumerated in that statute would be consolidated. The statutory definition of treason, however, differed little from the common law conception of the crime as elucidated in Bracton, *Fleta*, and *Britton*. The statute specified seven varieties of treason:

1. To compass or imagine the death of the king, queen or his eldest son.
2. To violate the queen, the king's eldest unmarried daughter or the wife of the king's son.
3. To wage war against the king.
4. To adhere to the king's enemies.
5. To counterfeit the king's seal or money.
6. To knowingly bring false money into the realm.
7. To slay the chancellor or any of the king's judges while in the performance of their duties.

The statute also specified what acts constituted the crime that would come to be known in the fifteenth century as petty treason: the killing of a husband by a wife, a master by a servant, a prelate by those both secular and religious who owed him obedience. As with the feudal felonies, the central theme linking the crimes listed by the Statute of 1352 is that all were deliberate acts which betrayed some bond of allegiance or trust.[46]

For the most part, the Statute of Treasons did little to change the manner in which traitors were punished. Cases indicate that drawing and quartering and hanging were still the conventional modes of dispensing with the traitor's body, while forfeiture was still the means by which his property was disposed of.[47] The statute merely made certain that there was no confusion about who gained the ultimate control of that property: the king.

---

[45] Yale, ed., in Bellamy, *The Law of Treason in the Later Middle Ages*, pp. vii–viii.

[46] For the text of the Statute of Treasons of 1352, see 25 Edward III, Statute 5, c. 2, *The Statutes of the Realm*, 1:319–20; see also Holdsworth, *A History of the English Law*, 2:449 n. 7; for a discussion of the relationship of the Statute of Treasons of 1352 to earlier formulations of the law of treason in England, see Holdsworth, *A History of English Law*, 3:287–93; Bellamy, *The Law of Treason in the Later Middle Ages*, pp. 59–101.

[47] See Bellamy's discussion of various treason trials from 1352 to 1485 and the punishments imposed on those convicted, in *The Law of Treason in the Later Middle Ages*, pp. 138–76; for examples of similar punishments imposed for treason, see Sayles, ed., *Select Cases in the Court of King's Bench*, 7:14, 95.

Chaucer appears to have had a general understanding of the nature of treason. He uses the terms "traitor" and "treason" and elements of the crime itself to evoke both moral and legal notions associated with the crime. Most instances of terms connected with treason in Chaucer's works occur in tandem with a breach of faith or "trouthe." This breach often happens in situations, such as those discussed in the preceding chapter, in which friends or lovers promise to be faithful to one another, seal that promise with a pledge of faith, and then, finally, break the promise. At other times, the terms associated with treason are linked with acts more often considered treasonous at law: breach of the bond of allegiance between king and subject or between lord and man. As will be shown, Chaucer's concept of treason is more philosophical than legalistic; it is rooted firmly in the idea that treason is a violation of the bond of "trouthe" between two people.

Chaucer probably based his conception of treason on popular ideas about the crime rather than on any particular legal text. W. R. J. Barron notes that in the popular imagination treason not only was the most heinous of offenses but also merited punishment often exceeding that levied by law.[48] He points out that the literature of the time was instrumental in perpetuating an extralegal image of the crime. In all likelihood, the layman was aware of the broad outlines of the crime, but not of the minute legal details of its statutory definition. In any event, an Englishman living in the last half of the fourteenth century had a number of opportunities to become acquainted with aspects of the law of treason. Treason trials were numerous during that period, and many involved prominent men.[49] For example, Nicholas Brembre, Robert Tresilian, and Thomas Usk, acquaintances of Chaucer, were convicted of treason by the parliament of 1388.[50]

In the following pages I deal with the concept of treason that emerges from an examination of Chaucer's use of terms associated with the crime. Political treason — violation of allegiance to one's lord or king — will be considered first. Chaucer adheres most closely to the legal definition of the crime when he is dealing with this type of treason. Thereafter, instances where Chaucer appropriates elements of

---

[48] See generally Barron, "The Penalties for Treason in Medieval Life and Literature."

[49] See the various treason cases discussed by Bellamy, *The Law of Treason in the Later Middle Ages*; and those in Sayles, ed., *Select Cases in the Court of King's Bench*, vol. 7, index, s.v. *treason*.

[50] See M. McKisack, *The Fourteenth Century, 1307–1399*, pp. 454–59.

the crime of treason to describe breach of trust between friends and lovers will be examined.

## ASPECTS OF THE LAW OF TREASON IN CHAUCER

*Political treason.* Two examples of political treason in Chaucer are the attack on Melibee by his enemies in *The Tale of Melibee* and Calkas's betrayal of Troy in *Troilus and Criseyde.* Although never explicitly stated in the tale, the treason in *The Tale of Melibee* seems to be treason against the feudal bond, that is, the old feudal felony. Calkas's treason, on the other hand, is treason against the crown. In fashioning both episodes, Chaucer added components of the crime and its punishment to his narrative to suggest the treasonous nature of the criminal acts described. It is important to note that the theme of treason was present, however, in Chaucer's sources for both *Melibee* and *Troilus.* *The Tale of Melibee* is a faithful translation of Chaucer's French source for the tale, *Le Livre de Mellibée et de Dame Prudence* of Renaud de Louens.[51] The elements of treason found in Chaucer's translation are borrowed directly from this source. For *Troilus and Criseyde,* however, Chaucer takes Boccaccio's suggestion that Calkas's betrayal of the Trojans is treason in the *Filostrato* and adds elements from the English law of treason. By adding these elements to his own version of the story, Chaucer not only emphasizes the treachery of Calkas's deed but also makes the consequences of his treason directly affect the fortunes of his daughter Criseyde.

What little there is of plot in *The Tale of Melibee* centers around an extended discussion about the course of action that Melibee should take to bring to justice the criminals who broke into his home and assaulted his family. Although there is no explicit evidence in the tale that a feudal bond was violated by the acts of these men, details in the French and Middle English versions regarding the type of punishment which they fear might be inflicted on them and which Melibee initially proposes to levy suggest that Chaucer's audience might have considered the crime treason. In the French and Middle English texts of the tale, the criminals, though persuaded by Prudence to submit to Melibee's

---

[51] See J. Burke Severs's discussion of Chaucer's source for *The Tale of Melibee* and his method of translation, in Bryan and Dempster, eds., *Sources and Analogues of Chaucer's Canterbury Tales,* pp. 560–67. All citations to *Le Livre de Mellibee et Prudence* are from Severs's edition in ibid., pp. 568–614; all citations to Albertanus of Brescia's *Liber consolationis et consilii* are from the edition by T. Sundby.

judgment, express their fears that his punishment of them may be excessively harsh. They ask Prudence to intercede with Melibee on their behalf so that "'we, ne oure freendes, be nat desherited ne destroyed thurgh oure folye'" (line 1750). This is part of a direct translation of the French lines: "'Et pour ce, plaise vous en ce fait avoir tel / advisement que nous et noz amis ne soyons / desheritez et perduz par nostre folie'" (lines 1049–50). There is no direct counterpart to these lines in the *Liber consolationis et consilii* of Albertanus of Brescia, the text from which the French version of Melibee was translated. Although Melibeus's adversaries express fear that the punishment he imposes might be harsh, the mode of punishment is never specified.[52]

When Melibee learns that his enemies will submit to his judgment, he explains how he intends to repay them for their attack (lines 1833–34):

> "I thynke and purpose me fully / to desherite hem of al that evere they han, and for to putte hem in exil for evere."

The French version is similar: "'je les entend a desheriter de tout ce qu'ilz ont / et les envoyer oultre mer senz retour'" (lines 1133–34). Melibeus's statement of the punishment his adversaries will receive is similar to that found in the French: "'Volo illos bonis omnibus spoliare illisque / praecipere, ut ad partes ultramarinas se transferant, ulterius huc non reversuri'" (p. 119, lines 19–21). All three versions mention exile as punishment. Although in England death was conventionally the punishment for treason, exile was an alternative. The crucial difference in the three versions of Melibee's intended punishment is that the French and Middle English specify that Melibee will "desherite" his enemies. That is, he will, in a general sense, dispossess them of their property but also, more specifically, deprive them of their feudal fief.[53] The Latin verb *spoliare*, "to despoil," of course, does not carry the same connotations as *desherite* or *desheriter*. *Spoliare* merely suggests that the criminal's possessions will be plundered, while the Middle English and French verbs suggest that their goods and land will be forfeited, as was customary in cases of treason.

Renaud seems to have modified his Latin source by adding elements which conformed to the French law of treason of the early fourteenth century. Chaucer possibly retained those modifications, not because he

52 See Albertanus of Brescia, *Liber consolationis et consilii*, p. 114, lines 7–17.
53 *Dictionnaire historique de l'ancien langage françois*, par La Curne de Sainte-Palaye, s.v. *desheriter* v., 3; *MED*, s.v. *disheriten* v., 1a; *OED*, s.v. *disherit* v., Obs., 1, 1b.

was blindly translating from the French but because he recognized
certain elements compatible with what he understood about the English law of treason. In both the Middle English and French versions,
the criminals fear that both they and their relatives might be disinherited because of their crime against Melibee. This feared punishment reflects sound English legal theory if not actual practice. Although Bracton held that a traitor's heirs should be disinherited and, in
certain cases, destroyed, in practice the punishment extended only to
the perpetrator. In France a similar theory of punishment held currency.[54] There it was thought that not only should the traitor be
punished by death or exile but his heirs should be killed as well. Legal
practice in France regarding divestment of the property of a traitor's
heirs seems to have followed theory more closely than in England.
According to J. G. Bellamy, in France the traitor lost all his property,
and his heirs were divested completely of their inheritance rights. Thus
the types of punishment that the foes fear might be levied upon them
and that Melibee proposes to levy appear to conform to both French
and English laws concerning punishment for treason against lordship:
execution and loss of property. Perhaps the elements of the anticipated
punishment in both versions would have suggested to Chaucer's audience that the adversaries' crime was treason against the feudal bond. In
any event, thanks to Prudence's intercession, the foes are spared
punishment and receive a pardon. Pardon was a viable alternative to
death in both France and England when the traitor made peace with his
lord.[55]

I should point out that Chaucer deals with treason against lordship,
or petty treason, in more original and humorous contexts than
*Melibee*.[56] Another act traditionally considered treason against one's
lord was adultery with the lord's wife. This act was a particularly
aggravated violation of the feudal bond. By analogy, a servant's adultery with his master's wife was a form of moral, if not legal, treason.
Thus when the narrator of *The Merchant's Tale* calls January's squire
Damyan "O servant traytour, false hoomly hewe" (line 1785) for his

---

[54] For a discussion of the punishments for treason in medieval France, see Cuttler, *The Law of Treason and Treason Trials in Later Medieval France*, pp. 116–31; for a comparison of French and English law on the punishments for treason, see Bellamy, *The Law of Treason in the Later Middle Ages*, pp. 12–13.

[55] See Bellamy, *The Law of Treason in the Later Middle Ages*, p. 173; Cuttler, *The Law of Treason and Treason Trials in Later Medieval France*, pp. 135–36.

[56] For a discussion of petty treason, see Bellamy, *The Law of Treason in the Later Middle Ages*, pp. 225–31.

pursuit of May, he is invoking a traditional idea about the types of acts which make one a traitor.

In *Troilus and Criseyde*, Chaucer deals with a form of treason which was delineated in the Statute of 1352 but which had its roots in the Roman crime of *laesa majestas*: the crime of adhering to the enemies of the king. The culprit, of course, is Calkas, who capitulates to the Greeks when his prognostications reveal that they are to win the Trojan War. Although Chaucer's description of Calkas's crime follows that of Boccaccio in the *Filostrato*, Chaucer takes special pains to make it clear that Calkas's crime is treason. While Boccaccio vaguely implies that Calkas acted like a traitor (1, st. 10), Chaucer specifically labels him a traitor (1.87). Also, Chaucer emphasizes the political nature of the crime by deliberately calling it treason (1.107, 117). Furthermore, Chaucer modifies Boccaccio's description of Calkas's treachery and Criseyde's subsequent pleas for protection by adding elements from the law of treason.

The Trojan mob's reaction to Calkas's defection is described as follows (1.85–91):

> The noise up ros, whan it was first aspied
> Thorugh al the town, and generaly was spoken,
> That Calkas traitour fled was and allied
> With hem of Grece, and casten to be wroken
> On hym that falsly hadde his feith so broken,
> And seyden he and al his kyn at-ones
> Ben worthi for to brennen, fel and bones.[57]

The mob describes Calkas's flight as a breach of faith, and the punishment they wish to inflict on him and his relatives, burning, was one associated with treason. Breach of faith, of course, was the primary element of treason, and, as previously mentioned, some legal writers thought that both the traitor and his family should be punished for the crime. Boccaccio's description lacks these important elements. He does

---

[57] Cf. Boccaccio, *Filostrato* 1.10: "Fu 'l romor grande quando fu sentito / per tutta la città generalmente / che Calcàs era di quella fuggito / e parlato ne fu diversamente, / ma mal da tutti, e ch'elli avea fallito / e come traditor fatto reamente, / né quasi per la più gente rimase / di non andargli col fuoco alle case." ("The outcry was great when it became generally known throughout the city that Calchas had fled. This was variously spoken of but condemned on all sides, and he was thought to have done wrong and committed an act of vile treachery. Indeed many people were almost inclined to go and set fire to his house.") All quotations from *Filostrato* are from Giovanni Boccaccio, *Tutte le opere di Giovanni Boccaccio*, ed. V. Branca, 2:17–228. All translations of passages from the *Filostrato* are from N. R. Havely, ed. and trans., *Chaucer's Boccaccio*; the passage above is on p. 25.

not term Calkas's act a breach of faith. Also, the crowd wants to burn down Calkas's house, not incinerate his kin, in the *Filostrato*.

Since Criseyde is Calkas's daughter, the public clamor for retribution is directed toward her in his absence. Wisely, she fears for her safety: "For of hire lif she was ful sore in drede" (1.95). Since her security in Troy is hardly guaranteed, she appeals to Hector for protection (1.106–12):

> This lady, which that alday herd at ere
> Hire fadres shame, his falsnesse and tresoun,
> Wel neigh out of hir wit for sorwe and fere,
> In widewes habit large of samyt broun,
> On knees she fil biforn Ector adown
> With pitous vois, and tendrely wepynge,
> His mercy bad, hirselven excusynge.[58]

Hector immediately grants her amnesty from prosecution for her father's treason (1.117–23):

> . . . "Lat youre fadres treson gon
> Forth with meschaunce, and ye youreself in joie
> Dwelleth with us, whil yow good list, in Troie.
>
> "And al th'onour that men may don yow have,
> As ferforth as youre fader dwelled here,
> Ye shul have, and youre body shal men save,
> As fer as I may ought enquere or here."

Hector assures Criseyde that her life and status in Troy will remain secure and also that her material welfare will not be jeopardized because of her father's treason. By clearly associating Calkas's crime and its consequences with ideas about treason prevalent in fourteenth-century England, Chaucer creates a plausible legal basis for Criseyde's fears of physical and material deprivation and for the necessity that she seek some sort of amnesty from Hector to keep her life and property secure.

In both *The Tale of Melibee* and *Troilus and Criseyde*, Chaucer employed elements of the law of treason, particularly the punishments associated with the crime, to give those works a semblance of legal verisimilitude. For *The Tale of Melibee*, he borrowed the material for treason from his source for the tale. For *Troilus and Criseyde*, however, Chaucer added details from the English law of treason to the hint of the crime in the *Filostrato* to emphasize the vile nature of Calkas's deed and

---

[58] Boccaccio, *Filostrato* 1.12–15.

to indicate that the ramifications of that act threatened his daughter's safety.

Chaucer also deals with a form of treason similar to the crime of *laesa majestas*, the violation of the bond between king and subject, in *The Man of Law's Tale*. In the tale, King Alla's vicious mother, Donegild, intercepts letters being exchanged between the king and his constable. She takes the letter addressed to the constable and replaces it with a letter that orders him to set Constance, Alla's wife, adrift at sea (lines 792–802):[59]

> Eft were his lettres stolen everychon,
> And countrefeted lettres in this wyse:
> "The king comandeth his constable anon,
> Up peyne of hangyng, and on heigh juyse,
> That he ne sholde suffren in no wyse
> Custance in-with his reawme for t'abyde
> Thre dayes and o quarter of a tyde;
>
> "But in the same ship as he hire fond,
> Hire, and hir yonge sone, and al hir geere,
> He sholde putte, and croude hire fro the lond,
> And charge hire that she never eft coome theere."

Upon discovering his mother's treachery, Alla has her put to death because "she traitour was to hire ligeance" (line 895). The tale clearly indicates, then, that Donegild's treachery was a violation of the loyalty she owed her king and was, therefore, treasonous. Interestingly enough, Gower's version of the tale of Constance specifies that the method by which Donegild was executed was the legal punishment for women guilty of treason: she was burned.[60]

Admittedly, Chaucer gets his material for *The Man of Law's Tale* from the Anglo-Norman *Chronicle* of Nicholas Trivet, and that source provides him with his material on treason. Trivet repeatedly terms Domylde's forgery "tresoun" and calls her "tretresce."[61] Indeed, both *The Tale of Melibee* and *The Man of Law's Tale* present problems in

---

[59] On the punishment of setting adrift, see J. R. Reinhard, "Setting Adrift in Mediaeval Law and Literature," *PMLA* 56 (1941): 33–68.

[60] See Gower, *Confessio Amantis* 2.1286–99: "And let a fyr do make tho, / And bad men forto caste hire inne; / Bot ferst sche told out al the sinne, / And dede hem alle forto wite / How sche the lettres hadde write, / Fro point to point as it was wroght. / And tho sche was to dethe broght / And brent tofore hire Sones yhe: / Wherof these othre, which it sihe / And herden how the cause stod, / Sein that the juggement is good, / Of that hir Sone hire hath so served; / For sche it hadde wel deserved / Thurgh tresoun of hire false tunge. . . ."

[61] See "Trivet's Life of Constance," ed. M. Schlauch, in Bryan and Dempster, eds., *Sources and Analogues of Chaucer's* Canterbury Tales, p. 176.

attempting to assess the extent of Chaucer's knowledge of technical aspects of the law of treason. Yet his use of treason in *Troilus and Criseyde* suggests that he did have a general understanding of the English law of treason and was not completely at the mercy of his sources when attempting to deal with treason in his works. What is clear from examining political treason in Chaucer's works is that he understood the broad outlines of the crime: that it was a crime committed by breaching one's faith to one's lord or king and that special forms of punishment were appropriate for the crime. A look at Chaucer's use of treason in his love poetry will shed further light on the extent of Chaucer's understanding of the crime.

*Treason in love.* Chaucer's use of treason in his love poetry suggests that he was intrigued by the metaphoric and symbolic connotations of the crime. For instance, on one level he equates treason with breach of faith between friends and lovers. Obviously he is playing with the notion that breach of faith was the fundamental component of treason. In *The Knight's Tale*, Palamon twice calls Arcite, his sworn brother, a "traitour." When he realizes that Arcite wants Emelye for himself Palamon says (lines 1129–30):

> "It nere," quod he, "to thee no greet honour
> For to be fals, ne for to be traitour. . . ."

Palamon again is moved to call Arcite a "false traytour" (line 1580) when he learns that Arcite has been spending time with Emelye while disguised as her chamberlain. Arcite has committed treason because, by pursuing Emelye, he has breached the pledge of faith which bound his vow to support Palamon as a brother in all he did. The idea behind Palamon's accusations of treason is that expressed in *Britton*: one commits treason even when he violates a bond of trust as simple as that shared between friends. This idea is also expressed in *The Parson's Tale* by the statement that one who gives wicked counsel is a traitor because he deceives one who trusts him (line 638):

> . . . he that wikked conseil yeveth is a traytour. For he deceyveth hym that trusteth in hym, *ut Achitofel ad Absolonem.*

Chaucer's point is that, even though breach of trust is not the legal equivalent of treason, it is at least the moral equivalent of the crime.
Chaucer also equates with traitors lovers who breach their vows of faithfulness to each other. This is evident particularly in the legends of

Hypsipyle and Medea in *The Legend of Good Women*. In these tales, Jason is singled out for his mendacity in love. In the prologue to these two legends, Jason is described as a criminal whose reputation should be publicized so that no other ladies can be injured by his treachery. He is labeled a faith breaker and a fraud (lines 1368–83):

> Thow rote of false lovers, Duc Jasoun,
> Thow sly devourere and confusioun
> Of gentil wemen, tendre creatures,
> Thow madest thy recleymyng and thy lures
> To ladyes of thy statly aparaunce,
> And of thy wordes, farced with plesaunce,
> And of thy feyned trouthe and thy manere,
> With thyn obeÿsaunce and humble cheere,
> And with thy contrefeted peyne and wo.
> There othere falsen oon, thow falsest two!
> O, often swore thow that thow woldest dye
> For love, whan thow ne feltest maladye
> Save foul delyt, which that thow callest love!
> Yif that I live, thy name shal be shove
> In English that thy sekte shal be knowe!
> Have at thee, Jason! now thyn horn is blowe!

The last line (1383) alludes to the horn blowing of the hue and cry, the procedure by which the commission of a crime was signaled.[62] As the prologue predicts, Jason uses lies and false promises to have his way with Hypsipyle, and then, after succeeding, he abandons her (lines 1542–58). He next moves to Medea and swears on his faith that he will marry her. When he leaves her, on winning the golden fleece, the narrator of the legends deems him a traitor for his treachery (lines 1656–59):

> For as a traytour he is from hire go,
> And with hire lafte his yonge children two,
> And falsly hath betraysed hire, allas!
> As evere in love a chef traytour he was; . . . .

From the preceding examples, it is clear that Chaucer uses the term "traytour" and its associations with treason to impute a greater degree

[62] For a discussion of the hue and cry, see Pollock and Maitland, *The History of English Law Before the Time of Edward I*, 2:578–80; this procedure is examined in greater detail later in this chapter. H. Schless, *Chaucer and Dante: A Revaluation*, pp. 164–67, has commented on the resemblance of these lines to aspects of the hue and cry. The term "sekte" (*The Legend of Good Women* 1382) has legal connotations. Technically it refers to compurgators or a legal action; for a discussion of the meaning of "sekte" here and elsewhere in Chaucer, see J. L. Baird, "*Secte* and *Suit* Again: Chaucer and Langland," *ChauR* 6 (1971): 117–19.

of reprehensibility to those who breach bonds of trust than is legally inherent in such acts. By equating a moral wrong with a legal wrong, Chaucer implies that the degree of ethical depravity imparted to perpetrators of both crimes against the heart and crimes against the king is equivalent. While there is certainly something unsavory about lovers who break their vows to one another, some irony is apparent in associating that act with the considerably more reprehensible crime of treason. In a few of his works, Chaucer draws more explicitly the connection between political treason and treason in love to exploit that irony.

Scholars have observed that language of the feudal contract was often used to characterize the relationship between lovers in the "courtly love" poetry of the Middle Ages.[63] In this poetry, the male typically took the role of vassal who served the woman who assumed the role of lord. By couching the lovers' bond in terms of the feudal bond, the poet metaphorically compared the love relationship to the feudal relationship between a lord and his man. Chaucer carries the metaphor a step further by having his lovers equate the breach of this bond with treason. To explore more fully the association of the breach of the bond between lovers with breach of the feudal bond, I examine the legal elements of the feudal contract before taking up Chaucer's use of those elements.

The standard form of the feudal contract was expressed in the vows of homage and fealty spoken by the prospective vassal to a lord. One form of these vows is recorded in *The Statutes of the Realm* under the heading "Modus faciendi Homagium et fidelitatem":

> When a Freeman shall do Homage to his Lord of whom he holdeth in Chief, he shall hold his Hands together between the Hands of his Lord, and shall say thus; "I become your Man from this Day forth, for Life, for Member, and for Worldly Honour, and shall owe you Faith for the Lands that I hold of you; Saving the Faith that I owe unto our Lord the King, and to mine other Lords."
>
> When a Freeman shall do Fealty to his Lord, he shall hold his Right Hand upon a Book, and shall say thus "Hear you my Lord R. that I, P., shall be to you both faithful and true, and shall owe my Fidelity unto you, for the Land that I hold of you, and lawfully shall do such Customs and Services, as my Duty is to you, at the Times assigned. So help me God, and all his Saints."[64]

[63] See M. Bloch, *Feudal Society*, trans. L. A. Manyon 1:233, 2:309; J. LeGoff, "The Symbolic Ritual of Vassalage," in *Time, Work, and Culture in the Middle Ages*," trans. A. Goldhammer, p. 262.

[64] *The Statutes of the Realm*, 1:227–28; for a general discussion of the elements of the feudal contract and the legal rights and duties generated by that contract, see Pollock and Maitland, *The*

Apart from a few minor details, the contractual ceremony described above was the same throughout feudal western Europe. Jacques LeGoff has analyzed the components of this ceremony and broken them down into three parts: the homage ceremony, the fealty oath, and the investiture of the fief.[65] The main feature of the homage ceremony was a statement of a desire to become the lord's man. This was made by the vassal while kneeling before the lord with his hands enclosed within the lord's clasped hands. This was followed by an oath of faithful service or fealty made to the lord and sealed by a kiss from the lord. Basically, the fealty oath was an elaborate pledge of faith. After the vassal became the lord's "man of mouth and hands," the lord invested him with a fief by bestowing on him a symbolic token representing the chattel or tenement he was to receive in exchange for becoming the lord's man. Two important aspects of the relationship generated by this ceremony were embodied in the terms "man" and "service."

In a number of places, Chaucer suggests a similarity between the bond between a man and his lady and the feudal bond and that the violation of the bond of "courtly love" is ironically equivalent to treason. For example, in *The Book of the Duchess*, a feudal relationship is suggested by the Black Knight's determination to love his lady " 'in my beste wyse, / To do hir worship and the servise / That I koude' " (lines 1097–99). The idea of faithful service was integral to the feudal bond between lord and man. When the Black Knight thinks that he is being asked to forsake his love, he equates such an action with treason by comparing such behavior to notorious treasons perpetrated in literature (lines 1115–25):

> "Repentaunce! nay, fy!" quod he,
> "Shulde y now repente me
> To love? Nay, certes, than were I wel
> Wers than was Achitofel,
> Or Anthenor, so have I joye,
> The traytor that betraysed Troy,
> Or the false Genelloun,
> He that purchased the tresoun
> Of Rowland and of Olyver.

---

*History of English Law Before the Time of Edward I*, 1:297–307; see also W. Ullmann, *The Individual and Society in the Middle Ages*, pp. 63–66, 84–91; Simpson, *A History of the Land Law*, pp. 15–16. Among the medieval English law books which discuss the homage and fealty ceremony, see Richardson and Sayles, eds. and trans., *Fleta*, 3:36–44; Sir Thomas Littleton, *Littleton's Tenures in English*, ed. and trans. E. Wambaugh, pp. 39–44.

[65] See LeGoff, "The Symbolic Ritual of Vassalage," pp. 239–48.

> Nay, while I am alyve her,
> I nyl foryete hir never moo."

In *The Parliament of Fowls*, service to the lady is stressed as an important element in considering which of the competing eagles is more worthy to become the formel's love. The royal eagle promises to serve her forever (line 419), while the second eagle argues that he has served her longer and is thus more worthy of her (lines 453–55). Both eagles indicate their willingness to be punished in a brutal fashion if they are ever found guilty of faithlessness to her. The punishments each eagle describes are very much like those inflicted on traitors. The royal tercel declares (lines 428–34):

> "And if that I to hyre be founde untrewe,
> Disobeysaunt, or wilful necligent,
> Avauntour, or in proces love a newe,
> I preye to yow this be my jugement
> That with these foules I be al torent,
> That ilke day that evere she me fynde
> To hir untrewe, or in my gilt unkynde."

As indicated previously, degradation of the body of a traitor was considered part of the punishment for treason. The second tercel proclaims that he ought to be hanged if he is found false to the formel and, also, that she should confiscate his property once he is found guilty (lines 456–62):

> "I dar ek seyn, if she me fynde fals,
> Unkynde, janglere, or rebel any wyse,
> Or jelous, do me hangen by the hals!
> And, but I bere me in hire servyse
> As wel as that my wit can me suffyse,
> From poynt to poynt, hyre honour for to save,
> Take she my lif and al the good I have!"

Hanging was a traditional punishment for treason, and confiscation by the feudal lord was the common method of disposing of the traitor's property.

These examples suggest how Chaucer ironically incorporates ideas connected with the feudal bond and treason into his love poetry by associating the most heinous of political crimes with violation of lovers' bonds. The most interesting and extensive use of the feudal bond as metaphor for the lovers' bond is found in *Troilus and Criseyde*. As indicated in an earlier chapter, Troilus and Criseyde seal their love for one another by exchanging promises of faithfulness to each other and securing those promises with pledges of faith. Chaucer complicates the symbolism of their relationship by also having them exchange promises which are similar to those recited in the ceremony forming a feudal contract and by associating Criseyde's subsequent violation of that contract with treason.[66]

The vows Troilus and Criseyde exchange explicitly mimic those exchanged by vassal and lord when they enter into a feudal contract: Troilus vows to become Criseyde's "man" and enter into her "service." Early in the poem, Troilus characterizes the kind of relationship he wants with Criseyde in language similar to that of the feudal contract. He states, "'. . . as hire man I wol ay lyve and sterve'" (1.427), and, ". . . myn estat roial I here resigne / Into hire hond, and with ful humble chere / Bicome hir man'" (1.432–34). Troilus seems to allude to the homage and fealty ceremony and the ritualistic gestures swich are part of that ceremony. Specifically, he refers to the portion of the ceremony whereby the vassal, in symbolic resignation of himself to his lord, places his hands between those of his lord and vows both to become his man and to serve him faithfully.

In book 3, Criseyde finally accepts Troilus into her service. This event occurs during their meeting at Deiphebus's house. After a bit of negotiation, the two lovers exchange promises that invoke terms of the feudal contract. Both Troilus and Criseyde stipulate terms to the agreement which the other must accept for it to take effect. The essence of Troilus's stipulations echoes the terms of a vassal's pledge of fealty to his lord: "'And thanne agreen that I may ben he, / Withouten braunche of vice on any wise, / In trouthe alwey to don yow my servise'" (3.131–33). Criseyde, addressing Pandarus, acknowledges that she accepts Troilus: "'And in swich forme as he gan now devyse, / [I] Receyven hym fully to my servyse'" (3.160–61). Subject to the condition that he must be careful always to maintain her honor, Criseyde makes Troilus her knight and kisses him (3.176–82):

---

[66] Meech, *Design in Chaucer's Troilus*, pp. 281–89, discusses the elements of the feudal contract in the promises exchanged between Troilus and Criseyde and the feudal aspect of their relationship. He observes that Chaucer puts more emphasis on the feudal quality of their relationship than his source did. Meech, however, does not connect Criseyde's betrayal of the terms of their feudal bond with treason. In fact, little has been written about treason in *Troilus and Criseyde*; but see W. F. Bolton, "Treason in *Troilus*," *Archiv* 203 (1966): 255–62. Bolton analyzes aspects of the theme of treason in the poem but does not deal with either the legal aspects of that crime in the work or Chaucer's use of elements of that crime to characterize Criseyde's defection to Diomede.

"And shortly, deere herte and al my knyght,
Beth glad, and draweth yow to lustinesse,
And I shal trewely, with al my myght,
Youre bittre tornen al into swetenesse;
If I be she that may yow do gladnesse,
For every wo ye shal recovere a blisse."
And hym in armes took, and gan hym kisse.

In Criseyde's speech, as in Troilus's, there are allusions to the feudal contract: the lord accepting the vassal as knight into his service and then sealing the pact with a kiss. The feudal nature of their relationship is reaffirmed later in book 3 when Criseyde once more asserts that she has accepted Troilus into her service as her knight.[67]

By having his characters recite language similar to that of the feudal contract when they seal their relationship, Chaucer metaphorically associates that relationship with a feudal relationship between a lord and his man. Thus, when Criseyde abandons Troilus for Diomede in book 5, she violates both her pledges of "trouthe" to Troilus and the terms of the symbolic feudal contract which oblige her to remain loyal to Troilus. If the feudal metaphor that characterizes their relationship is extended to cover Criseyde's actions in book 5, then, her violation of her vows to Troilus is symbolically treason. Theoretically, either party to the feudal contract, lord or man, could be guilty of treason if he violated the contract; if the lord caused the breach, the offense was more reprehensible because his obligation was to support and protect the vassal in exchange for the vassal's services.[68] Pandarus even terms her faithlessness treason: "'. . . and of this tresoun now, / God woot that it a sorwe is unto me!'" (5.1738–39). In the parallel passage in the *Filostrato*, Pandaro calls Criseyda's defection to Diomedes merely a *gran fallire*, a great wickedness.[69] Chaucer, on the other hand, intentionally has Pandarus label her betrayal of Troilus "tresoun." Pandarus's verdict regarding Criseyde's guilt is justified because Chaucer has made sure that her defection fits the facts of treason throughout the poem: she has not only breached her faith but also breached the terms of the feudal contract that defined her relationship with Troilus. From Pan-

---

[67] Cf. the following speeches by Criseyde: "'Lo, herte myn, as wolde the excellence / Of love, ayeins the which that no man may / Ne oughte ek goodly make resistence; / And ek bycause I felte wel and say / Youre grete trouthe and servise every day, / And that youre herte al myn was, soth to seyne, / This drof me for to rewe upon youre peyne. / And youre goodnesse have I founde alwey yit, / Of which, my deere herte and al my knyght, / I thonke it yow. . .'" (3.988–97). "'But lat us falle awey fro this matere, / For it suffiseth, this that seyd is heere, / And at o word, withouten repentaunce, / Welcome, my knyght, my pees, my suffisaunce!'" (3.1306–1309).

[68] See Barron, "The Penalties for Treason in Medieval Life and Literature," p. 188.

[69] Boccaccio, *Filostrato*, 8.23.

darus's viewpoint, her crime is more reprehensible than the real treason of her father because her symbolic role in her relationship with Troilus was as lord; Calkas's treachery was simply that of a vassal. Ironically, Pandarus misses the larger picture—Calkas's treason is ultimately far more devastating to the larger world of Troy in which he dwells.

As the preceding discussion has indicated, in his love poetry Chaucer works with the theme of treason on several different levels. Sometimes a lover's treason consists only of a breach of faith, a moral though not a legal type of treason. In poems like *Troilus and Criseyde*, however, Chaucer more clearly relates the breach of faith to the crime of treason by couching the promises exchanged between lovers in terms similar to those of the feudal contract. The violation of those promises is thus ironically equated with the treasonous act of breaching a feudal contract. The unifying theme running throughout Chaucer's use of ideas connected with treason is that the crime is a violation of a bond of trust and fidelity between two people. Whether the actions constituting that breach of faith accord with actual acts considered treason at law does not dictate Chaucer's character's denomination of the act as treason; rather, the existence of a breach of faith is the determining factor. This allows Chaucer to use treason in a broad fashion as both a thematic and a symbolic device in his poetry.

## ASPECTS OF CRIMINAL PROCEDURE IN CHAUCER: ARREST AND TRIAL

In addition to his use of aspects of the law of felony and treason, Chaucer also makes use of various elements of criminal procedure. By criminal procedure I mean the rules which dictate the proper procedure to be followed in accusing and arresting a criminal suspect and then in conducting his trial. Naturally, the first step in bringing any criminal to justice is catching the miscreant and detaining him until he can be handed over to the authorities. In Chaucer's day catching criminals was, as I have mentioned, a community affair. A witness to a crime or its victim was required to raise the hue and cry and pursue the culprit.[70]

[70] For examinations of the history and function of the hue and cry, see R. F. Hunnisett, *The Medieval Coroner*, pp. 10–11, 56; Pollock and Maitland, *The History of English Law Before the Time of Edward I*, 2:578–79. For a survey of the handling of the subject in medieval English legal works, see Schneebeck, "The Law of Felony in Medieval England from the Accession of Edward I Until the Mid-Fourteenth Century," 1:50–52. In the Statute of Winchester (1285), Edward I

The hue and cry was the outcry the victim or witness to the crime made to summon the neighborhood to join in and help catch the perpetrator. If, upon discovering the perpetration of a crime, a person neglected to raise the hue and cry, he was amerced, that is, fined. Maitland thought that the cry raised was "Out, out." He noted that "haro" was also a common cry. Both "out, out" and "harrow" are used in Chaucer when the hue and cry is raised. Upon hearing the hue and cry, the neighbors were to turn out with weapons, shouting and blowing horns in pursuit of the suspect. Chaucer often uses the hue and cry in quite comic ways. For example, in *The Nun's Priest's Tale*, the widow raises the hue and cry upon seeing Chauntecler being spirited away by the murderous fox. She and her daughters, along with a herd of barnyard animals, give pursuit. Included in the description of the chase are details like shouting and horn blowing which were commonly associated with raising the hue and cry (lines 3375–82, 3393–3401):[71]

> This sely wydwe and eek hir doghtres two
> Herden thise hennes crie and maken wo,
> And out at dores stirten they anon,
> And syen the fox toward the grove gon,
> And bar upon his bak the cok away,
> And cryden, "Out! harrow! and weylaway!
> Ha! ha! the fox!" and after hym they ran,
> And eek with staves many another man.

> So hydous was the noyse, a, *benedicitee*!
> Certes, he Jakke Straw and his meynee
> Ne made nevere shoutes half so shrille

---

required that all witnesses of the commission of a felony raise the hue and cry and give pursuit; see *The Statutes of the Realm*, 1:96–98. The terms of this statute are reiterated in an ordinance of 1285 recorded in *The Liber Albus*. This ordinance required citizens of London to raise hue and cry upon observing the commission of a breach of the king's peace or a felony; see *The Liber Albus*, pp. 280–81.

[71] *Britton* describes the procedure to be followed in raising hue and cry: "2. And for the maintaining of peace, we will that when a felony is committed, every one be ready to pursue and arrest the felons, according to our Statutes of Winchester, with the company of horns and voices from township to township, until they are either taken or have been pursued as far as the chief town of the county or franchise." Nichols, ed. and trans., *Britton*, pp. 42–43. Although the cry "Harou" is raised and pursuit is given when it is discovered that Renart the fox has abducted Chantecler in *Le Roman de Renart*, a possible source for this part of *The Nun's Priest's Tale* (see Bryan and Dempster, eds., *Sources and Analogues of Chaucer's* Canterbury Tales, pp. 655–56), Chaucer's description of the pursuit of the fox incorporates a larger array of details linked with the raising of the hue and cry, for example, the shouting and blowing of horns. For a more serious use of the hue and cry in *The Nun's Priest's Tale*, recounted in Chauntecler's account of the man who dreams of a companion's murder and then finds his body in a dung cart the next day, see lines 3032ff.

> Whan that they wolden any Flemyng kille,
> As thilke day was maad upon the fox.
> Of bras they broghten bemes, and of box,
> Of horn, of boon, in whiche they blewe and powped,
> And therwithal they skriked and they howped.
> It semed as that hevene sholde falle.

Compared with the Jews in *The Prioress's Tale*, who do their best to suppress evidence of a murder, these creatures are ideal citizens intent on fulfilling their civic duty by thwarting the perpetration of a horrible felony and bringing the felon to speedy justice.

In *The Miller's Tale*, the hue and cry is also used for comic effect. When Nicholas first fondles Alison, she threatens to cry "out, harrow" (line 3286) unless he lets her be.[72] Later in the tale, after John the carpenter has mistaken Nicholas's cries of pain for the signal to cut himself down from the rafters and float about in Noah's new flood, Alison and Nicholas summon the neighbors by raising the hue and cry. Their quick thinking causes enough confusion to prevent John from discovering them in flagrante delicto (lines 3824–29):

> Up stirte hire Alison and Nicholay,
> And criden "out" and "harrow" in the strete.
> The neighebores, bothe smale and grete,
> In ronnen for to gauren on this man,
> That yet aswowne lay, bothe pale and wan,
> For with the fal he brosten hadde his arm.

In both *The Nun's Priest's Tale* and *The Miller's Tale*, Chaucer gives humorous and yet probably fairly accurate examples of the operation of the hue and cry in medieval England.[73] After a crime had been committed and the suspect apprehended, there were two methods by which he could be accused and brought to trial: by appeal or by presentment of what amounted to an indictment by a jury.[74] Before dealing with this phase of criminal procedure in Chaucer's works,

---

[72] For a survey of the different interpretations of "harrow" and its possible derivation, see *A Variorum Edition of the Works of Geoffrey Chaucer*, gen. ed. P. G. Ruggiers, vol. 2, *The Canterbury Tales*, pt. 3, *The Miller's Tale*, ed. T. W. Ross, p. 157 n. to line 3286. Though Ross equates the cry here with some sort of cry of distress, he does not identify it with the hue and cry. I think, however, that the context surrounding the use of "harrow" in both *The Miller's Tale* and *The Nun's Priest's Tale* indicates that the cry "harrow" was associated with the hue and cry.

[73] For other examples of the use of the hue and cry in Chaucer, see *The Merchant's Tale* 2366 and *The Reeve's Tale* 4072, 4307.

[74] For an excellent discussion of the various types of proof required for trial by appeal and trial by jury, see Milsom, *Historical Foundations of the Common Law*, pp. 406–13.

however, the distinction between appeal and presentment should be examined.

An appeal was the accusation made by the victim of a crime or, in a case of homicide, by his family against the suspect. This procedure, also known as the appeal of felony, is outlined by Bracton and his redactors.[75] A thirteenth-century Anglo-Norman tract, the *Placita corone*, is devoted exclusively to detailing both the manner in which an appeal for the vaious types of felonies should be brought and the methods one could use to defend against such appeals.[76] Several steps had to be precisely followed for an appeal to be successful. Upon being robbed, assaulted, or otherwise victimized, the prospective appellor had to raise the hue and cry and make suit to the four nearest townships and to the local coroner. He then had to show the coroner that the hue and cry had been raised and pursuit given and affirm a desire to prosecute. Next he recited his appeal; that is, he accused a suspect and described the commission of the crime in as precise detail as possible. The coroner enrolled all of this in his rolls. At trial, the appellor again had to recite his appeal following the formula as it had been recorded in the coroner's rolls. If he varied the original language of the appeal, the appeal failed. The accused was allowed to challenge the appeal with a denial and an offer to vindicate himself by battle. Likewise, the appellor had to swear to the truth of his accusation and be prepared to support his oath by entering into battle with the accused if the appeal was challenged.[77] Battle was the traditional procedure for determining the truth of an appeal; by Chaucer's day, however, even though defen-

---

[75] For the rules outlining the procedure for conducting appeals for the different types of felonies, see Bracton, 2:385–435; Richardson and Sayles, eds. and trans., *Fleta*, 2:79–99; Nichols, ed. and trans., *Britton*, pp. 81–105.

[76] J. M. Kaye, ed. and trans., *Placita corone*, pp. 1–2, gives general details regarding the proper procedure to follow in making an appeal; the rest of the work deals with appeals for the different types of felonies.

[77] For the form of the oaths that the appellor and appellee had to swear, see Bracton, 2:399; see also Kaye, ed. and trans., *Placita corone*, p. 4. What follows is based on the formulas for the oaths found in *Placita corone*: "Both the appellor and the appellee had to swear on a holy book as to the truth of their respective appeal and denial. *Appellee*: Hear you this, man whom I hold by the hand, who call yourself_____ by name of baptism, that I never (here he recites the particulars of the accusation made against him), as you accuse me of doing, may God and the holy relics assist me. *Appellor* (stands on the right of the accused and holds his right hand in his left and a holy book in his right): Hear you this, man whom I hold by the hand who call yourself_____, that you are perjured, that you (here he recites his appeal), feloniously, as I accuse you of doing, may God and these holy relics assist me. After this, battle is begun."

dants occasionally offered battle, juries commonly determined the outcome of the trial.[78]

The other method of accusation was by presentment jury.[79] When this procedure was employed, the suspect was accused on the basis of suspicion of guilt rather than by a witness to the crime. A jury made up of members of a particular community was assembled to bring indictments against those suspected of criminal activity. Since no individual brought the accusation, the accused could not prove his denial of the accusation by battle. Instead, he had to present evidence that a trial jury could assess in determining the truthfulness of his denial.

Whether or not the defendant had the burden to prove the truth of his denial depended on the mode of accusation and trial employed. In an appeal, the burden of proof lay with the appellor. He swore to the truth of the facts as set out in his appeal. Before Chaucer's day, the truthfulness of that oath was commonly determined by battle. When accusation was brought by the presentment jury, the burden of proof fell on the accused. He denied committing the crime and then swore to the truth of that denial. Before the edicts of the Fourth Lateran Council in 1215, the defendant's oath was tested either by compurgation or by ordeal. Ordeal, however, became obsolete as a mode of proof in England soon after the council's edicts forbidding priests from conducting ordeals went into effect.[80] Thereafter, the defendant had to

[78] The records show that Chaucer had some connection with at least one trial started by appeal of felony. In 1390, Chaucer was robbed by a group of men. Richard Brierley confessed to the crime, turned king's approver, and appealed his accomplices; see *LR*, pp. 478–89. The culmination of Brierley's career as an approver for the king is noteworthy as an illustration that trial by battle was not totally obsolete by Chaucer's day. Brierley appealed Adam Clerk as his accomplice in another robbery that he committed in 1390. Adam denied the accusation and challenged Brierley to trial by battle. Adam defeated Brierley in the judicial duel, and Brierley was hanged; see *LR*, pp. 482–83. The rules for conducting the judicial battle are presented by Bracton, 2:399–402; Richardson and Sayles, eds. and trans., *Fleta*, 2:83–86; Nichols, ed. and trans., *Britton*, pp. 84–91. For a recent study of the use of trial by battle in England and a good survey of sources dealing with that procedure, see M. J. Russell, "II. Trial by Battle and the Appeals of Felony," *Journal of Legal History* 1 (1980): 135–64; see also Russell, "I. Trial by Battle and the Writ of Right," in ibid., pp. 111–34. As noted earlier, it appears that by Chaucer's day appeals were rarely decided by battle except in special types of appeals such as those made by king's approvers; see Bellamy, *Crime and Public Order in England in the Later Middle Ages*, pp. 127–29.

[79] This discussion of the presentment jury and the different modes of proof required for different types of trials is based on Milsom, *Historical Foundations of the Common Law*, pp. 407–13.

[80] For a brief treatment of the effects of the decrees of the Fourth Lateran Council on the use of the ordeal in England, see Milsom, *Historical Foundations of the Common Law*, p. 410; P. R. Hyams, "Trial by Ordeal: The Key to Proof in the Early Common Law," in M. S. Arnold et al., eds., *On the Laws and Customs of England: Essays in Honor of Samuel E. Thorne*, pp. 123–24.

prove the truth of his denial before a jury.

There is an interesting allusion to ordeal and compurgation as procedures for determining the truth in book 3 of *Troilus and Criseyde*. When Criseyde tries to prove to Troilus that his jealousy is unfounded, she states (lines 1045–49):

> "But, for my devoir and youre hertes reste,
> Wherso yow list, by ordal or by oth,
> By sort, or in what wise so yow leste,
> For love of God, lat preve it for the beste;
> And if that I be giltif, do my deye!"[81]

Criseyde is saying that she will put the truth of her denial of Troilus's charges of infidelity to the test of ordeal, compurgation, or sortilege, the use of divination to reveal the truth or some other hidden matter. All three of these modes of proof were appeals to a supernatural authority to disclose the truth. The ordeal and compurgation were distinctly legal modes of proof, the latter surviving in English courts up to the late Middle Ages.[82] Compurgation was the method by which a defendant could prove the truth of his oath denying charges against him by producing neighbors who would swear to his credibility. The supernatural element in compurgation was that one incurred the wrath of God if he swore falsely. Thus even though the defendant or his compurgators might circumvent earthly justice by perjuring themselves, at the judgment that mattered they would receive retribution. The ordeal placed a greater burden on God to intervene to confirm the truth of a defendant's denial. The two types of ordeal popular in England before 1215 were the ordeals by fire and water. With the ordeal by fire, the defendant was given a hot iron that had previously been blessed by a priest. If he was innocent, God would prevent the iron from burning him. With the ordeal by water, a priest prayed over a body of water so that it would reject the defendant if he was innocent. If God kept the defendant from sinking once he was lowered into the

---

[81] See Robinson's note to 3.1046 of *Troilus and Criseyde*, *The Works of Geoffrey Chaucer*, p. 825. For a general discussion of the ordeal and oath, see Pollock and Maitland, *The History of English Law Before the Time of Edward I*, 2:598–601; for a more elaborate study of the ordeal in England, see Hyams, "Trial by Ordeal," pp. 90–126.

[82] For a discussion of the survival of compurgation in medieval English courts, see Bellamy, *Crime and Public Order in England in the Later Middle Ages*, pp. 142–44. Bellamy notes that compurgation was not used in the king's courts in criminal matters after the Assize of Clarendon (1166), but it continued to be used in those courts with regard to certain civil matters, debt and detinue, until the late fifteenth century. In local courts compurgation continued to be used as a mode of proof in both civil and criminal cases until very late in the Middle Ages.

water, then he was found not guilty. Thus, by stating her willingness to submit to the ordeal or compurgation, Criseyde actually is asserting willingness to let a supernatural power determine the veracity of her protestations of fidelity.

In *The Man of Law's Tale*, Chaucer uses elements of the appeal of felony in depicting Constance's trial for the murder of Hermengyld: the appeal, the oath attesting to the truth of that appeal, and trial by battle. Chaucer found most of these elements in his source for the scene. The knight's accusation of Constance, his appeal, and his oath to the truth of that accusation are from Trivet's account of the perils of Constance in his *Chronicle*. In fact, Trivet explicitly indicates that the procedure for accusing Constance and determining the truth of that accusation is the appeal by terming the accusation an "appeal." When the knight accused Constance of the crime, he "apela la pucele de tresoun."[83] That is, he appealed (*apela*) the lady of treason. Elsewhere the murder is termed a "felonie." The reference the narrator of *The Man of Law's Tale* makes to trial by battle, however, is not based on anything in Trivet's account of Constance's trial.

M. Hamilton has commented on the procedural elements in this scene in "The Dramatic Suitability of 'The Man of Law's Tale.'"[84] Because her findings differ from mine, I shall look briefly at her conclusions regarding the nature of the procedural elements in this scene before examining those elements as components of the appeal of felony.

Hamilton thinks that Chaucer incorporated elements of Anglo-Saxon legal procedure into this scene to render it more accurate historically.[85] Although she is correct that something of a judicial inquest (a mode of procedure not necessarily restricted to the Anglo-Saxon period) is begun by Alla to look into the murder of Hermengyld before the knight formally accuses Constance, she is inaccurate in relegating the procedural details of the trial to Anglo-Saxon times. For instance, although she correctly identifies the narrator's lament at Constance's

---

[83] The quotation from Chaucer's source for *The Man of Law's Tale* is from "Trivet's Life of Constance," in Bryan and Dempster, eds., *Sources and Analogues of Chaucer's Canterbury Tales*, p. 171. "Apela" in this passage is a legal term meaning "appeal" or "accuse"; see *Anglo-Norman Dictionary*, ed. L. W. Stone, W. Rothwell, and T. B. W. Reid, s.v. *apeler*, *app-* v.a., where this passage is cited to illustrate the legal meaning of "apeler."

[84] M. Hamilton, "The Dramatic Suitability of 'The Man of Law's Tale,'" in M. Brahmer, S. Helsztynski, and J. Kryzanowski, eds., *Studies in Language and Literature in Honor of Margaret Schlauch*, pp. 153–63.

[85] Ibid., p. 158–63.

lack of an earthly champion (lines 631–35) as an allusion to trial by battle, Hamilton assumes that the judicial battle was an Anglo-Saxon method of trial. Trial by battle, however, is generally considered to have been introduced to England by the Normans.[86]

Hamilton also detects an allusion to the ordeal in Constance's prayer to God for mercy (lines 638–44) after the knight has accused her of murder. Hamilton sees in Constance's prayer a resemblance to formulaic prayers recited by the accused before undergoing the ordeal.[87] Like the inquest, however, the ordeal as a form of legal procedure was not limited to the Anglo-Saxon period. Upon closer scrutiny, the procedural details of Constance's trial most resemble the appeal of felony rather than Anglo-Saxon modes of procedure.[88] Breslin, in fact, has reached this same conclusion, but she has confused matters by also accepting Hamilton's account of the law in the scene; for instance, she terms the knight's oath supporting his accusation of Constance (lines 662–72) an "ordeal."[89]

Because of the confusion surrounding the form of legal procedure in this passage, the elements of the appeal of felony therein will be considered briefly. Constance's trial is begun by the appeal that the knight makes against her (lines 619–27):

> This false knyght, that hath this tresoun wroght,
> Berth [Constance] on hond that she hath doon thys thyng.
> But nathelees, ther was greet moornyng
> Among the peeple, and seyn they kan nat gesse
> That she had doon so greet a wikkednesse;

> For they han seyn hire evere so vertuous,
> And lovynge Hermengyld right as hir lyf.
> Of this baar witnesse everich in that hous,
> Save he that Hermengyld slow with his knyf.

[86] See Pollock and Maitland, *The History of English Law Before the Time of Edward I*, 1:39.

[87] Hamilton, "The Dramatic Suitability of 'The Man of Law's Tale,'" pp. 161–63.

[88] Most of Chaucer's additions to Trivet's version of this trial scene seem to be rhetorical tropes rather than legal details; see W. Scheps, "Chaucer's Man of Law and the Tale of Constance," *PMLA* 89 (1974): 285–95, esp. pp. 288–92. Scheps, however, accepts Hamilton's conclusions about the nature of the legal material that Chaucer added.

[89] Breslin, "Justice and Law in Chaucer's *Canterbury Tales*, pp. 95, 99–101. Actually, the knight's oath is just that: an oath attesting to the truth of his accusation of Constance. Since the appeal of felony was defended by battle, the appellor or accuser had the burden of proof and, consequently, had to swear to the truth of his accusation. If the mode of trial in the tale had been ordeal, then the burden of proof would have fallen on Constance, the defendant, and she would have had to defend her denial of the knight's charges by submitting to the ordeal. The accuser never had to submit to the ordeal because the ordeal was resorted to only when accusation was made by presentment jury rather than by an individual.

The narrator of the tale next alludes to the mode of proof employed in an appeal, battle, when he laments that Constance has no champion to defend her but Christ (lines 631–35):

> Allas! Custance, thou hast no champioun,
> Ne fighte kanstow noght, so weylaway!
> But he that starf for our redempcioun,
> And boond Sathan (and yet lith ther he lay),
> So be thy stronge champion this day!

Constance contends that she is innocent of "this felonye" (line 643). Finally, Alla, believing in Constance's innocence, requires the knight to swear to the truth of his accusation. This was the part of the appeal that preceded wager of battle. Accordingly, Alla orders a book to be brought for the knight to swear upon. Unfortunately for the knight, the book happens to be a holy book (lines 662–72):

> "Now hastily do fecche a book," quod he,
> "And if this knyght wol sweren how that she
> This womman slow, yet wol we us avyse
> Whom that we wole that shal been oure justise."
>
> A Britoun book, written with Evaungiles,
> Was fet, and on this book he swoor anoon
> She gilty was, and in the meene whiles
> An hand hym smoot upon the nekke-boon,
> That doun he fil atones as a stoon,
> And bothe his eyen broste out of his face
> In sighte of every body in that place.

As it turns out, Christ indeed proves to be Constance's champion by striking down the false knight and, in a graphic representation of the way modes of proof based on appeals to the supernatural should work, proves that the knight perjured himself. When the knight fails to meet the burden of proof required of him in an appeal by not proving the truth of his accusation, Constance is acquitted. Alla has the knight slain for his perjury.[90] Although the procedure for the appeal of felony is not followed precisely in the description of Constance's trial, both the elements of the trial that Chaucer borrowed from Trivet and his own additions indicate that the appeal of felony and not an Anglo-Saxon

---

[90] Punishment of a false appeal by death seems to have been an accepted form of punishment for the deed; see Sayles, ed., *Select Cases in the Court of King's Bench Under Richard II, Henry IV, and Henry V*, 7:132. The writ printed therein and dated 1402 records that a certain party found guilty of bringing a false appeal of treason was hanged.

mode of procedure was the method of trial on which this passage was modeled.

Chaucer also incorporates elements of the appeal of felony into his account of the trial of the rapacious knight in *The Wife of Bath's Tale*. After the knight rapes the maiden, the king learns of the offense (lines 889–92):

> For which oppressioun was swich clamour
> And swich pursute unto the kyng Arthour,
> That dampned was this knyght for to be deed,
> By cours of law. . . .

As Breslin has observed, the procedure followed in bringing the knight to trial, "clamour" and "pursute," was probably the hue and cry.[91] The *Placita corone* states that it was essential for the success of an appeal that the appellor, here the victim, had raised the hue and cry and at least instigated the pursuit of the rapist.[92] Breslin also correctly noted that the trial in an appeal of rape was by inquest rather than battle and suggested that the reason there is no battle in the knight's trial was because Chaucer was attempting to portray faithfully the procedure for the appeal of rape.[93]

The outcome of this particular appeal, the conviction of the knight is forestalled, however, by the queen's offer of clemency if the knight can discover what it is that women desire most of all. An interesting aspect of her offer of pardon is the time limit that she sets for him to carry out his task (lines 908–10):

> "Yet wol I yeve thee leve for to gon
> A twelf-month and a day, to seche and leere
> An answere suffisant in this mateere; . . . ."

Although in chivalric romances a year and day was traditionally the time period given for knights to perform their feats of glory and honor, that period of limitation was also significant in English law.[94] A year

---

[91] Breslin, "Justice and Law in Chaucer's *Canterbury Tales*, pp. 115–18.

[92] For the procedure for an appeal of rape, see Kaye, ed. and trans., *Placita corone*, pp. 7–9.

[93] For the rules relating to women and battle in an appeal, see Nichols, ed. and trans., *Britton*, p. 87; Richardson and Sayles, eds. and trans., *Fleta*, 2:88–89.

[94] For a discussion of the year and day limitation period in medieval English law and a convenient list of the different circumstances under which this limitation period came into play, see F. W. Maitland, "Possession for Year and Day," in *The Collected Papers of Frederic William Maitland*, 2:61–80, esp. pp. 66–73. The legal background of this limitation with regard to the "twelmonyth and a day" time period within which Gawain must meet the Green Knight to receive his blow to the neck has been discussed in R. J. Blanch, "The Legal Framework of 'A Twelmonyth and a Day' in *Sir Gawain and the Green Knight*," *NM* 84 (1984): 347–52.

and a day was the period set by law within which a person must exercise certain legal rights or claims or forever lose the right to exercise them. It was also the time period during which certain events must occur or fail to occur for a change in legal status to result. For instance, a year and a day was the period within which a widow or heir must make an appeal of homicide for the appeal to be valid. Likewise, one could not be appealed of homicide if the injured man lived beyond a year and a day after the injury was inflicted. It was the time period within which those who claimed ownership of land adjudged to belong to another had to advance their claim, and the period within which judgments against defendants had to be executed by the plaintiff for the judgment to stand. In certain cases, a year and a day was the period that had to elapse for an intruder to gain legal possession of land. It was also the time within which a lord had to claim a villein who had deserted the manor and taken refuge on the ancient demesne or in a chartered town; if a year and a day lapsed and the villein had not been claimed, then he was declared free. These examples show how the year-and-a-day limitation period functioned as a legally significant time frame within which certain rights had to be exercised if they were to remain legally valid. In *The Wife of Bath's Tale*, the "twelf-month and a day" imposed by the queen operates in the same manner; it is the time period within which the knight must fulfill the condition precedent to his receiving the pardon or forever lose the right to that pardon.

## PROCEDURE BY BILL IN *THE PHYSICIAN'S TALE*

Chaucer's use of legal procedure is not limited to the hue and cry and the appeal of felony. For instance, in *The Tale of Melibee*, as I have indicated earlier, Chaucer uses aspects of the law dealing with bail and sureties. Bruce Cowgill has observed that the procedure for the tournament in *The Knight's Tale* closely adheres to that followed in conducting a trial by battle.[95] Also, *The Parliament of Fowls* contains a mock trial in which the competing eagles present before Nature their cases on which should win the formel by "pletynge" (line 495), while the other birds deliver the "verdit" (line 503) on whom they think to be most

---

[95] B. K. Cowgill, "Chaucer and the Just Society: Conceptions of Natural Law and the Nobility in the *Parliament of Fowls*, the *Knight's Tale*, and the Portraits of Miller and Reeve" (Ph.D. dissertation, University of Nebraska, 1970), pp. 74–138; see also G. A. Lester, "Chaucer's Knight and the Medieval Tournament," *Neophil* 66 (1982): 460–68.

worthy of the honor.[96] In these works Chaucer uses a variety of procedural terms to suggest, and at times to demonstrate explicitly, that legal or quasi-legal procedure is being employed to adjudicate these different fictitious disputes. The care that Chaucer takes in ensuring that his trials contain elements of legal procedure implies not just a concern with verisimilitude but also an understanding of the important function that these procedural formalities play in both bringing about justice and maintaining the social order. As the trial in *The Wife of Bath's Tale* shows, however, Chaucer is not so naive to assume that procedural formalities are not subject to manipulation or even circumvention by those in a position of power. In *The Physician's Tale*, he employs another type of legal procedure, procedure by bill, to show how legal formalities can be adhered to and injustice still result when the forms are manipulated by a judge with evil motives. Although in the following discussion I examine Chaucer's use of bill procedure in *The Physician's Tale*, I also deal, in a peripheral manner, with his use of that procedure in *An ABC* and *The Complaint unto Pity*.[97] First, however, I undertake a survey of the function of bill procedure in the law courts of Chaucer's day.

Not all crimes in medieval England were serious enough to be classified as felonies. Many were lesser offenses either against the king's peace or against a citizen and could be prosecuted either in the name of the king or in the name of the injured citizen. Unlike cases involving prosecution for felony, these "personal injury" cases — what modern law would consider "civil," as opposed to "criminal," suits — were concerned as much with compensating the victim for his injury as with punishing the accused.[98] Basically, actions of this type could be begun in two ways: by writ or by bill. Which method one used to begin a lawsuit, however, depended on the type of court in which the plaintiff wanted to try the suit. Writs were the standard method of beginning actions in

[96] Cf. Geoffrey Chaucer, *The Parlement of Foulys*, ed. D. S. Brewer, nn. 485, 495. Brewer does not think that "ple," "pletynge," or "verdit" as used in these lines has a "legal flavour." In light of the discussion later in the poem of the proper mode that might be used to decide which eagle has a right to the formel and the suggestion that battle might be one means of reaching a decision (lines 519–53) — that is, a discussion which refers to methods of legal procedure — it is certainly possible that Chaucer intended these terms to convey a "legal flavour."

[97] Chaucer's use of bill procedure in *The Complaint unto Pity* has been examined by C. J. Nolan, "Structural Sophistication in 'The Complaint unto Pity,'" *ChauR* 13 (1979): 363–72.

[98] The law of torts as we think of it was still intermixed with criminal law in medieval England. For an examination of the lesser crimes in English law and the rise of the law of torts out of the criminal law, with special emphasis on the role the writ of trespass played in that development, see Milsom, *Historical Foundations of the Common Law*, pp. 283–313, 403–405.

royal courts: the court of common pleas and county courts in cases over which the king's justices exercised jurisdiction.[99] Essentially orders, writs performed many functions in the royal bureaucracy. A writ instigating a lawsuit commanded a defendant to appear before a certain court and answer a plaintiff's charges. The writ also served as the warrant which authorized the presiding justice to hear the dispute. Writs, however, were cumbersome devices for starting up the legal process. Before any legal proceedings could be begun, the plaintiff had to present his complaint to the chancellor, who would then sell him a writ designed to begin an action covering the type of wrong about which the plaintiff complained. Furthermore, writs were available to begin only a limited number of specific actions. When the circumstances of the wrong did not conform to those for which writs were available to begin the action, in some instances the lawsuit could be initiated by presenting a bill or plaint directly to the court of the chancellor.[100]

A bill was a less circuitous method of beginning a lawsuit; it could be drafted by the plaintiff and presented directly to the court. Basically, the bill was a petition alleging that a certain person had committed some wrong against the complainant and requesting that the court provide a remedy for the wrong. Traditionally, the plaint, or *querela*, was presented orally. Later it became standard practice to present the complaint in the written form of a bill.[101] As already suggested, bills were more flexible means of instigating lawsuits than writs. Although bills were formulaic to a certain extent, the formulas did not rigidly confine the format of the document's content and thus prevent it from being used to begin certain types of actions as was the case with writs.

Procedure by bill was used in certain courts to the exclusion of procedure by writ, and in some royal courts it was an alternative to writ procedure when writs were not available to start a particular type of lawsuit. The bill was recognized by the king's bench as a method of

---

[99] For a brief examination of the role of writs and the distinction between procedure begun by writ and that begun by bill in English law, see ibid., pp. 33–36.

[100] My account of procedure by bill is based on the following sources: W. P. Baildon, ed., *Select Cases in Chancery, A.D. 1364 to 1471*; W. C. Bolland, ed., *Select Bills in Eyre, A.D. 1292–1333*; I. S. Leadam and J. F. Baldwin, eds., *Select Cases Before the King's Council, 1243–1482*. For a discussion of the early history of procedure by bill in England, see Richardson and Sayles, eds., *Select Cases of Procedure Without Writ Under Henry III*, pp. xlv–clv; for a convenient examination of procedure by bill in medieval England, see A. Harding, "Plaints and Bills in the History of English Law, Mainly in the Period 1250–1350," in DaFydd Jenkins, ed., *Legal History Studies 1972*, pp. 65–86.

[101] See generally Harding, "Plaints and Bills in the History of English Law."

beginning lesser criminal actions.[102] It was also the standard method of starting civil and some types of criminal suits before the king's council, the court of chancery,[103] and local courts such as the mayor's court of London.[104]

Since the range of remedies a bill could request was unlimited, bills were often used because they could petition for forms of redress normally unavailable at law. Courts faced with an action begun by bill would have to look to an amorphous body of principles called equity to provide these extralegal remedies. In general, equity was the principle of justice which allowed a court to weigh the merits of each litigant's case, regardless of legal rules, to reach a just decision in instances where strict application of the letter of the law would produce an unfair result. Some scholars think that procedure by bill was naturally associated with equitable remedies in certain courts, especially in the king's council and court of chancery.[105] Because the nature of equitable principles brought into play by beginning an action with a bill is relevant to a discussion of bill procedure in *The Physician's Tale*, below I consider briefly how courts applied equitable principles and how Chaucer would have understood the term "equity."

In the fourteenth century, equitable jurisdiction was not invested in a single court, although later the court of the chancellor became the sole dispenser of equitable remedies in England.[106] Instead, some form of equity was practiced by all English law courts to a certain

[102] See Sayles, ed., *Select Cases in the Court of King's Bench Under Edward II*, 4:lxxxv.

[103] An excellent introduction to the form and function of chancery bills, also known as petitions, and an edition of examples of such bills in the vernacular is found in J. H. Fisher, M. Richardson, and J. L. Fisher, eds., *An Anthology of Chancery English*; see also Baildon, ed., Introduction, *Select Cases in Chancery*; Leadam and Baldwin, eds., Introduction, *Select Cases Before the King's Council, 1243–1482*.

[104] For the use of bills and plaints in the mayor's court of London, see A. H. Thomas, ed., *Calendar of Early Mayor's Court Rolls, 1298–1307*, pp. xxvii–xxviii; Thomas, ed., *Calendar of Select Pleas and Memoranda of the City of London*, 3:xv, xxv. Bills were also brought before justices of the peace; see Harding, "Plaints and Bills in the History of English Law," pp. 77–80.

[105] Although the king's bench heard cases brought before it by bill, Sayles thinks that the remedies prayed for and received had little to do with equity (see Sayles, ed., *Select Cases in the Court of King's Bench Under Edward II*, 4:lxxxv); but see Harding, "Plaints and Bills in the History of English Law," p. 75, who observes that the "plaintiff who took his bill to the justices [of the king] was relying less on definite rights in private law than on the king's known concern for justice and public order."

[106] For a discussion of theories about equity, the practice of equity in medieval English law courts, and the gradual separation of courts with jurisdiction over equitable matters from those with jurisdiction over legal matters, see Milsom, *Historical Foundations of the Common Law*, pp. 82–96; W. S. Holdsworth, *A History of English Law*, vol. 1, 7th ed., rev. and ed. A. L. Goodhart and H. G. Hanbury, Introduction and additions by S. B. Chrimes, pp. 446–49.

degree. In the fourteenth century, "equity," in its legal sense, referred to the application of reason and a sense of fairness to reach a just decision in a dispute between two people.[107] In a broader sense, equity was the use of reason to attain "Truth."[108] The earliest English treatise to deal exclusively with the applications of equity in English courts is St. German's sixteenth-century work *Doctor and Student*.[109] St. German's work reflects ideas about equity common to two seminal writers on the subject, Aristotle and John of Salisbury, and thus offers a definition of equity that may suggest something of the way Chaucer understood the concept:

Equytye is a [ryghtwysenes] that consideryth all the pertyculer cyrcumstaunces of the dede / the whiche also is temperyd with the swetnes of mercye. And [such an equytye] must alway be obseruyd in euery lawe of man / and in euery generall rewle therof / & that knewe he wel that sayd thus. Lawes couet to be rewlyd by equytye. And the wyse man sayth: be not ouer moch ryghtwyse for the extreme ryghtwysenes is extreme wronge / [as who sayth yf thou take all that the wordes of the law gyueth then thou shalte sometyme do agaynst the lawe]. And for the playner declaracyon what equytie is thou shalt vnderstande that syth the dedes and actes of men for whiche lawes ben ordayned happen in dyuers maners infynytlye. It is not possyble to make any generall rewle of the lawe / but that it shall fayle in some case. And therfore makers of lawes take hede to suche thynges as may often come and not to euery particuler case / for they coulde not though they wolde And therfore to folowe the wordes of the lawe/ were in some case both agaynst Iustyce & the common welth: wherefore in some cases it is *good and even* necessary to leue the wordis of the lawe / & to folowe that reason and Justyce requyreth / & to that intent equytie is ordeyned / that is to say to tempre and myttygate the rygoure of the lawe. And it is called also by some men epicaia. The whiche is no other thynge but an excepcyon of the lawe of god / or of the lawe of reason / from the generall rewles of the lawe of man: when they by reason of theyr generalytye wolde in any partyculer case luge agaynste the lawe of god / or the lawe of reason / the whiche excepcion is secretely vnderstande in euery generall rewle of euery posytyue lawe.[110]

The association of equity with divine law as well as with the application of reason to mitigate the harshness of the letter of the law is

---

[107] *MED*, s.v. *equite* n., 1, defines equity as "what is just, fair, or right"; definition 3 states that equity is "general principles of justice"; see also *OED*, s.v. *equity* n., I, 1, and II, 3.

[108] Cf. the use of "equyte" in the penitential treatise *Jacob's Well*, ed. Arthur Brandeis, pp. 272–79. There equity is described as the quality that unites reason and will so that man can function in the world according to God's commandments.

[109] *Doctor and Student* is a treatise composed of two dialogues that examine the relationship between English law and equity, or conscience. The first dialogue was published in Latin in 1523. The second was published in English in 1530: see Christopher St. German, *St. German's Doctor and Student*, ed. T. F. T. Plucknett and J. L. Barton, pp. xiv–xv.

[110] W. A. Dunning, *A History of Political Theories Ancient and Mediaeval*, pp. 54, 186; the passage from St. German, *Doctor and Student*, is at pp. 95–97.

implicit in Chaucer's use of the term in poems other than *The Physician's Tale*. For instance, in *The Clerk's Tale*, Griselda is said to be equitable, fair, and merciful in the way she resolves disputes between Walter's subjects (lines 435–41):

> Though that hire housbonde absent were anon,
> If gentil men or othere of hire contree
> Were wrothe, she wolde bryngen hem aton;
> So wise and rype wordes hadde she,
> And juggementz of so greet equitee,
> That she from hevene sent was, as men wende,
> Peple to save and every wrong t'amende.

When Chaucer is accused of heresy by the God of Love in the *Prologue* to *The Legend of Good women*, Alceste comes to his defense by arguing that Chaucer is innocent and by lecturing the God of Love on the responsibility of a lord to apply equity in judging his subjects (G 383–85):

> In noble corage oughte ben arest,
> And weyen every thing by equite,
> And evere han reward to his owne degre.

In both examples, "equitee" is viewed as a principle of fairness and justice.

Chaucer's use of bills in other works indicates that he viewed a bill as a request for mercy or justice. In *An ABC*, Mary is portrayed as an advocate who presents man's bill petitioning for mercy to God (lines 109–10):

> From his ancille he made the maistresse
> Of hevene and erthe, oure bille up for to beede.[111]

As C. J. Nolan has shown, the complaint in *The Complaint unto Pity* mirrors an actual bill that the narrator wishes to present to Pity begging for mercy in love. This "bille" is structured according to the general formulas of bills presented before the king's council.[112] Chaucer also uses the term "bille" in other places to imply complaint or petition for

[111] The reference to "bille" seems to be Chaucer's addition; there is no correlative passage in the *Pèlerinage de la vie humaine* on which these lines are based. A convenient comparison of Chaucer's version with that of the Old French is provided by Skeat in his edition of *The Complete Works of Geoffrey Chaucer*, 1:267.

[112] Although Nolan, "Structural Sophistication in 'The Complaint unto Pity,'" deals only with bills brought before the king's council and does not examine the use of procedure by bill in other English courts, generally bills brought before the king's council shared formulaic and structural similarities with bills brought before other English courts.

"justice." For example, in *The Merchant's Tale*, Damyan's appeal to May for mercy in love is called a "bille" (lines 1937, 1971). Although this bill is actually a letter, because it asks for a remedy to be granted, it performs a function similar to that of a legal bill.

As Nolan noted in his discussion of Chaucer's "bille" to Pity, bills usually had three distinct parts: an address, a statement of grievance, and a prayer for remedy.[113] A bill began with an introductory address to the justice presiding over the court. As an address from a bill presented to the chancellor in 1393 indicates, most addresses were deferential in tone and described the justice to whom the bill was presented in the most exalted of terms:

A tresreuerent piere en Dieu et tres gracious seignur, l'Euesque d'Excestre, Chaunceller d'Engleterre. . . .[114]

[To the most reverend Father in God, and most Gracious Lord, the Bishop of Exeter, Chancellor of England. . . .]

After the address, the plaintiff set forth his grievance. The complaint usually began with a formulaic statement that the petitioner "humbly beseecheth" (*supplie humblement*) that or "humbly showeth how" (*mostre tres humblement coment*) the defendant injured him in a certain terrible manner.[115] In his statement of the wrong done to him which followed, the petitioner presented in great detail how he was injured by the wrongdoer. Often the statement of injury was embellished to emphasize the immoral and illegal nature of the offense and the grievous hardship that the plaintiff had to suffer because of it. For example, a bill presented by William Burton before the chancellor in 1420 complained of the abduction of his seven-year-old daughter and claimed that the girl had been ravished and detained by Ludovic Greville "wrongfully, and against law, right and good conscience, and against the will of the said suppliant."[116]

---

[113] See generally ibid. and Leadam and Baldwin, eds., *Select Cases Before the King's Council, 1243–1482*, p. xxxv. Fisher, Richardson, and Fisher, eds., *An Anthology of Chancery English*, break the structure of chancery bills and petitions to Parliament into five parts: the address, the identification of the petitioner, the exposition (statement of grievance), the petition (prayer for remedy), and the valediction; see *An Anthology of Chancery English*, p. 21. While the bills in this edition are, of course, in English, many bills were presented before the court in Anglo-Norman French.

[114] Baildon, ed., *Select Cases in Chancery*, A.D. *1364 to 1471*, p. 48.

[115] See generally the bills printed in ibid. and in Fisher, Richardson, and Fisher, eds., *An Anthology of Chancery English*.

[116] Baildon, ed., *Select Cases in Chancery*, A.D. *1364 to 1471*, p. 119; the original bill is in French.

The final part of the bill contained the prayer for a remedy. There the plaintiff detailed the form of remedy he desired. For example, William Burton prayed for the return of his daughter. The prayer often closed with a formula stressing the righteousness of the plaintiff's claim in the form of a request that the remedy be granted as "law and conscience," "law and reason," "law and right" demanded or "for God and in the way of charity."[117] At the bottom of most bills was attached an endorsement by several witnesses or pledges who swore to the truth of the allegations in the bill.

Because bills often asked judges to set right a wrong for which there was no remedy at law, justices could grant a variety of extralegal remedies under the guise of furthering the ends of justice. This sort of freedom might prove dangerous in the hands of unscrupulous judges. Chaucer's *Physician's Tale* is a fiction about a corrupt judge who uses bill procedure to pervert justice rather than to enforce it. Crazed with desire for Virginia, Appius concocts a scheme that will allow him to use his judicial powers to have his way with her. Accordingly, he has his henchman, Claudius, bring a bill before him which claims that the girl is actually a servant stolen from him by Virginius.

Claudius's bill to Appius is quite faithful to the formulas followed in legal bills.[118] It begins with an address to Appius. The address is followed by a grievance which begins with the formulaic "sheweth" (lines 178–87):

> "To yow, my lord, sire Apius so deere,
> Sheweth youre povre servant Claudius
> How that a knyght, called Virginius,
> Agayns the lawe, agayn al equitee,
> Holdeth, expres agayn the wyl of me,
> My servant, which that is my thral by right,
> Which fro myn hous was stole upon a nyght,
> Whil that she was ful yong; this wol I preeve
> By witnesse, lord, so that it nat yow greeve.
> She nys his doghter nat, what so he seye."

Claudius's grievance contains other traces of language found in the bills to the chancellor mentioned previously. For instance, Claudius's bill

---

[117] For a list of other formulaic expressions of this kind found in bills, see ibid., p. xxx.

[118] The idea for Claudius to begin his action by bill was probably suggested by the analogous passage in *Le Roman de la Rose*; there the action is begun by a *fausse querele* (line 5591), a false complaint. The *querele* is recited by Appius's *sergent* at lines 5600–14 of Guillaume de Lorris and Jean de Meun, *Le Roman de la Rose*, ed. E. Langlois, 2:263–64. Although there are similarities in the substance of the *querele* in *Le Roman de la Rose* and the bill in *The Physician's Tale*, Chaucer adds formulas associated with the legal bill not found in the *querele* recited by Appius's *sergent*.

states that Virginia is being held against his will and was taken from him by Virginius in violation of law and equity.

Finally Claudius's bill requests a remedy (lines 188–90):

> "Wherfore to yow, my lord the juge, I preye,
> Yeld me my thral, if that it be youre wille."
> Lo, this was al the sentence of his bille.

In a recitation of the bill earlier in the tale (and in lines 185–86 of the bill itself) Claudius offers to prove his allegations by producing witnesses (lines 169–70):

> "I wol it preeve, and fynde good witnesse,
> That sooth is that my bille wol expresse."

Clearly, Claudius's bill follows the standard formulas found in legal bills in Chaucer's day even down to the endorsement by witnesses which usually graced the end of the bill and which Claudius alludes to when he states that he will find witnesses to prove that his bill is true.

The obvious irony in Chaucer's use of procedure by bill as the mode of procedure for Appius's court is that, while bills were often employed to ask for equitable remedies, in *The Physician's Tale* a most inequitable result is reached through the use of this procedure. Yet, even though Appius perverts all notions of right and justice in his handling of Claudius's bill, if one were to go by appearances alone, justice seems to have been done. An astute jurist, Appius makes sure that proper procedure is followed in conducting most of the brief trial against Virginius. For example, when Claudius first presents his bill and requests that right be done, Appius claims that he cannot pass judgment upon the case unless the defendant, Virginius, is present (lines 165–73). Appius ironically confides to Claudius, though, that "'Thou shalt have al right, and no wrong heere'" (line 174). Likewise, Appius's decision in favor of Claudius is fair and right given the facts presented in Claudius's bill. Indeed, the trial is a model of procedural propriety. Unfortunately, the procedure masks the fraud that Appius and Claudius perpetrate.

Virginius recognizes that justice will be perverted if Appius is allowed to decide the case, but he is prevented from proving his innocence by Appius's speedy resolution of the matter in Claudius's favor (lines 191–98):

> Virginius gan upon the cherl biholde,
> But hastily, er he his tale tolde,

And wolde have preeved it as sholde a knyght,
And eek by witnessyng of many a wight,
That al was fals that seyde his adversarie,
This cursed juge wolde no thyng tarie,
Ne heere a word moore of Virginius,
But yaf his juggement, . . . .

Virginius's desire to prove his case as a knight is possibly a reference to trial by battle, while the reference to witnesses may be either to compurgation or to jury trial—two modes of proof practiced in medieval English courts, but not allowed, in this instance, in Appius's.

By the end of the tale, justice is achieved somewhat, but too late for poor Virginia, who loses her head at the thought of having to submit to the advances of Appius. While the justice of the tale's ending is not complete, what is complete and successful is Chaucer's critique of law. By using bill procedure and stressing concepts of right and equity in the brief scene detailing Claudius's complaint, Chaucer pointedly demonstrates how a procedure designed to facilitate justice can easily be manipulated to subvert it by judges whose motive is personal gain.

# Conclusion

Contractual language is often used by Chaucer to make a character's promises appear to have some legal force, and legal ideas like the pledge of faith or treason often play major roles in developing the plot or theme of a particular work. An examination of these legal elements also shows that Chaucer was conscious of the prominent position of law in the lives of the people of his day and that he understood the different ways law was administered by medieval English courts.

It seems safe to conclude that he did not have, or at least did not wish to display, an extraordinary mastery of esoteric or technical aspects of the law. His allusions to law are of the sort that probably would have been readily understood by the civil servants and courtiers who made up his audience. Many of his allusions to criminal law are general, derived either from his sources or from popular notions about certain crimes. His use of contractual formalities suggests, however, a certain mastery of the nuances of the law of agreements. His acquaintance with this area of the law can obviously be attributed to his mercantile background. His exposure to commercial transactions both through his duties as a civil servant and in his business dealings as a private citizen would necessarily have provided him with a broader command of the facets of commercial law than with other areas of law.

Chaucer, however, rarely employs extremely technical legal details, such as those only a lawyer would know. When he does use technical material, as in his use of formulas associated with bills or the details concerning procedure in church courts, it is an exception. In any case, this "technical material" may not have been so technical in Chaucer's day. Since the layman of Chaucer's England probably knew something about how to start a lawsuit by bill in the local courts and the sorts of actions that a church court would hear, the material appears technical only from a twentieth-century perspective. What can be concluded from the law found in Chaucer's works, then, is that they reflect the facility with and apprehension of law that one would expect of a man who had occasional dealings with the law both as a civil servant and a private citizen: a competent but not extraordinary command of the subject.

Chaucer's knowledge of law was eclectic rather than systematic. He was capable of taking legal material from different legal systems and fitting it into his literary works. Although this material would not have been beyond the ken of his medieval audience, much of it may be unfamiliar to the modern reader. I have attempted to reclaim legal allusions that might otherwise be lost on the reader who possesses little or no knowledge of law in Chaucer's day. Perhaps I have also provided some insight into the extent of Chaucer's command of law and how he understood law to operate.

# Bibliography

Adams, N., and C. Donahue, eds. *Select Cases from the Ecclesiastical Courts of the Province of Canterbury, c. 1200–1301.* Selden Society, vol. 95. London: Selden Society, 1981.

Adams, R. "The Concept of Debt in *The Shipman's Tale.*" *SAC* 6 (1984): 85–102.

Albertanus of Brescia. *Albertani Brixiensis liber consolationis et concilii, ex quo hausta est fabula gallica de Melibeo et Prudentia.* Ed. T. Sundby. London: Williams and Norgate, 1873.

Alford, J. A. "Literature and Law in Medieval England." *PMLA* 92 (1977): 941–51.

———, and D. Seniff. *Literature and Law in the Middle Ages: A Bibliography of Scholarship.* New York: Garland, 1984.

———. "Scriptural Testament in *The Canterbury Tales*: The Letter Takes Its Revenge." In D. L. Jeffrey, ed. *Chaucer and Scriptural Tradition.* Ottawa: University of Ottawa Press, 1984, pp. 197–203.

Allmand, C. T. "The Civil Lawyers." In C. H. Clough, ed. *Profession, Vocation and Culture in Later Medieval England.* Liverpool: Liverpool University Press, 1982, pp. 155–80.

*Anglo-Norman Dictionary.* Ed. L. W. Stone, W. Rothwell, and T. B. Reid. London: Modern Humanities Research Association, 1977–.

Arnold, M. S. "Fourteenth-Century Promises." *Cambridge Law Journal* 35 (1976): 321–34.

———, ed. *Year Books of Richard II, 2 RII, 1378–79.* London: Ames Foundation, 1975.

Baildon, W. P., ed. *Select Cases in Chancery, A.D. 1364 to 1471.* Selden Society, vol. 10. London: Bernard Quaritch, 1896.

Baird, J. L. "Law and the *Reeve's Tale.*" *NM* 70 (1969): 679–83.

———. "*Secte* and *Suit* Again: Chaucer and Langland." *ChauR* 6 (1971): 117–19.

Baker, J. H. "The Inns of Court in 1388." *Law Quarterly Review* 92 (1976): 184–87.

———. "The Law Merchant and the Common Law Before 1700." *Cambridge Law Journal* 38 (1979): 295–322. Reprinted in J. H. Baker, *The Legal Profession and the Common Law: Historical Essays.* London: Hambledon Press, 1986, pp. 341–68.

161

Barron, W. R. J. "The Penalties for Treason in Medieval Life and Literature." *Journal of Medieval History* 7 (1981): 187–202.

———. *"Trawthe" and Treason: The Sin of Gawain Reconsidered.* Manchester: Manchester University Press, 1980.

Bateson, M., ed. *Borough Customs.* Vol. 2. Selden Society, vol. 21. London: Bernard Quaritch, 1906.

Baugh, A. C. "Chaucer's Serjeant of the Law and the Year Books." In *Mélanges de langue et littérature du moyen âge et de la renaissance offerts à Jean Frappier — par ses collègues, ses élèves et ses amis.* Geneva: Droz, 1970, 1:65–76.

Bellamy, J. G. *Crime and Public Order in England in the Later Middle Ages.* London: Routledge and Kegan Paul, 1973.

———. *The Law of Treason in England in the Later Middle Ages.* Ed. D. E. C. Yale. Cambridge: Cambridge University Press, 1970.

Berman, Harold J. *Law and Revolution: The Formation of the Western Legal Tradition.* Cambridge, Mass.: Harvard University Press, 1983.

Blanch, R. J. "'Al Was This Land Fulfild of Fayerye': The Thematic Employment of Force, Willfulness, and Legal Conventions in Chaucer's *Wife of Bath's Tale.*" SN 57 (1985): 41–51.

———. "The Legal Framework of 'A Twelmonyth and a Day' in *Sir Gawain and the Green Knight.*" NM 84 (1984): 347–52.

———, and J. N. Wasserman. "Medieval Contracts and Covenants: The Legal Coloring of *Sir Gawain and the Green Knight.*" Neophil 69 (1984): 598–610.

———. "To 'Ouertake your wylle': Volition and Obligation in *Sir Gawain and the Green Knight.*" Neophil 70 (1986): 119–29.

Bland, D. S. "Chaucer and the Inns of Court: A Re-Examination." ES 33 (1952): 145–55.

Blenner-Hassett, R. "Autobiographical Aspects of Chaucer's Franklin." *Speculum* 28 (1953): 791–800.

Bloch, M. *Feudal Society.* Trans. L. A. Manyon. 2 vols. Chicago: University of Chicago Press, 1961.

Boccaccio, Giovanni. *Filostrato.* In *Tutte le opere di Giovanni Boccaccio.* Ed. V. Branca. •• vols. Milan: Mondadori, 1964, 2:17–228.

Bøgholm, N. "A Rash Promise." SN 15 (1942): 41–42.

Bolland, W. C., ed. *Select Bills in Eyre, A.D. 1292–1333.* Selden Society, Vol. 30. London: Bernard Quaritch, 1914.

Bolton, W. F. "Treason in *Troilus.*" *Archiv* 203 (1966): 255–62.

Bowden, M. *A Commentary on the* General Prologue *to the* Canterbury Tales. New York: Macmillan, 1949.

Boyle, L. E. "The Fourth Lateran Council and Manuals of Popular Theology." In T. J. Heffernan, ed. *The Popular Literature of Medieval England.* Knoxville: University of Tennessee Press, 1985, pp. 30–43.

Bracton, Henry de. *Bracton de legibus et consuetudinibus angliae.* Ed. G. E. Woodbine. Trans. and rev. S. E. Thorne. 4 vols. Cambridge, Mass.: Belknap Press, Harvard University Press, 1968–77. [Bracton]

Breslin, C. A. "Justice and Law in Chaucer's *Canterbury Tales.*" Ph.D. dissertation, Temple University, 1978.

Brewer, D. S. *Chaucer.* 3d ed. London: Longmans, 1973.

———. *An Introduction to Chaucer.* London: Longmans, 1984.

————. Review of H. A. Kelly. *Love and Marriage in the Age of Chaucer*. *RES* 28 (1970): 194–97.

Brusendorff, Aage. *The Chaucer Tradition*. Oxford: Oxford University Press, 1925.

Bryan, W. F., and G. Dempster, eds. *Sources and Analogues of Chaucer's Canterbury Tales*. Chicago: University of Chicago Press, 1941.

Burrow, J. A. *A Reading of* Sir Gawain and the Green Knight. London: Routledge and Kegan Paul, 1965.

Cahn, K. S. "Chaucer's Merchants and the Foreign Exchange: An Introduction to Medieval Finance." *SAC* 2 (1980): 81–119.

Caldwell, R. A. "Joseph Holand, Collector and Antiquary." *MP* 40 (1943): 295–301.

Cam, H. "The Law-Courts of Medieval London." In *Law-Finders and Law-Makers in Medieval England*. London: Merlin Press, 1962, pp. 85–94.

————, ed. *The Eyre of London, 14 Edward II, A.D. 1321*. Vol. 1. Selden Society, vol. 85. London: Bernard Quaritch, 1968.

Carr, C., ed. *Pension Book of Clement's Inn*. Selden Society, vol. 78. London: Bernard Quaritch, 1960.

Chaucer, Geoffrey. *The Complete Poetry and Prose of Geoffrey Chaucer*. Ed. J. H. Fisher. New York: Holt, Rinehart and Winston, 1977.

————. *The Complete Works of Geoffrey Chaucer*. Ed. W. W. Skeat. 7 vols. Oxford: Clarendon Press, 1894–97.

————. *The Parlement of Foulys*. Ed. D. S. Brewer. London: Nelson, 1960.

————. *The Text of the* Canterbury Tales. Ed. J. M. Manly and E. Rickert. 8 vols. Chicago: University of Chicago Press, 1940, vol. 1.

————. *A Variorum Edition of the Works of Geoffrey Chaucer*. P. G. Ruggiers, gen. ed. Vol. 2, *The Canterbury Tales*. Pt. 3, *The Miller's Tale*. Ed. T. W. Ross. Norman: University of Oklahoma Press, 1983.

————. *The Workes of ovr Antient and lerned English Poet, Geffrey Chavcer, newly Printed*. Ed. T. Speght. London, 1598.

————. *The Works of Geoffrey Chaucer*. Ed. F. N. Robinson. 2d ed. Boston: Houghton Mifflin, 1957.

Chute, M. *Geoffrey Chaucer of England*. New York: Dutton, 1946.

Cohen, H. *A History of the English Bar and the "Attornatus" to 1450*. London: Sweet and Maxwell, 1929.

Cotter, J. F. "The Wife of Bath and the Conjugal Debt." *ELN* 6 (1969): 169–72.

Cowgill, B. K. "Chaucer and the Just Society: Conceptions of Natural Law and the Nobility in the *Parliament of Fowls*, the *Knight's Tale*, and the Portraits of Miller and Reeve." Ph.D. dissertation, University of Nebraska, 1970.

Crow, M. M., and C. C. Olson, eds. *Chaucer Life-Records*. Oxford: Clarendon Press, 1966. [*LR*]

Cuttler, S. H. *The Law of Treason and Treason Trials in Later Medieval France*. Cambridge: Cambridge University Press, 1981.

David, A. *The Strumpet Muse*. Bloomington: Indiana University Press, 1976.

Davies, R. T. Review of H. A. Kelly. *Love and Marriage in the Age of Chaucer*. *MLR* 73 (1978): 871–74.

Davis, N., et al., eds. *A Chaucer Glossary*. Oxford: Clarendon Press, 1979.

Dawson, J. P. *The Oracles of the Law*. 1968. Reprint. Westport, Conn.: Greenwood Press, 1978.

Delany, S. "Sexual Economics, Chaucer's Wife of Bath, and *The Book of Margery Kempe.*" *MinnR*, n.s., 5 (1975): 104–15.

*Dictionnaire historique de l'ancien langage françois.* Par la Curne de Sainte-Palaye. 10 vols. Paris, 1875–82.

Donahue, C. "The Policy of Alexander the Third's Consent Theory of Marriage." In S. Kuttner, ed. *Proceedings of the Fourth International Congress of Medieval Canon Law.* Vatican City: Biblioteca Apostolica Vaticana, 1976, pp. 251–81.

———. "Roman Canon Law in the Medieval English Church: Stubbs vs. Maitland Reexamined After 75 Years in the Light of Some Records from the Church Courts." *Michigan Law Review* 72 (1974): 647–716.

Dunleavy, G. W. "Natural Law as Chaucer's Ethical Absolute." *TWA* 52 (1963): 177–87.

Dunning, W. A. *A History of Political Theories Ancient and Modern.* New York: Macmillan, 1930.

Emden, A. B. *A Biographical Register of the University of Oxford to A.D. 1500.* Oxford: Clarendon Press, 1959, vol. 3.

Esmein, A. *Le Mariage en droit canonique.* Vol. 1. 2d ed. Rev. R. Génestal. Paris: Recueil Sirey, 1929.

Fifoot, C. H. S. *History and Sources of the Common Law: Tort and Contract.* London: Stevens, 1949.

Fisher, J. H. *John Gower: Moral Philosopher and Friend of Chaucer.* New York: New York University Press, 1964.

———, M. Richardson, and J. L. Fisher. *An Anthology of Chancery English.* Knoxville: University of Tennessee Press, 1984.

Fortescue, Sir John. *De laudibus legum anglie.* Ed. and trans. S. B. Chrimes. Cambridge: Cambridge University Press, 1942.

Friedburg, E., ed. *Corpus juris canonici.* 2 vols. Leipzig: B. Tauchnitz, 1879–81.

Furnivall, F. J., ed. *Child-Marriages, Divorces, and Ratifications, etc. in the Diocese of Chester, A.D. 1561–6.* EETS, o.s., vol. 108. London: Kegan Paul, Trench, Trübner, 1897.

Galway, M. "Geoffrey Chaucer, J.P. and M.P." *MLR* 36 (1941): 1–36.

Gaylord, A. T. "The Promises in the *Franklin's Tale.*" *ELH* 31 (1964): 331–65.

Golding, M. R. "The Importance of Keeping 'Trouthe' in *The Franklin's Tale.*" *MÆ* 39 (1970): 306–12.

Gower, John. *The Complete Works of John Gower.* Ed. G. C. Macaulay. 4 vols. Oxford: Clarendon Press, 1901, vols. 2–3.

Gratian. *Decretum Gratiani seu verius decretorum canonicorum collectanea.* Paris, 1561.

Green, R. F. *Poets and Princepleasers.* Toronto: University of Toronto Press, 1980.

Green, T. A. "The Jury and the English Law of Homicide, 1200–1600." *Michigan Law Review* 74 (1976): 413–99.

———. "Societal Concepts of Criminal Liability for Homicide in Mediaeval England." *Speculum* 47 (1972): 669–94.

Gross, C., ed. *Select Cases Concerning the Law Merchant.* Vol. 1. Selden Society, vol. 23. London: Bernard Quaritch, 1908.

Guillaume de Lorris and Jean de Meun. *Le Roman de la Rose.* Ed. E. Langlois. 5 vols. Société des Anciens Textes Français, no. 63. Paris: Firmin Didot etc., 1914–24.

Guth, D. J. "Enforcing Late-Medieval Law: Patterns in Litigation During Henry VII's

Reign." In J. H. Baker, ed. *Legal Records and the Historian*. London: Royal Historical Society, 1978, pp. 80–96.

de Haas, E. *Antiquities of Bail: Origin and Historical Development in Criminal Cases to the Year 1275*. New York: Columbia University Press, 1940.

Hahn, T., and R. W. Kaeuper. "Text and Context: Chaucer's *Friar's Tale*." *SAC* 5 (1983): 67–102.

Hall, H., ed. *Select Cases Concerning the Law Merchant*. Vols. 2, 3. Selden Society, vols. 46, 49. London: Bernard Quaritch, 1930, 1932.

Hamilton, M. "The Dramatic Suitability of 'The Man of Law's Tale.'" In M. Brahmer, S. Helszyynski, and J. Kryzanowski, eds. *Studies in Language and Literature in Honor of Margaret Schlauch*. Warsaw: Pantstowe, 1966, pp. 153–63.

Hammond, E. P. *Chaucer: A Bibliographical Manual*. New York: Macmillan, 1908. Reprint. Gloucester, Mass.: Peter Smith, 1933.

Harding, A. "Plaints and Bills in the History of English Law, Mainly in the Period 1250–1350." In DaFydd Jenkins, ed. *Legal History Studies 1972*. Cardiff: University of Wales Press, 1975, pp. 65–86.

Havely, N. R., ed. and trans. *Chaucer's Boccaccio*. Cambridge: D. S. Brewer, 1980.

Hazeltine, H. D. "The Formal Contract of Early English Law." *Columbia Law Review* 10 (1910): 608–17.

Helmholz, R. H. "Assumpsit and *Fidei Laesio*." *Law Quarterly Review* 91 (1975): 406–32.

———. *Marriage Litigation in Medieval England*. Cambridge: Cambridge University Press, 1974.

———. "The Writ of Prohibition to Court Christian Before 1500." *MS* 43 (1981): 297–314.

Hennedy, H. L. "The Friar's Summoner's Dilemma." *ChauR* 5 (1971): 213–17.

Henrici de Segusio, Cardinalis Hostiensis. *Summa aurea*. 1574. Reprint. Turin: Bottega d'Erasmo, 1963.

Henry, R. L. *Contracts in the Local Courts of Medieval England*. London: Longmans, Green, 1926.

Hermann, J. P. "Dismemberment, Dissemination, Discourse: Sign and Symbol in the *Shipman's Tale*." *ChauR* 19 (1985): 302–37.

Herrtage, S. J. H., ed. *Catholicon Anglicum: An English-Latin Wordbook, Dated 1483*. EETS, o.s., vol. 75. London: Trübner, 1881.

Holdsworth, W. S. *A History of English Law*. Vol. 1. 7th ed. Rev. and ed. A. L. Goodhart and H. G. Hanbury. Introduction and additions by S. B. Chrimes. London: Methuen, 1956.

———. *A History of English Law*. Vol. 2. 4th ed. 1936. Reprint. London: Methuen, 1966.

———. *A History of English Law*. Vol. 3. 5th ed. 1942. Reprint. London: Methuen, 1966.

———. *A History of English Law*. Vol. 4 3d ed. London: Methuen, 1945.

Hulbert, J. R. *Chaucer's Official Life*. Menasha, Wis.: Collegiate Press, 1912.

Hunnisett, R. F. *The Medieval Coroner*. Cambridge: Cambridge University Press, 1961.

Hussey, S. S. *Chaucer: An Introduction*. London: Methuen, 1971.

Hyams, P. R. "Trial by Ordeal: The Key to Proof in the Early Common Law." In M. S.

Arnold et al., eds. *On the Laws and Customs of England: Essays in Honor of Samuel E. Thorne*. Chapel Hill: University of North Carolina Press, 1981, pp. 90–126.

Ingram, M. "Spousals Litigation in the English Ecclesiastical Courts c. 1350–1640." In R. B. Outhwaite, ed. *Marriage and Society: Studies in the Social History of Marriage*. London: Europa, 1981, pp. 35–57.

Ives, E. W. "The Common Lawyers." In C. H. Clough, ed. *Profession, Vocation and Culture in Later Medieval England*. Liverpool: Liverpool University Press, 1982, pp. 181–217.

————. *The Common Lawyers of Pre-Reformation England: Thomas Kebbell, a Case Study*. Cambridge: Cambridge University Press, 1983.

*Jacob's Well*. Ed. A. Brandeis. EETS, o.s., vol. 115. London: K. Paul, Trench, Trübner, 1900.

Jenkinson, H., and B. E. R. Formoy, eds. *Select Cases in the Exchequer of Pleas*. Selden Society, vol. 48. London: Bernard Quaritch, 1932.

Johnson, C., ed. *Registrum Hamonis Hethe, Diocesis Roffensis*. Ed. C. Johnson. Vol. 2. Canterbury and York Society, vol. 49. Oxford: Oxford University Press, 1948.

Johnson, D. R. "'Homicide' in the *Parson's Tale*. *PMLA* 57 (1942): 51–56.

Johnson, L. S. "The Prince and His People: A Study of Two Covenants in the *Clerk's Tale*." *ChauR* 10 (1975): 17–29.

Kane, G. *Chaucer*. Oxford: Oxford University Press, 1984.

Kaye, J. M. "The Early History of Murder and Manslaughter." *Law Quarterly Review* 83 (1967): 365–95, 569–601.

————, ed. and trans. *Placita corone*. Selden Society, supp. ser, vol. 4. London: Bernard Quaritch, 1966.

Keiser, G. R. "Language and Meaning in Chaucer's *Shipman's Tale*." *ChauR* 12 (1978): 147–61.

Kelly, H. A. "Clandestine Marriage and Chaucer's 'Troilus.'" In J. Leyerle, ed. *Marriage in the Middle Ages*. *Viator* 4 (1973): 435–57.

————. *Love and Marriage in the Age of Chaucer*. Ithaca, N.Y.: Cornell University Press, 1975.

Kemp, E. W. *An Introduction to Canon Law in the Church of England*. London: Hodder and Stoughton, 1957.

Kuhl, E. P. "Some Friends of Chaucer." *PMLA* 29 (1914): 270–76.

Kuttner, S. *Repertorium der Kanonistik (1140–1234)*. Vatican City: Biblioteca Apostolica Vaticana, 1937.

Langland, William. *Piers Plowman: The B Version*. Ed. G. Kane and E. T. Donaldson. London: Athlone Press, 1975.

Leadam, I. S., and J. F. Baldwin, eds. *Select Cases Before the King's Council, 1243–1482*. Selden Society, vol. 35. Cambridge, Mass.: Harvard University Press, 1918.

Le Bras, G. *The Legacy of the Middle Ages*. Ed. C. G. Crump and E. F. Jacob. 1926. Reprint. Oxford: Clarendon Press, 1951.

LeGoff, J. "The Symbolic Ritual of Vassalage." In *Time, Work and Culture in the Middle Ages*. Trans. A. Goldhammer. Chicago: University of Chicago Press, 1980, pp. 237–87.

Lenaghan, R. T. "The Irony of the *Friar's Tale*." *ChauR* 7 (1973): 281–94.

Lester, G. A. "Chaucer's Knight and the Medieval Tournament." *Neophil* 66 (1982): 460–68.

*The Liber Albus.* Vol. 1 of *Munimenta Guildhallae Londoniensis.* Ed. H. T. Riley. Rolls Series, vol. 12. London: Longman, Brown, Green, Longmans, and Roberts, 1859–60.

Littleton, Sir Thomas. *Littleton's* Tenures *in English.* Ed. and trans. E. Wambaugh. Washington, D.C.: J. Byrne, 1903.

Lounsbury, T. R. *Studies in Chaucer.* 3 vols. 1892. Reprint. New York: Russell, 1962.

Lyndwood, W. *Provinciale (seu constitutiones angliae).* Oxford, 1679.

McGovern, W. M. "Contract in Medieval England: The Necessity for Quid pro Quo and a Sum Certain." *American Journal of Legal History* 13 (1969): 173–201.

————. "The Enforcement of Informal Contracts in the Later Middle Ages." *California Law Review* 59 (1971): 1145–93.

————. "The Enforcement of Oral Covenants Prior to Assumpsit." *Northwestern University Law Review* 65 (1970): 576–614.

McKisack, M. *The Fourteenth Century, 1307–1399.* Oxford: Clarendon Press, 1959.

Maguire, J. "The Clandestine Marriage of Troilus and Criseyde." *ChauR* 8 (1974): 262–78.

Maitland, F. W. "The Beatitude of Seisin." In *The Collected Papers of Frederic William Maitland.* Ed. H. A. L. Fisher. Cambridge: Cambridge University Press, 1911, 1:407–57.

————. "The Mystery of Seisin." In *The Collected Papers of Frederic William Maitland.* Ed. H. A. L. Fisher. Cambridge: Cambridge University Press, 1911, 1:358–84.

————. "Possession for Year and Day." In *The Collected Papers of Frederic William Maitland.* Ed. H. A. L.. Fisher. Cambridge: Cambridge University Press, 1911, 2:61–80.

————, ed. *Select Pleas in Manorial and Other Seignorial Courts.* Selden Society, vol. 2. London: Bernard Quaritch, 1888.

————, and W. P. Baildon, eds. *The Court Baron.* Selden Society, vol. 4. London: Bernard Quaritch, 1891.

Makowski, E. M. "The Conjugal Debt and Medieval Canon Law." *Journal of Medieval History* 3 (1977): 99–114.

Manly, J. M. *Some New Light on Chaucer.* New York: Henry Holt, 1926. Reprint. Gloucester, Mass.: Peter Smith, 1959.

Mann, J. *Chaucer and Medieval Estates Satire.* Cambridge: Cambridge University Press, 1973.

Meech, S. *Design in Chaucer's* Troilus. Syracuse, N.Y.: Syracuse University Press, 1959.

*Middle English Dictionary.* Ed. H. Kurath, S. M. Kuhn, and J. Reidy. Ann Arbor, Mich.: University of Michigan Press, 1952–. [*MED*]

Milsom, S. F. C. *Historical Foundations of the Common Law.* 2d ed. London: Butterworth, 1981.

————. "Reason in the Development of the Common Law." *Law Quarterly Review* 81 (1965): 496–517.

Mitchell, W. *An Essay on the Early History of the Law Merchant.* Cambridge: Cambridge University Press, 1904.

Montgomery, F. "A Note on the Reeve's Prologue." *PQ* 10 (1931): 404–405.

Myers, L. M. "A Line in the Reeve's Prologue." *MLN* 49 (1934): 222–26.

Nicholas, B. *An Introduction to Roman Law.* Oxford: Clarendon Press, 1962.

Nichols, F. M., ed. and trans. *Britton.* Washington, D.C.: J. Byrne, 1901.

Nolan, C. J. "Structural Sophistication in 'The Complaint unto Pity.'" *ChauR* 13 (1979): 363–72.

Noonan, J. T. *Contraception*. Cambridge, Mass.: Belknap Press, Harvard University Press, 1965.

Olson, P. "The *Reeve's Tale*: Chaucer's *Measure for Measure*." *SP* 59 (1962): 1–17.

Orme, N. "The Education of the Courtier." In V. J. Scattergood and J. W. Sherborne, eds. *English Court Culture in the Later Middle Ages*. London: Duckworth, 1983.

Owen, D. "Ecclesiastical Jurisdiction in England, 1300–1550: The Records and Their Interpretation." In D. Baker, ed. *Material, Sources and Methods of Ecclesiastical History*. Studies in Church History 11 (1975): 199–21.

*The Oxford English Dictionary*. Ed. Sir J. A. W. Murray et al. 13 vols. Oxford: Clarendon Press, 1933 [*OED*]

Pantin, W. A. *The English Church in the Fourteenth Century*. Cambridge: Cambridge University Press, 1955.

Passon, R. H. "'Entente' in Chaucer's *Friar's Tale*." *ChauR* 2 (1968): 166–71.

Payne, R. O. *Geoffrey Chaucer*. 2d ed. Boston: Twayne, 1986.

Petersen, K. O. *The Sources of the* Parson's Tale. Boston: Ginn, 1901.

Pike, L. O. *A History of Crime in England*. 2 vols. London: Smith, Elder, 1873–76.

Plucknett, T. F. T. *A Concise History of the Common Law*. 5th ed. London: Butter-worth, 1956.

Pollack, F., and F. W. Maitland. *The History of English Law Before the Time of Edward I*. 2d ed. 2 vols. 1898. Reissured with Introduction by S. F. C. Milson. Cambridge: Cambridge University Press, 1968.

Post, J. B. "Ravishment of Women and the Statutes of Westminster." In J. H. Baker, ed. *Legal Records and the Historian*. London: Royal Historical Society, 1978, pp. 150–64.

———. "Sir Thomas West and the Statute of Rapes, 1382." *Bulletin of the Institute of Historical Research* 53 (1980): 24–30.

Putnam, B. H., ed. *Proceedings Before the Justices of the Peace in the Fourteenth and Fifteenth Centuries*. London: Spottingwoode, Ballantyne, 1938.

Ranulf de Glanville. *The Treatise on the Laws and Customs of the Realm of England Commonly Called Glanvill*. Ed. and trans. G. D. G. Hall. London: Nelson, 1965.

Rastell, J. *An Exposition of Certaine Difficult and Obscure Wordes and Termes of the Lawes of this Realme*. 1579. Reprint. New York: Da Capo Press, 1969.

Raymond de Pennaforte. *Summa Sancti Raymundi de Peniaforte de poenitentia, et matrimonio cum glossis Joannis de Friburgo*. Rome, 1603.

Reinhard, J. R. "Setting Adrift in Mediaeval Law and Literature." *PMLA* 56 (1941): 33–68.

Reisner, T. A. "The Wife of Bath's Dower: A Legal Interpretation." *MP* 71 (1974): 301–302.

Richardson, H. G. *Bracton: The Problem of His Text*. Selden Society, supp. ser., vol. 2. London: Selden Society, 1965.

———, and G. O. Sayles, eds. and trans. *Fleta*. Vol. 2. Selden Society vol. 72. London: Bernard Quaritch, 1955. Vol. 3. Selden Society, vol. 89. London: Selden Society, 1972.

———, and ———, eds. *Select Cases of Procedure Without Writ Under Henry III*. Selden Society, vol. 60. London: Bernard Quaritch, 1941.

Rickert, E. "Was Chaucer a Student at the Inner Temple?" In *The Manly Anniversary*

*Studies in Language and Literature*. Chicago: University of Chicago Press, 1923, pp. 20–31.

Robertson, D. W., Jr. "'And for My Land Thus Hastow Mordred Me?' Land Tenure, the Cloth Industry, and the Wife of Bath." *ChauR* 14 (1980): 403–20.

Ross, C. D. "Forfeiture for Treason in the Reign of Richard II." *English Historical Review* 71 (1956): 560–75.

Roxburgh, R. F. "Lawyers in the New Temple." *Law Quarterly Review* 88 (1972): 414–30.

———. "Lincoln's Inns of the Fourteenth Century." *Law Quarterly Review* 94 (1978): 363–82.

———. *The Origins of Lincoln's Inn*. Cambridge: Cambridge University Press, 1963.

Ruggiers, P. G. *The Art of the* Canterbury Tales. Madison: University of Wisconsin Press, 1965.

Russell, M. J. "I. Trial by Battle and the Writ of Right." *Journal of Legal History* 1 (1980): 111–34.

———. "II. Trial by Battle and the Appeals of Felony." *The Journal of Legal History* 1 (1980): 135–64.

St. German, Christopher. *St. German's Doctor and Student*. Ed. T. F. T. Plucknett and J. L. Barton. Selden Society, vol. 91. London: Selden Society, 1974.

Salter, E. *Fourteenth-Century English Poetry*. Oxford: Clarendon Press, 1983.

Sanborn, F. R. *Origins of the Early English Maritime and Commercial Law*. New York: Century, 1930.

Sayles, G. O., ed. *Select Cases in the Court of King's Bench Under Edward II*. Vol. 4. Selden Society, vol. 74. London: Bernard Quaritch, 1955.

———, ed. *Select Cases in the Court of King's Bench Under Richard II, Henry IV and Henry V*. Vol. 7. Selden Society, vol. 88. London: Bernard Quaritch, 1971.

Scattergood, V. J. "The Originality of the *Shipman's Tale*." *ChauR* 11 (1977): 210–31.

Scheps, W. "Chaucer's Man of Law and the Tale of Constance." *PMLA* 89 (1974): 285–95.

Schless, H. *Chaucer and Dante: A Revaluation*. Norman, Okla.: Pilgrim Books, 1984.

Schneebeck, H. N. "The Law of Felony in Medieval England from the Accession of Edward I Until the Mid-Fourteenth Century." 2 vols. Ph.D. dissertation, University of Iowa, 1973.

Schneider, P. S. "'Taillynge Ynough': The Function of Money in the *Shipman's Tale*." *ChauR* 11 (1977): 201–209.

Schulz, F. "Bracton and Raymond de Peñafort." *Law Quarterly Review* 61 (1945): 286–92.

Schwertner, T. M. *Saint Raymond of Pennafort*. Ed. and rev. C. M. Antony. Milwaukee, Wis.: Bruce, 1935.

Shanks, E., ed. *Novae narrationes*. Selden Society, vol. 80. London: Bernard Quaritch, 1963.

Shaw, J. "Corporeal and Spiritual Homicide, the Sin of Wrath, and the 'Parson's Tale.'" *Traditio* 38 (1982): 281–300.

———. "The Influence of Canonical and Episcopal Reform on Popular Books of Instruction." In T. J. Heffernan, ed. *The Popular Literature of Medieval England*. Knoxville: University of Tennessee Press, 1985, pp. 44–60.

Sheehan, M. M. "The Formation and Stability of Marriage in Fourteenth-Century England: Evidence of an Ely Register." *MS* 33 (1971): 228–63.

―――. *The Will in Medieval England from the Conversion of the Anglo-Saxons to the End of the Thirteenth Century.* Toronto: Pontifical Institute of Mediaeval Studies, 1963.

Shoaf, R. A. "The *Franklin's Tale*: Chaucer and Medusa." *ChauR* 21 (1986): 274–90.

―――. *The Poem as Green Girdle: "Commercium" in "Sir Gawain and the Green Knight."* Gainesville: University of Florida Monographs, 1984.

Shook, L. K. Review of H. A. Kelly. *Love and Marriage in the Age of Chaucer. Speculum* 52 (1977): 701–702.

Silverman, A. H. "Sex and Money in Chaucer's *Shipman's Tale*." *PQ* 32 (1953): 329–36.

Simpson, A. W. B. "The Early Constitutions of the Inns of Court." *Cambridge Law Journal* 28 (1970): 241–56.

―――. *A History of the Common Law of Contract: The Rise of the Action of Assumpsit.* Oxford: Clarendon Press, 1975.

―――. *A History of the Land Law.* 2d ed. Oxford: Clarendon Press, 1986.

*Sir Gawain and the Green Knight.* Ed. J. R. R. Tolkien and E. V. Gordon. Rev. N. Davis. Oxford: Oxford University Press, 1967.

Skeat, W. W., ed. *Chaucerian and Other Pieces.* Oxford: Oxford University Press, 1897.

Smith, L. T., ed. *The Boke of Brome: A Common-Place Book of the Fifteenth Century.* London: Trübner, 1886.

Spendal, J. R. "The Fifth Pentad in 'Sir Gawain and the Green Knight.'" *N&Q*, n.s., 23 (1976): 147–48.

Spies, F. *De l'Observation des simples conventions en droit canonique.* Paris: Librarie du Recueil Sirey, 1928.

Spurgeon, C. F. E. *Five Hundred Years of Chaucer Criticism and Allusion, 1357–1900.* 3 vols. Cambridge: Cambridge University Press, 1925.

*The Statutes of the Realm.* Vols. 1–2. 1810–16. Reprint. London: Dawsons, 1963.

Stock, B. *The Implications of Literacy.* Princeton, N.J.: Princeton University Press, 1983.

Strohm, P. "Chaucer's Fifteenth-Century Audience and the Narrowing of the 'Chaucer Tradition.'" *SAC* 4 (1982): 3–32.

Teetaert, A. "Raymond De Penyafort." *Dictionnaire de théologie catholique.* Ed. A. Vacant et al. 15 vols. Paris: Librairie Letouzey et Ane, 1903–46.

Themblay, F. A., ed. "The Latin-Middle English Glossary 'Medulla Grammatice.'" Ph.D. dissertation, Catholic University of America, 1968.

Thomas, A. H., ed. *Calendar of Early Mayor's Court Rolls, A.D. 1298–1307.* Cambridge: Cambridge University Press, 1924.

―――, ed. *Calendar of Select Pleas and Memoranda of the City of London, A.D. 1381–1412.* Vol. 3. Cambridge: Cambridge University Press, 1932.

Thorne, S. E. "The Early History of the Inns of Court with Special Reference to Gray's Inn." *Graya* 50 (1959): 79–96. Reprinted in S. E. Thorne. *Essays in English Legal History.* London: Hambledon Press, 1985, pp. 137–54.

Thynne, F. *Animadversions upon Speght's First (1598 A.D.) Edition of Chaucer's Works.* Ed. G. H. Kingsley. Rev. F. J. Furnivall. EETS, o.s., vol. 9. London: Trübner, 1875.

―――. "Discourse of the Antiquity of the Houses of Law." In T. Hearne, ed. *A Collection of Curious Discourses.* London, 1771, 1:66–77.

Toner, B. *The Facts of Rape*. London: Arrow Books, 1977.

Tout, T. F. *Chapters in the Administrative History of Mediaeval England*. Vol. 3. Manchester: Manchester University Press, 1928.

———. "Literature and Learning in the English Civil Service in the Fourteenth Century." *Speculum* 4 (1929): 365–89.

Ullmann, W. *The Individual and Society in the Middle Ages*. Baltimore, Md.: Johns Hopkins University Press, 1966.

Way, A., ed. *Promptorium parvulorum sive clericorum*. Camden Society, vol. 89. London: Camden Society, 1865.

Wentersdorft, K. P. "Some Observations on the Concept of Clandestine Marriage in *Troilus and Criseyde*." *ChauR* 15 (1980): 101–26.

———. "The *Termes* of Chaucer's Sergeant of the Law." *SN* 53 (1981): 269–74.

Wenzel, S. "The Source of Chaucer's Seven Deadly Sins." *Traditio* 30 (1974): 351–78.

Whiting, B. J., ed. (with H. W. Whiting). *Proverbs, Sentences, and Proverbial Phrases from English Writings Mainly Before 1500*. Cambridge, Mass.: Harvard University Press, 1968.

Wood, C. *The Elements of Chaucer's Troilus*. Durham, N.C.: Duke University Press, 1984.

Woodcock, B. L. *Medieval Ecclesiastical Courts in the Diocese of Canterbury*. Oxford: Oxford University Press, 1952.

# Index